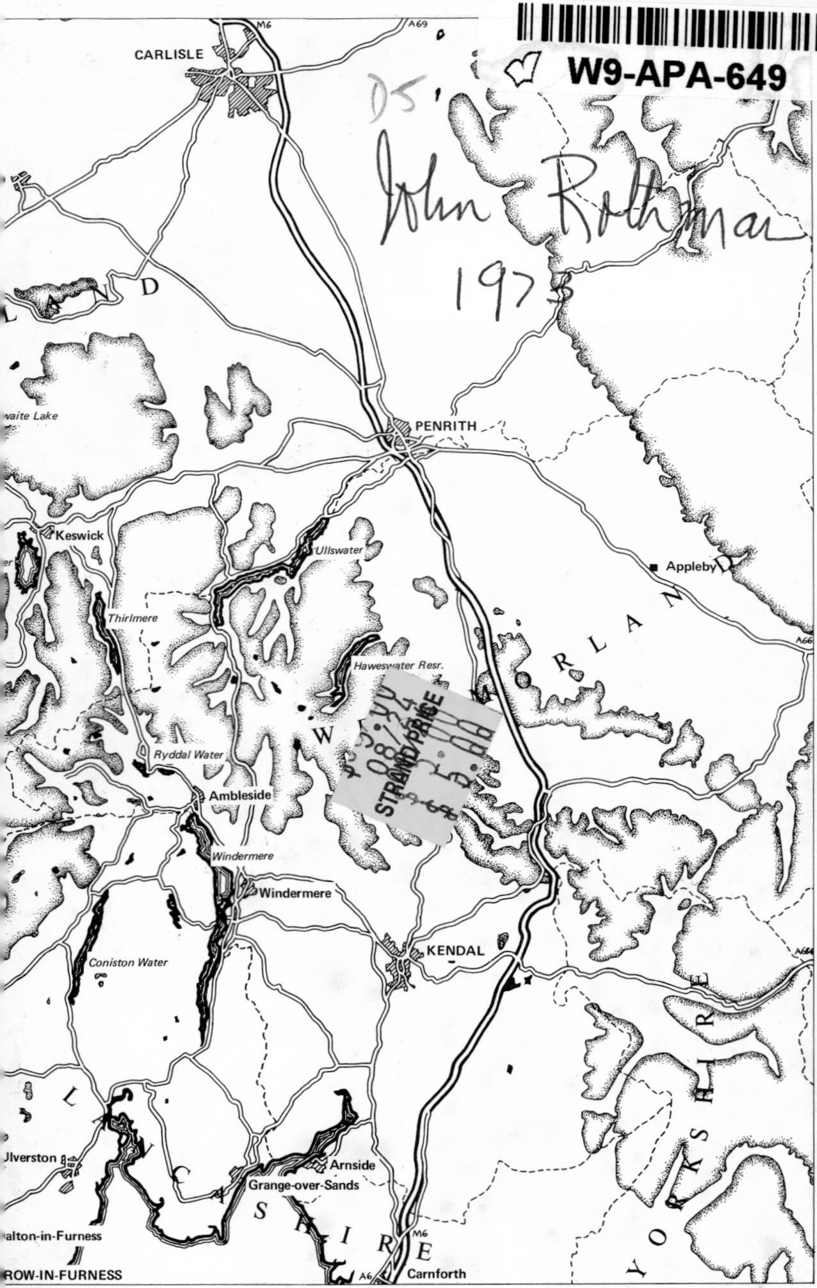

John Rothman
1973

COMPANION INTO LAKELAND

Also in this series

Companion into Buckinghamshire by Maxwell Fraser
Companion into Berkshire by R. P. Beckinsale
Companion into Sussex by Norman Wymer
Companion into Surrey by L. Collison Morley

MIDDLE FELL BUTTRESS, ABOVE THE OLD DUNGEON GHYLL HOTEL

COMPANION INTO LAKELAND

by
MAXWELL FRASER

WITH 16 PLATES AND AN ENDPAPER MAP

SPURBOOKS LTD.

First published by Methuen & Co., Ltd.
This edition, with new photographs and
endpaper map by
SPURBOOKS LTD.,
1 Station Road, Bourne End, Bucks.
1973.

SBN 0 902875 22 1

Printed offset litho by
Biddles Ltd., Guildford, Surrey.

ACKNOWLEDGMENTS

Where use has been made in the following pages of information contained in other books on the Lake District, due acknowledgment has been made in the text, with the exception of *The Lake District History*, by the late W. G. Collingwood, which proved an invaluable work of reference on all matters relating to the early history of the district.

Among those who have helped by supplying information or checking data, I should especially like to mention Mrs. Eleanor Rawnsley, Mrs. Elizabeth Johnstone, Dr. B. R. Johnstone and Mr. and Mrs. Telford of Grasmere; Miss Russell of Applethwaite; Mr. Varty of the *Lake District Herald*; Mr. Herbert Bell, Mr. Edward Tyson and Mr. Bernard Horrax, of Ambleside; Mr. Tom Sarginson of the *Cumberland and Westmorland Herald* and Mr. Gilpin of the Penrith Library; Mr. W. Scott of the Ullswater Navigation & Transit Co., Mr. T. Moore of the *Westmorland Gazette*, Mr. H. W. Jones, and Mr. B. Alexander the Mayor of Kendal; Miss M. C. Fair of Eskdale; Mr. G. G. Carter of the *Whitehaven News*; Mr. Thomas Watson of Windermere; Mrs. E. D. Gregory of Finsthwaite; Mr. Jameson, Engineer in Charge, Haweswater; Mr. H. S. West of Lancaster; Major L. S. Hoggarth for the authentic story of the Levens curse; the late Mr. G. Loftus Allen of the L.M.S. Railway; and Sir S. H. Scott of the Yews, Windermere.

I should like to take this opportunity of saying that where incidents, persons or places are either omitted or only briefly dealt with, it is because the Lake District has such a wealth of beauty and interest it is impossible to deal with everything in one book; and although as far as possible even the best-known facts are alluded to, preference has been given to details which are not so generally known. The detailing of instructions for walks, climbs and drives has been entirely omitted owing to the numerous admirable guide-books on these subjects already in print; similarly the preference shown for quoting little-known and often doggerel verse, implies no disrespect to the celebrated Lake Poets, but a recognition of the reality of their fame, which has resulted in every one making at least a passing acquaintance with their works during school-days.

M.F.

CONTENTS

PART I

WESTMORLAND

PART II

CUMBERLAND

ILLUSTRATIONS

PART I

WESTMORLAND

Chapter I

KENDAL

I

KENDAL has innumerable claims upon the interest and affection of visitors and townsfolk alike, and Kendalians have reason to be proud of the indomitable spirit with which their forefathers carried on their work despite continual ravages by the Scots during long centuries of Border warfare, and the equally destructive ravages of floods and storms. Kendalians turned so readily from fighting to manufacturing that Kendal archers and Kendal Green were equally famous, whilst the town also produced so many notable scholars that the critical De Quincey said he witnessed in Kendal 'more interesting conversations, as much information and more natural eloquence in conveying it' than was to be found 'usually in literary cities or in places professedly learned'.

Curiously enough, Kendal owes much of its present charm to one of its greatest sources of tribulation—the raids by the Scots—for it was the attempt to defend their property that led to the building of the castle and to the style of domestic building peculiar to the Border country: houses grouped round a yard, reached by a gateway from the street, which could be securely bolted and barred at night. Nowhere do these yards survive in greater numbers than in Kendal—there are nearly 100 of them, and although some are modern, a large number still show traces of the bolts and bars which once secured the entrances, to prove their antiquity.

There is nothing more fascinating than the perpetual glimpses of these yards in passing up and down the ancient streets of Kendal. Many are narrow even for a wheelbarrow to pass through, and a closer examination reveals their variety and interest. The present houses, although old, are later than the strenuous days of the Border warfare, but are built on the original foundations. Some of the yards have cobbled passages; others flag-stones; and yet others grass plots and flower beds. Some of the houses have the date of their origin clearly marked, and others bear the signs of their age in a picturesque gable or latticed window.

The Report of the Royal Commission on the Historical Monuments of Westmorland lists no less than forty seventeenth century houses surviving in Kendal, and numerous others dating from the eighteenth century, in addition to outstanding buildings of earlier date, and the majority of these buildings are in extremely good condition, with beautiful examples of panelling and plaster work.

Around the Market Place the shop fronts have been modernized, but the upper storeys are old, and a bell-tower over one marks the site of the old Moot Hall. The original seventeenth century first floor front is preserved in the timber-framed No. 28 Highgate; the seventeenth century Fleece Inn, also in Highgate, has its first floor next the street built out over the pavement and held up by pillars, the last remnant of the days when the shoppers of Kendal could pass all along the streets sheltered from the rain; a house up the Rainbow Yard has a galleried front of the old type; the unusually large arch of the Woolpack Inn in Stricklandgate is reminiscent of the days when the great wagons piled high with wool were brought to the staplers in the yard; several houses have the quaint long flight of outside stone stairs to the upper floor; and a house in one of the Stramongate yards, near the Quakers' Meeting House, has a long staircase window going up three full storeys, a type rarely seen outside Westmorland and gradually vanishing from the county.

No. 20 Market Place, now converted into a shop, was the old Football Inn where the local tradesmen held the meetings of the curiously-named 'Fastossity Society', whose minutes, contained in a handsome oak box, are now in the Kendal Museum.

The Museum also has a very good model of St. George's Chapel of Ease, which stood for a hundred years on the site now occupied by the War Memorial, but was pulled down in 1854 to make room for the Market. The chapel stood over the vaults of a wine-merchant, which gave rise to a verse said to have been inscribed over the door:

'There's a Spirit above; and a Spirit below;
A Spirit of Love, and a Spirit of Woe,
The Spirit above is the Spirit Divine,
And the Spirit below is the Spirit of Wine.'

The survival of so many ancient buildings, and of the distinctive yards, may perhaps be due to a Corporation town planning scheme of 1577, found in Kendal's 'Boke Off Recorde':

'The Alderman and Burgesses of this Boroughe off Kirkbie-kendall at this pnte (present) not onelye seinge and thoroughlie pceyvinge by sundrye Examples the manyfest hurte and Inconvenyence alredye come to this Boroughe by great streitninge off the Markett places within the Same. . . . But also dowbtinge that the lyke or worse heareafter should ensewe & be attemptyd & doone by others to the ffurther piudice (prejudice) thereoff, Iff spedie remodie, foresight, and redresse should not in time be had & pvided therein—

'Therefore it is nowe Ordeyned & Constitutid by the Alderman & the xij head Burgesses off the same Boroughe at this tyme beinge, That no manner off person or persons whatsoever ffrome hencfurthe shall or may Improve, Incroche, stopp, streytten, or take vpp any ffrount roweme or ground to buyld vpon in any parte, place, circuyte, or precincte off the Markett place within this Boroughe off Kirkbie-kendall withowte the speciall apoyntemt., & Assignem^{t}. off the Alderman & Burgesses off the Same . . . vpon payne to losse & fforfeitte to the Chamber off this Boroughe . . . xx^{lr}. . . . And iff it be done in any other part or place wth in this borugh owte off the Markett places where m'kethe is not kept Then . . . x^{lr}.'

One is inclined to suspect the measure was introduced less with any eye to the well-being of the townspeople than because the aldermen and burgesses themselves held much of the property, and were disinclined to make alterations, particularly as they were careful to include a clause exempting themselves from the fines, in case they should wish to make any alterations jointly or severally.

II

Although 'Kentdale' was granted by William Rufus to his powerful baron, Ivo de Taillebois, the Barony probably did not exist until 1189, when Richard I granted all the forest of Kendal and Furness, and a weekly market at Kendal, to Gilbert Fitz-Reinfred, who had married Helewise, daughter of the second William de Lancaster, who was descended from Elftred (or Eldred), a great Anglian Thane. The early history of the Barony is so confused that almost every historian who has written about it has differed from his predecessors in some point or other, but all are agreed that the Barony passed in the female line on more than one occasion. Ivo de Taillebois had no legitimate issue, but the family continued to hold various lands, until, in 1861, nearly seven centuries after Ivo took possession of Kentdale, the last of this once-powerful family, Emily Taillebois, a girl of eighteen, died a pauper in Shrewsbury workhouse.

It was in the very year that the Barony was created that Kendal experienced such a terrible massacre by the Scots under Duncan, Earl of Fife, that it was recorded as 'one of the bloodiest and most lamentable days ever known in Kendal', and it was probably this raid that led to the building of Kendal Castle and its earthwork, although none of the masonry now standing appears of earlier date than the thirteenth century, and the greater part dates from the fourteenth century.

The castle is chiefly famous in the present day as the birthplace of Katherine Parr, the last of Henry VIII's wives, and of her brother William, created Lord Parr and Ross, of Kendal, in 1539, and Marquis of Northampton in 1543.

The exact date of Katherine's birth is uncertain, but was probably 1512, as it is calculated she was about thirty-five or thirty-six at the time of her death. In her short life she was married four times, and her hand was first sought in marriage when she could not be more than eleven years of age. The long and interesting correspondence which passed between Lord Dacre, chosen as negotiator on account of his relationship with both the parties involved; Lord Scroop, father of the proposed bridegroom; and Katherine's mother, are printed in full in Nicholson's *Annals of Kendal* and in Dr. Whitaker's history of the Scroops of Bolton. Katherine's first husband was, however, Edward Burgh, a widower, with children, far older than his young bride, whom he left a widow when she was about sixteen years of age. Her second husband, Lord Latimer, was also an elderly widower with children. She married King Henry in 1543, when she was about thirty years of age, and lived with him three and a half years. Lastly she married Lord Seymour of Sudeley, and died soon after the birth of her first child, a daughter, Mary Seymour, who was disinherited in 1549 by Act of Parliament, in consequence of her father's intrigues against his brother, the Lord Protector, for which he was beheaded in that year. Queen Katherine's Book of Devotion is to be seen at Kendal in the Mayor's Parlour; and specimens of her exquisite needlework are preserved at Sizergh Castle.

Kendal Castle was probably partially destroyed after the attainder of the Marquis of Northampton in 1553, for espousing the cause of Lady Jane Grey, although he was acquitted, and in 1559 Queen Elizabeth restored him to all his former estates and honours. He died without heirs in 1571. Edward VI called him his 'honest uncle', and Henry VIII 'his integrity', whilst Elizabeth also thought highly of him. Kendal Castle was described as in a state of decay in a survey made in July, 1572, and Camden, writing in 1586, described it as 'almost ready to fall down with age', so that it is quite impossible there should be any truth in a once popular local tradition that Cromwell erected his guns on Castle How to bombard the castle, particularly as it is fairly certain Cromwell never came to Kendal. The poet Gray wrote a description of the castle on his visit in 1769, which West amended in his *Guide to the Lakes* published ten years later.

With the death of the Marquis of Northampton the Barony of Kendal returned to the Crown, and was conferred successively on various great nobles or members of the Royal family, except on the occasion when the third son of James II was created *Duke* of Kendal, and again when the title of Duchess of Kendal was conferred by George I on his mistress, the Countess Ehrengard Melusina von der Schulenberg, in 1719. In 1784, the old title of Baron of Kendal was made hereditary in the family of the Earls of Lonsdale.

The building known as the Castle Dairy, a delightful old house open to the public, is probably contemporary with the present castle, but was reconditioned in the sixteenth century and extended in the early seventeenth century. The rooms are beautifully panelled in sixteenth century woodwork, and have oak-beamed ceilings. Some of the windows have stained glass, and there is some fine contemporary furniture.

In view of the fact that the ancient name of Kendal was 'Cherchebie' or 'Kirkbie' in Kentdale, and that Ivo de Taillebois granted the church of Kentdale to the Abbey of St. Mary in York in 1087, it is certain there was a church on the site from early times, and the discovery of part of an eighth century cross suggests there may have been a building on the site at that period. The present church dates from the thirteenth century, with the chapels of the Bellinghams, Stricklands and Parrs added in the late fifteenth or early sixteenth centuries. Although the body of the church has been drastically restored, the brasses and monuments in the chapels are of much interest, and among the fittings are the ancient cross-shaft and a coffin-lid of the late thirteenth century. A basket-hilted sword and a helmet hanging in the church near the Bellingham Chapel is conjectured by Nicholson to commemorate Sir Roger Bellingham, who was a Knight Banneret, but tradition says they commemorate an incident of the Civil War described in an old ballad, 'Robin the Devil', which tells how Col. Briggs, a magistrate of Kendal and an officer in Cromwell's army, besieged Major Robert Philipson, a Cavalier known as Robert the Devil, who lived on Belle Isle in Lake Windermere. The siege was raised after a few days by Colonel Philipson, Robert's elder brother, and the following Sunday Robert rode into Kendal with a troop of horse, determined on having his revenge, and actually rode into the parish church, during the service. The astonishment and consternation of the congregation can well be imagined when the horseman rode up

TARN HOWS

the chancel in search of his enemy who, fortunately, was not there. All accounts agree so far, but there is a certain amount of confusion about what followed. All that emerges definitely is that one of the townsmen attempted to stop the Major and was cut down for his pains, and that in his hurry to escape Robert lost his helmet and possibly his sword.

The incident has been used by Scott in his poem *Rokeby*, Canto VI, and has been described many times. William Gilpin, in his *Guide to the Lakes*, published in 1787, concludes his account of the incident by sententiously saying: 'Such are the calamities of Civil War! After the direful effects of public opposition cease; revenge, and private malice, long keep alive the animosity of individuals.'

Thomas West, author of the *Antiquities of Furness*, and of a guide to the Lakes published in the early eighteenth century, is buried in the church, but the best-known monument owes its fame to its quaint inscription:

'Here vunder lyeth ye body of Mr. Ravlph Tirer, late vicar of Kendall, Batchler of Divinity, who dyed the 4th day of Jvne, Ano Dni. 1627.

'London bredd me, Westminster fedd me,
Cambridge sped me, my sister wed me,
Study taught me, Living sought me,
Learning brought me, Kendall caught me,
Labour pressed me, sickness distressed me,
Death oppressed me, and grave possessed me,
God first gave me, Christ did save me,
Earth did crave me, and heaven would have me.'

There are several other seventeenth century memorials bearing long verses extolling the virtues of those they commemorate.

The complete set of colours borne by the Westmorland Regiment since it was raised in 1755 is preserved in the church, together with the Imperial Chinese Dragon Flag captured by Lieutenant Butler during the Chinese War.

Kendal church is one of the few in this country to possess five aisles, and is of such splendid proportions that its breadth of 103 ft. makes it the fifth widest in England, and is only 3 ft. short of the width of York cathedral.

Probably few congregations have had quite so many disastrous events take place in their church. Those who fled to the church for sanctuary during the massacre of 1189 were actually put to death in the building, and even if the story of 'Robin the Devil's' exploit is not true, there is a long chapter of accidents on record. In February, 1762, there was a violent storm during which some of the lead from the roof was torn off and fell into the church in the middle of the service, and the congregation 'left in confusion'. Five years later the congregation had another scare during the service with an earthquake shock. Among other vicissitudes, the River Kent 'came into the vestry' and on another occasion the river swept over the churchyard wall in the seventeenth century and 'itt left much ffish' on the graves. In the same century the whole of the Communion Plate was stolen and never recovered, whilst during the following century one of the tower pinnacles fell and broke a woman's leg.

One of the most interesting of the ancient houses surviving in Kendal is Collin Field, which dates back to the early part of the seventeenth century and has a Latin inscription over the door which has been translated: 'Now mine, soon his; but afterwards I know not whose. 1663.' It was acquired in 1668 by George Sedgwick, secretary of Anne, Countess of Pembroke, on his retirement. He records in his memoirs:

'After eighteen years' service with this good lady, she began to mind me of myself, and my future well-being in the world; often repeating to me a verse of Mr. Samuel Daniel, the famous poet and historiographer, who had been her instructor in her childhood and youth:

"To have some silly home I do desire,
Loth still to warm me by another's fire."

She further declared her noble intention to me, that when I met with some small habitation, she would give me £200 towards the purchase, which she punctually performed.

'Within awhile God directed me to Collin Field, a small estate held under Queen Katherine, as part of her jointure . . . where by God's blessing I enjoy a quiet and retired life to my contentment; having oftentimes the society of several of my worthy friends and neighbours from the town of Kendal, having lived here above 14 years at the writing hereof, 1682.'

The battened door of Collin Field still has a wooden padlock with the initials of the Countess—one of several she had made for houses where she was likely to visit, or gave as signs of her affection for her friends. These locks were made for the Countess by George Dent of Appleby, and cost £1 each. One dated 1670 is preserved at Great Ashby rectory, and another is kept at Rose Castle, Carlisle.

Among other ancient houses surviving in Kendal are Bellingham House in Stramongate, once the town house of the owners of Levens Hall; Wattsfield, Birk Hag, and Raysholme, dating back to the seventeenth century; and Abbot Hall, built in 1759. The two bridges across the River Kent, although widened in the eighteenth century and again later, preserve the earlier bridges in the centre of each—probably dating from the seventeenth century in each case—and if anyone regrets the alteration to the original bridges, let them think of the day in November, 1806, when the waters of the Kent came down in a flood at three o'clock in the morning, and swept away a post-chaise which was crossing by the old ford at Nether Bridge, and drowned all the occupants.

III

One of the most fascinating things about exploring Kendal and delving into its past history is the way in which the two dovetail, owing partly to the number of ancient buildings surviving, and partly to that mine of information, Kendal's 'Boke off Recorde'. Queen Elizabeth, who was Lady of the Barony of Kendal, granted a charter of incorporation in 1575 under which the chief magistrate of the borough was known as an alderman, the term of mayor not being used until the town received a second charter from Charles I. Kendal was distinctly unfortunate in its first holders of office. Robert Briggs, the first recorder, was deprived of his office within a year, and Henry Wilson, the first alderman, was deprived of his burgess-ship and of the office of justice of the peace in 1579, for misconducting himself with Jeanette Eskrigge, wife of one of the townsmen. Black Hall, which was for centuries the home of the Wilson family, still stands in Stricklandgate, and is easily distinguished by the model of a large black hog, the sign of the Brush Company who use the old mansion for their factory. Alderman Wilson's nephew, George, married the daughter of Sir Thomas Braithwaite of Burneside Hall.

If the first alderman was not satisfactory, later holders of the office, and their successors, the Mayors of Kendal, gave convincing proofs of their probity and generosity. One magistrate, when presiding over a case brought against himself, had no hesitation in deciding it against himself. Thomas Sandes, who was Mayor in 1647, founded the Sandes Hospital in Highgate for eight widows. The original Gatehouse block, which was built eleven years before the formal foundation in 1670, is still standing, although the almshouses were rebuilt in 1852. Thomas Sandes also founded a blue-coat school for boys eleven years before his death. Grandy Nook Hall, in Low Fellside, has a stone bearing the initials of Thomas Sandes and his wife Katherine, and an oak panel with the date 1659. Cornelius Nicholson, the Kendal historian, was Mayor in 1846.

Among other entries in the 'Boke off Recorde' is one made on the occasion of a 'stranger' being deported to his birthplace—Sedbergh, which is only 10½ miles from Kendal; Kendalians regarded everyone as 'strangers' and 'forrainers' if they were not born in the town, even if they only came from Hutton, less than four miles away!

When James I passed through Kendal on his way south to claim the English throne, he spent the night in Brownsword House, afterwards the Pack Horse Inn, which stood opposite Black Hall. As the accession of King James caused the Union of England and Scotland and the cessation of Border warfare, the townspeople should have given him a rapturous welcome!

In 1652 Kendal had a very different kind of visitor in the person of George Fox, who records in his diary that he 'spake through Kendal on a market-day. . . . So dreadful was the power of God upon me, that people flew like chaff before me into their houses and shops. I warned them of the mighty day of the Lord, and exhorted them to hearken to the voice of God in their own hearts, who was now come to teach His people Himself.' One of the earliest Meeting Houses of the Society of Friends was built in Kendal about 1688, and rebuilt on the same site in Stramongate in 1815. Kendal was a great centre for the Quakers, and it was probably largely due to their influence that Kendal took so little part in the Civil War and the Rebellions of 1715 and 1745. Curiously enough, however, there is no record of their having made any notable protest against the custom of bull-baiting, although it may have been due to their influence that the Corporation put a stop to the practice in 1790. The Kendal bull ring stood on a green at the High Beast Banks.

During the Rebellion of the '45 Prince Charles lodged in the town on his way south, and spent another night there on his retreat. No. 95 Stricklandgate is still known locally as 'Prince Charlie's House'. On his retreat the Prince was followed so closely by the Hanoverian troops that two nights after his second visit the Duke of Cumberland slept on the same couch.

The Kendalians were strongly in favour of the 'Revolution' of 1688 which placed the Protestant William of Orange on the throne. When a rumour spread that James II was lying off the Yorkshire coast ready to land in an endeavour to regain his crown, the Lord Lieutenant of Westmorland called out the 'Posse Comitatus', comprising all able-bodied men from sixteen to sixty. Kendal's inhabitants met in a field called Miller's Close, near the town, and marched to Kirkby Lonsdale, where they heard that they would not be required and therefore returned home, the incident being celebrated in the rhyme:

'Eighty-eight was Kerby feight,
When never a man was slain;
They yatt their meaat, an' drank their drink,
An' sae kom merrily haem again.'

Exactly a hundred years after the accession of William of

Orange the Kendalians set up the obelisk on Castle How, with the inscription 'Sacred to Liberty'.

IV

In spite of its castle, Kendal was never a feudal dependency, but from very early times had a trade and industry of its own, and was ever a peaceful industrial town when the Scots gave opportunity for the development of its manufactories. It is a Kendal tradition that letters of protection—the first ever given to a foreign cloth weaver—were granted by Edward III to John Kemp of Flanders, who established himself so successfully in the town that it is said his daughter became the reigning beauty, and married the then Baron of Kendal, but this has since been disproved.

The ancient motto of Kendal, 'Wool is my Bread,' is an indication of the importance of the Kendal woollen trade. 'Kendal Green' was famous for centuries, and was frequently mentioned in medieval ballads. Shakespeare lovers will remember that in *King Henry IV* Falstaff speaks of 'three misbegotten knaves in Kendal green', and many other such references might be quoted.

The Kendal woollen trade has lost its ancient fame, and the name of Kendal green is only a memory, but for those who are interested the Museum has a card showing specimens of wool dyed in yellow, blue and green to show the blue obtained from the woad plant (*Isatis tinctoria*) and the yellow of Dyer's broom (*Genista tinctoria*) from which the green was obtained, and the resulting colour, which is an attractive shade of bottle green, similar to that used as a uniform by one of the leading schools in Kendal to-day. The houses in the narrow lanes climbing Fellside are said to have been built for the handloom weavers, and many of these houses have rooms showing traces of the primitive old machine fixtures.

Kendal was also famous for its 'milk-white' cloth, which was also supplied in pieces with hand-coloured spots in blue, red or green called 'ermines' or 'spotted cottons'. One old ballad of the Battle of Flodden Field tells how:

'The left-hand wing with all his rout
The lusty Lord Dacre did lead
With him the bows of Kendal stout
With milke-white coats and crosses red;
There are the bows of Kendal bold
Who fierce will fight, and never flee.'

A letter addressed by the Earl of Surrey to Cardinal Wolsey in 1523, shows that the ballad did no more than justice to the valour of the Kendal bowmen, for in his account of the Border campaign he mentions that 'the said Kendal men were so handled that they proved hardy men that went noo foote back for theym'.

In the seventeenth century Kendal began to achieve fame for a new manufacture—that of snuff. In the present day although Kendal's woollen trade has lost its supreme importance, the town is manufacturing more snuff than it has ever done, and 'Kendal Brown' is still pre-eminent. Kendal mint and Kendal parkin, which have superseded the old 'Kendal black drop', are also world-famous, and have been included in the supplies for expeditions to the Arctic, Antarctic, and Everest. A wide range of other industries help to maintain the ancient fame and prosperity of Kendal as an industrial centre without detracting in the slightest from the charm of the town.

Every writer who visited Kendal in the seventeenth and eighteenth centuries paid a tribute to its industry and its attractions, and their descriptions are substantially true in the present day. Sir Daniel le Fleming, of Rydal, writing in 1671, said: 'It is the chief town for largeness, neatness, buildings and trade in this county, and is most pleasantly seated . . . a place of excellent manufacture and for civility, ingenuity, and industry so surpassing that in regard thereof it deservedly carrieth a great name.' At the beginning of the following century the *Tour of the whole Island of Great Britain*, attributed to Daniel Defoe, said: 'Kendal is a rich and populous Town, esteemed the Beauty of the County, has a free school well endowed, and drives a great trade in Woolen cloth, cottons, druggets, serges, hats and stockens. . . .'

As late as the early part of the twentieth century Kendal was practically equal in size and importance to Carlisle and Lancaster, and in compensation for being outstripped by these towns it can now claim its age-old charm is quite unspoiled and the beauty of its situation is unimpaired. The surrounding hills, whether grass-clad or covered with woods, are untouched, and such new houses as are built stand close to the town and main road, and are of grey stone or roughcast, which blends successfully with the rest of the town and its surroundings. The castle ruins are effectively isolated on their grassy hill, and the steep lanes of Fellside lead up to the delightful Serpentine Woods with the old T well, now disused, but once celebrated as a cure for all eye-troubles. Even more unusual and fortunate, there is a tree-shaded path running beside the river, and the houses do not crowd so close as to mar its attractions, as in so many ancient river towns.

V

Kendal has been celebrated for its educational facilities since the foundation of the Grammar School in 1588. The original building is still in existence, although no longer used as a school since a larger building was provided in 1888. Among those who gave donations towards the original building was Bernard Gilpin, who was born in the neighbouring valley of Kentmere. Among its most famous scholars was James Pennington, who was born at Kendal in 1777, and was regarded as one of the leading authorities of his day on currency and finance. He was consulted by Sir Robert Peel during the preparation of the Bank Act of 1844, and constantly placed his knowledge at the disposal of the Government. Many of the articles he wrote on currency are of permanent value.

Thomas Shaw, the son of a shearman-dyer of Kendal, was another pupil of the Grammar School. He was appointed chaplain to the British factory at Algiers in 1720 and during his thirteen years residence there made a series of expeditions to Egypt, the Holy Land, Cyprus and Northern Africa, often in circumstances of great danger, as a result of which he wrote valuable observations of natural history and geography. Wordsworth referred to him in *Social Life in the English Universities*, and a botanical species was named 'Shawia' in his honour.

Ephraim Chambers, usually called the 'first encyclopædist', was born at Kendal about 1680, and also received his early education in the Grammar School. His encyclopædia was published in 1728 and brought him many honours. Barnaby Potter, another pupil, was the son of a Mercer and alderman of Highgate in Kendal. He became provost of Queen's College, Bishop of Carlisle, and Chaplain to Charles I when Prince of Wales. Two of his daughters—'Handsome' Mistress Grace, and Amye—were celebrated by Herrick in *The Hesperides.* Another Bishop of Carlisle, Edmund Law, also received his education in Kendal Grammar School.

Richard Braithwaite or Brathwaite, the poet, who was born at the neighbouring mansion of Burneside, may also have been educated at Kendal Grammar School, for his father, Thomas Braithwaite, was a barrister and recorder of Kendal in the sixteenth century, and the poet says in *Drunken Barnabee's Itinerary:* 'Now to Kendall . . . Where I had my native breeding.'

The Kendal Quaker School, which stood in Stramongate on the site now occupied by the Senior Boys School, was also famous in its day. A distinguished pupil of this school was John Gough, born at Kendal in 1721, who wrote the standard *History of the Society of Friends*, and other books, and is specially remembered for his work at Lisburn in Ireland, where he removed in 1774. Another and more famous John Gough, born in Kendal in 1757, was descended from General William Goffe, the regicide, and was known as 'The Blind Philosopher', owing to the fact that his sight was destroyed by small-pox when he was scarcely three years old. He was an intimate of the Lake poets, and Wordsworth refers to him in the seventh book of *The Excursion*, and Coleridge pays tribute to him in his essay on *The Soul and its organs of Sense*, saying: 'The every way amiable and estimable John Gough of Kendal is not only an excellent mathematician but an infallible botanist and zoologist . . . the rapidity of his touch appears fully equal to that of sight, and its accuracy greater.' Many tales are told of his industry, his prodigious memory, and his knowledge of botany.

William Hudson, who was born at the White Lion Inn, which was kept by his father, in 1730, was also a famous botanist. He was resident sub-librarian at the British Museum for a year, and published his *Flora Anglica* the year after he was elected a Fellow of the Royal Society. According to the best authorities this book 'marks the establishment of Linnaean principles of botany in England'.

The Quaker School achieved its greatest prosperity under Jonathan and John Dalton, who were assistants in the school until they succeeded their cousin George Bewley in its management in 1785. Robert Barnes of Cockermouth, who was sent to their school in 1794, says in his Autobiography: 'The Pedagogue (Jonathan Dalton) under whose government I was now placed excelled in nothing so much as in that of handling a cane or birch rod, and these I must confess he could manage in a very masterly style, and no thanks to him for he had abundance of practice. Although I never came under his correction but once, I believe I shall remember it as long as I live.' He goes on to describe the flogging which ended in a doctor being called to attend to his lacerated back—and he was only twelve years old at the time! He paints a more pleasant picture of John Dalton, who was then at Manchester, but 'came to spend the vacation of his academy with my master at Kendal; and, at the same time, took the opportunity to deliver a course of lectures on Astronomy, Chemistry, Electricity, Hydraulics, Hydrostatics, and Pneumatics, and I had the good fortune to be chosen for his assistant, in going through the various experiments belonging to each of these sciences. I never in my life enjoyed anything so much, and am confident that I received more information from him in six weeks than from his brother in two years'.

During the twelve years John Dalton spent in Kendal he became acquainted with Gough, the Blind Philosopher, who assisted him in his studies, and suggested his meteorological journal, which Dalton commenced in 1789, and kept so carefully for fifty-seven years that he recorded 200,000 observations. Many valuable discoveries arose from his observations at Kendal and those carried out simultaneously by his friend, Peter Crosthwaite, at Keswick. He gained a European reputation with his discoveries, which were the direct cause of meteorology being constituted a science, and also published valuable essays on Chemistry. He received many honours and awards from English and Foreign societies.

Anthony Askew, the classical scholar and physician, was born in Kendal in 1722. He gathered together such an extensive and valuable library that the sale after his death lasted twenty days, among the principal purchasers being the kings of England and France, and the British Museum.

George Romney, although born at Dalton-in-Furness, had many associations with Kendal. Both he and his son John married Kendal girls. The house where George Romney lived in Redmayne's Yard at the beginning of his career is marked with a plaque, and also the house in Kirkland where he died, and there is a wall tablet in Kendal parish church to his memory, although he is buried at Dalton. Romney's first recorded work, a hand posting a letter, painted as a sign for the post office at Kendal, is now in the Kendal Town Hall with other specimens of his work.

Close to Romney's home in Redmayne's Yard is the birthplace of Thomas Stewardson who, after a short apprenticeship with John Fothergill, a Kendal painter, went to London and became the pupil of Romney, who painted his portrait. Stewardson became portrait painter to George IV and Queen Caroline, and painted many of the notabilities of his day. Specimens of his work now hang in the National Portrait Gallery.

The Lake Poets had many acquaintances among the Kendalians, to whom they made references in their works—among others, James Patrick, who is buried near the Presbyterian Meeting House where Wordsworth worshipped, and who was the original of 'The Wanderer' in *The Prelude*.

Wordsworth, Southey, Professor Wilson, Dr. Thomas Gough—son of the Blind Philosopher—Lord Brougham, John Dalton, Professor Adam Sedgwick, Dr. Birkbeck and other distinguished people were honorary members of the Kendal Literary and Scientific Society. The Museum formed by this society was the nucleus of the present

Museum which, as befits a town that has produced such distinguished botanists and scientists, has one of the finest botanical, natural history and geological sections possessed by any local museum in the Kingdom.

De Quincey's association with Kendal was even closer than that of the Lake Poets, for he was on the staff of the *Westmorland Gazette* from its foundation, and was Editor from 1819 to 1820.

Even if Kendal had no associations with the Lake Poets, and no other claims upon the interest of tourists to the Lakes, it would be worth their while to see the many interesting Lake Country relics in the Museum, or to consult the magnificent collection of Lake Country books in the Carnegie Library there.

Chapter II

LAKELAND DEFENCES AROUND KENDAL

SOUTH: ROMAN WATERCROOK: THE PELE-TOWERS OF SIZERGH, LEVENS, DALLAM, HAZELSLACK, BEETHAM AND ARNSIDE

I

THE vast and easily navigable Bay of Morecambe, with its three great estuaries of the Kent, Lune, and Leven was ever a source of anxiety to those bent on defending the approaches to the Lake District. The Britons had numerous camps on the hilltops overlooking the Kent Valley; the Romans built Watercrook; and later comers set up many pele-towers. The district south of Kendal consequently has much interest for thoughtful tourists, and the development of the pele-towers into mansions, which can be seen to perfection at Sizergh and Levens, has an even wider appeal. Levens Hall, which is frequently open to the public, draws sightseers of all classes, from all parts of the country.

The old Roman road to the north followed approximately the same route as the modern railway line, to the east of the present highway, and the Roman station at Watercrook did not command any through route, but was designed to defend the valley of the Kent against invaders from the sea. Watercrook stands on a small peninsula formed by a deep bend in the river Kent, a mile south of Kendal, and was almost certainly used by the division of Agricola's army which came to the Lake District in A.D. 79. Although invariably called Concangium by earlier historians, and so marked on the Ordnance Survey, it is identified by W. G. Collingwood and other modern investigators with Alone. It was excavated in 1930 and the pottery, coins, altar, monument and statue found there are now in the Kendal museum.

The pele-towers of the district originally consisted of a small square tower, with very thick walls, a vaulted store-room on the ground floor, a narrow-windowed chamber above, and a still higher room used by the women-folk or as a living-room. In time of raids the villagers left their wattle-built houses at the mercy of the marauders, and crowded into the tower with their valuables, driving the cattle into a small walled yard, or other safe hiding-places, and so lying low until the raiders had departed. The earliest of these towers south of Kendal were Sizergh, Levens, and Arnside, which were built during the fourteenth century, soon after a disastrous raid by the Scots under Robert the Bruce, and the remainder were built about a century later.

Some of the earliest documents in the possession of the Kendal corporation are letters concerning the defence of the English border against the inroads of the Scots, and several of them are proclamations issued by the Lord Warden of the Western Marches ordering watch to be kept for the firing of beacons at critical times. The beacon hills of Westmorland were Barbon, Stainmore, Orton Scar, Whinfell, Farleton Knot, and Helton, and only too often must they have flamed in warning to the unfortunate inhabitants. Another order issued in connexion with the defence of the Border was that yew trees must be planted in or near all churchyards to provide bows for the archers, and another result of the warfare was that the inhabitants held their lands on 'Border tenure', by which all able-bodied members of each family, between the ages of sixteen and sixty, were bound to give their aid in repelling invaders whenever required.

Sometimes reprisals were carried out, and Sir Thomas, afterwards Lord, Wharton of Westmorland, was one of the most active and vigilant Wardens of the Marches. In the thirty-fourth year of the reign of Henry VIII he issued a letter of proclamation, calling to his aid all those subject to border service within the bounds of the West Marches. Among those who responded were Walter Strickland of Sizergh, with twenty-two horse; Sir John Lowther with a hundred horse and forty foot; and Sir James Leyburne of Cunswick with twenty horse. It is possibly this muster which carried out the foray which lasted from 2nd July to 17th November, 1544, when the amount of damage done in Scotland was computed in Haine's State Papers as:

Towns, towers, stedes, parish churches &c. cast down and burned	192
Scots slain	403
Prisoners taken	816
Nolt (i.e. horned cattle) taken	10,386
Sheep	12,492
Nags and geldings	1,296
Goats	200
Balls of Corn	890

Insight (i.e. household furniture) not reckoned.

II

Sizergh Castle, which lies three miles south of Kendal, has a special interest as the home of the same family for seven hundred years. It came into the possession of the Strickland family, of Strickland Hall in the parish of Morland, on the marriage of William de Strickland or Strikland, with Elizabeth, daughter and heiress of Sir Ralph Dreincourt of Sizergh. William Strickland, Bishop of Carlisle, who died in 1419, was probably one of the Stricklands of Sizergh. He was married before he took orders, and his daughter Margaret married Robert de Lowther, ancestor of the Earls of Lonsdale, who quarter Margaret

Strickland's arms—which are the same as those of the Sizergh Stricklands, with the addition of a border engrailed.

The Stricklands served in Parliament as Knights of the Shire for Westmorland seventeen times between the reign of Edward II and the Restoration, and Sir Thomas Strickland was created a Knight banneret by King Charles in person at the battle of Edgehill in 1642, and was later privy purse to Charles II. His son Walter, who died at the age of about nine in 1656, is commemorated by a beautiful tomb in the Strickland Chapel of Kendal church. It has an effigy of the boy and a long inscription. Although Agnes Strickland, the nineteenth century historian born at Reydon Hall, Suffolk, frequently claimed a connexion with the Sizergh Stricklands, the claim is unsupported by documentary evidence. The Sizergh Stricklands were the earliest influential patrons of Romney, and friends of West, the historian.

The earliest part of Sizergh Castle is the pele-tower at the south end of the main block, which dates from the second half of the fourteenth century, and contains the 'Queen's room' in which Katherine Parr frequently stayed on visits to the Stricklands before her royal marriage. The room has fine sixteenth century panelling and a fireplace with a richly carved overmantel bearing the royal arms and the date and inscription '1559. Vivat Regina', sometimes mistaken for a reference to Katherine Parr, but as the date proves, actually referring to Queen Elizabeth, in whose reign Sir Walter Strickland added two long west wings and much of the panelling for which the castle is famous. The room above the Queen's chamber is said to be haunted.

The castle is not open to the public, but this is mitigated by the fact that it is close to the highway, from which it can be seen clearly in all the beauty of bright flower-beds glowing against the ancient grey walls; whilst the finest of the panelling was taken from the Inlaid Chamber in 1891, and can now be seen in the Victoria and Albert Museum. The panelling was replaced by sixteenth century hangings of Flemish Tapestry.

Sizergh Castle stands in the parish of Helsington, whose church dates from 1726, and the village has several sixteenth and seventeenth century houses, including a seventeenth century inn. The church also serves the charming little village of Brigster, with its attractive cottages and still more delightful woods where the lily of the valley grows wild, and the damson orchards blossom gloriously in their season. A lane near the south-eastern entrance to Sizergh Park leads to Hawes Bridge which spans one of the most beautiful reaches of the River Kent, and about two miles further down the river is Force Bridge and the long reach of Force Fall, where the river foams and cascades over great boulders before flowing beneath Levens Bridge and through the grounds of Levens Hall.

III

The history of Levens Hall can be traced back even further than that of Sizergh, but does not show a similar unbroken possession. The Manor of Levens was bought from the Baron of Kendal by Henry de Redeman, or Redman, in 1189, the original deed being preserved in the house. During the three hundred years they were seated at Levens there were many distinguished members of the Redman family, whose deeds are fully described in Greenwood's *Chronicles of the Redmans of Levens and Harewood.* Sir Matthew Redman, who died in 1360, sat for Westmorland in the parliaments of 1357 and 1358. His son, also Sir Matthew, served in France and Spain under John of Gaunt; was warden of Roxburghe in 1381 and appointed commissioner to treat with the Scottish envoys in 1389. His son, Sir Richard Redman, was granted leave to hold a tournament at Carlisle about 1393.

Sir Richard became Speaker of the House of Commons, and married Elizabeth, widow of Sir Bryan Stapleton, and daughter of William de Aldburgh, in whose right he became lord of the manor of Harewood and other estates in Yorkshire. His son Matthew, who predeceased him, was probably the grandfather of Richard Redman who was born in the chapelry of Levens, became abbot of Shap and afterwards Bishop of St. Asaph, where he restored the cathedral; then Bishop of Exeter, and afterwards of Ely. He was

noted for his wealth and profuse liberality. The Redmans sold Levens to Alan Bellingham of Burneside, in 1489, and removed to their manor of Harewood, now the home of the Earl of Harewood and the Princess Royal.

Alan Bellingham was the younger son of Sir Robert Bellingham of Burneside, or Burneshead Manor, which lies two miles north of Kendal, and it was his grandson, Sir James, who in 1585 converted the Plantagenet pele-tower into a splendid Elizabethan mansion. Apart from some alterations made by Col. Grahme soon after he bought Levens from the Bellinghams in 1690, the mansion stands to-day as Sir James Bellingham planned it.

Col. Grahme was born in Yorkshire, and received his first commission from Louis XIV in 1671, and in 1673 was appointed by Charles II to the captaincy of a company of foot commanded by the Earl of Carlisle. His handsome face, fine figure, and engaging manners made him a great favourite at court, where he fell in love with Dorothy Howard, grand-daughter of the first Earl of Berkshire, who was then maid of honour to the Queen. Evelyn says in his diary, under the date 1675, that Grahme was 'exceedingly in love. . . . I could not but pity them both, the mother not much favouring it. This lady was not only a great beauty but a most virtuous and excellent creature and worthy to have been wife to the best of men. My advice was required and I spake to the advantage to the young gentleman, more out of pity than that she deserves no better match; for though he was a gentleman of good family, yet there was great inequality.'

Through the good offices of John Evelyn, the marriage took place in 1675, and as Col. Grahme was high in the royal favour he received a succession of good appointments. On the accession of James II he became the King's Privy Purse and intimate friend. He was appointed Master of the harthounds and buckhounds, and Deputy-Lieutenant of the castle and forest of Windsor in 1683, with the lease of a lodge in Bagshot Park. Evelyn visited Mrs. Grahme there, and described the house and park in his diary. Col. Grahme was at this time also one of the Members of Parliament for Carlisle, and the great silver-gilt mace he presented to the borough is still in the possession of the Corporation.

When James II fled to France in 1689, Col. Grahme was left in charge of his affairs in England, but although he was a faithful friend to the absent King, he was at first also in the good graces of William III. On the arrest of his brother, Viscount Preston, with treasonable papers, Col. Grahme also came under suspicion, and was arrested three times, during one of his imprisonments at the Fleet being visited by Evelyn.

When finally pardoned, Col. Grahme settled quietly at Levens, which he had purchased some years before, and speedily became one of the most popular men in the county. In 1717 he was elected Mayor of Appleby and in 1722 became Deputy-Lieutenant for Westmorland. He was especially noted for his lavish hospitality, and Bishop Ken was a frequent visitor to Levens, the room he occupied being known still as the Bishop's Room.

Col. Grahme was exceedingly generous in helping his many Jacobite friends, and when Monsieur Beaumont, the gardener of James II, who designed the grounds at Hampton Court, failed to get an appointment under the new King, he was taken into the Colonel's service and remained at Levens for many years, designing and supervising the laying out and planting of the topiary work and flower gardens which are the glory of Levens, and the finest of their kind now in existence. A small painting of Beaumont is preserved at Levens, and a book made in 1928 which has drawings of the innumerable designs for the clipped yews is also to be seen at the Hall. Among the designs are a crowned lion, many varieties of birds, a barrister's wig, pyramids, and summer-houses.

Col. Grahme was twice married, but left no male heir. His daughter Catherine married her first cousin, Henry Bowes Howard, fourth Earl of Berkshire, who succeeded in the right of his wife to the Levens estate, and for two hundred years Levens passed only in the female line, until the time of Sir Josceline Fitzroy Bagot, who succeeded in 1885, and whose grandson is the present owner. There is a tradition in the family that someone who had asked for refreshment at Levens Hall some 200 years ago and had been refused, cursed the lady of Levens of that time, saying that 'a male heir would never be born to Levens until the river Kent ran dry and a white stag should be born in the Park'. This curse was fulfilled until 1895, when the river Kent was frozen solid, and a light-coloured stag was born in the park, and on February 20th, 1896, Alan Desmond Bagot was born.

The Royal Commission on the Historical Monuments of Westmorland says that Levens is 'perhaps the most interesting 16th century house in the county'. The magnificent succession of rooms, with their richly-carved panelling, plaster-work, family portraits, contemporary furniture, and hangings of tapestry and stamped leather-work more than justify such a pronouncement. Even the servants' hall is panelled in sixteenth century woodwork, and has a handsome stone fireplace. The chimney piece of one room is supported by carved figures representing Samson and Hercules, with the Seasons, Elements and five Senses represented emblematically above, and an inscription cut into the oak:

> 'Thus the five Sences stand portrated here
> The elements four, and seasons of the year.
> Samson supports the one side as in rage;
> The other, Hercules, in like equipage.'

It is said that the carving in this room alone, at the pre-1914 standard of wages, would have cost £3,000, yet the effect is never ostentatious, but indicative of the most exquisite good taste allied to a love for beautiful things, making the perfect counterpart of the quaintly formal gardens with their long beech alleys and vistas, their bowling greens, bright flower-beds, and 'carved' yews.

The owners of Levens for centuries kept up the custom instituted by Col. Grahme of entertaining the Mayor and Corporation of Kendal on their return from Milnthorpe fair. As one account says, they used to 'eat reddishes and drink Morrocco till the sun went to bed', and toasted the owner, wishing him luck 'While Kent flowed'. The Morocco was an exceedingly strong ale, said to have been brewed only at Levens, and kept twenty-one years before use. The Morocco had to be drunk at one draught, and its potency sometimes had the most amusing effect on those who afterwards competed in the sports.

The novel *Helbeck of Bannisdale* was written by Mrs. Humphry Ward whilst staying at Levens, and 'Bannisdale' is apparently a combination of Sizergh and Levens, with a considerable amount of 'poetic licence'.

The countryside around has also furnished the setting for *The Lonely Plough*, *Crump Folk Going Home*, and *The Old Road from Spain*—three famous novels by Constance Holme.

IV

The picturesque sixteenth century mansion of Nether Levens, which belonged to the Preston family from 1452 to the end of the seventeenth century, lies about half a mile to the west of Levens Hall.

Southward from Levens the main road runs through the pleasant village of Heversham to Milnthorpe, a tranquil and delightful town which has seen many centuries of existence. In the immediate neighbourhood are Dallam Tower, entirely rebuilt by Daniel Wilson in 1720; Hazelslack Tower, built in the late fourteenth century and allowed to fall into ruin during the seventeenth century; Beetham and Arnside.

Beetham Hall is now a barn and the remains form an interesting example of a fourteenth century semi-fortified house. There is a famous natural beauty spot at Beetham, known as the Fairy Steps, where the limestone outcrop has taken the form of a narrow staircase decked with many ferns, and commanding a widespread view of the great estuary of the Kent, whose scenery backed by the peaks of Lakeland is as lovely as that of any of the lakes, when the tide is in. The defaced effigies of the last of the Beethams, who was knight of the shire for Westmorland in 1425, is in Beetham church, which is one of the oldest in the district.

There is a delightful walk from Beetham to Arnside, the last of the pele-towers on the Westmorland shore of Morecambe Bay. Although still regarded as a good example of the larger pele-towers of the district, its great attraction for the majority of tourists lies in its beautiful situation, whilst at Whitsuntide its appeal is completely overshadowed by the attractions of Arnside Woods, for when the lilac blooms it is a sign that the wild lilies-of-the-valley are waiting to be picked in their thousands.

NORTH: TOLSON HALL; BURNESIDE; SELSIDE; CUNSWICK AND SKELSMERGH; KENTMERE

I

Tolson Hall stands beside the main road between Kendal and Windermere, and is easily identified by the arch formed of the jaw bones of a whale which stands opposite the entrance to its drive. The Hall was built by Thomas Tolson, a tobacco merchant of Kendal, in 1630, and preserved in the house are some quarries of painted glass depicting pipes and plugs of tobacco. One bears the inscription: 'God by this meanes hath sent, what I on this house have spent T.T. 1638,' and the other the same inscription with the addition of the words: 'All prayses be unto His name that gave me meanes to build the same.' The inscriptions indicate the early origin of Kendal's still flourishing tobacco industry.

Between Tolson Hall and the village of Burneside, which lies off the main road, is Ellergreen, once the home of James Cropper, who was descended from old Viking stock, for his name is found in the *Landnama Bók* of Iceland. He founded a scholarship at Lady Margaret Hall, and gave other practical proofs of his interest in education for women. He died in 1900 and is buried at Burneside. The village is sheltered on the north by Potter Fell, and Burneside Hall stands apart on a tongue of land formed by the junction of the Kent and the Spring, but contrary to the general impression, does not derive its name from this fact. 'Burns', in the sense of rivers, are unknown in Lakeland, and the name is derived from the Norse 'Bronolf's Head'. The manor was for centuries known as Burneshead, and to this day, though so corrupted, is pronounced in three syllables. The Hall is an interesting example of a fourteenth century defensive dwelling, with a walled enclosure for cattle, and a gatehouse added in the late sixteenth or early seventeenth century.

The manor was originally in the possession of the de Burneshead family, the last of whom to reside there was Gilbert de Burneshead, who bought Lambrigg, a few miles to the north, about 1283, and whose daughter and heiress, Margaret, married Richard Bellingham of Tindale in Northumberland. The Bellinghams came to live at Burneshead in the reign of Edward II, and remained there until the time of Sir Robert Bellingham, about the middle of the sixteenth century. During that time Sir Henry Bellingham was attainted in the reign of Edward IV for having sided with the house of Lancaster, but his lands were apparently restored to the family later, as several of his desendants are styled 'of Burneside'. Sir Roger Bellingham, Knight Banneret, who died in 1533, is buried with his wife in the Bellingham Chapel of Kendal church, which he built. It was his son, Sir Robert, who sold Burneside, and his grandson Alan who bought Levens, whilst his granddaughter became the wife of Sir William Thornburgh of Selside.

After being bought and sold on three further occasions, Burneside came into the possession of Richard Braithwaite of Ambleside, whose son, Thomas Braithwaite of Burneside, became recorder of Kendal and father of Richard Braithwaite the poet. The family spelled their name in six different ways, and the poet himself used three different spellings. Richard was born in 1588 and wrote innumerable poems, essays and stories during his eighty-five years of life, but the only one really well known in the present day is *Drunken Barnabee's Itinerary*, a bi-lingual poem of which the Latin original is generally considered incomparably superior to the English version, although both are by Braithwaite. The poem was not especially popular when it first appeared, but has run through many editions since then, the last of which came out as recently as 1932 and included another of his bi-lingual poems, *Bessie Bell*. When the seventeenth edition appeared in 1818 Southey pronounced it to be the best example of rhymed Latin of the day.

Richard Braithwaite was a staunch Royalist, and one of his sons followed Charles II into exile. Another son, Sir Stafford Braithwaite, was killed in the ship *Mary*, commanded by Sir Roger Strickland, during a fight with Algerian pirates.

Richard Braithwaite, popularly known as 'Dapper Dick', became Deputy-Lieutenant of Westmorland and a justice of peace until his removal into Yorkshire at the time of his second marriage, when he sold the Burneside estate. It has passed through various hands since, and is now a farm.

Selside Hall, to which Thomasine Bellingham removed on her marriage to Sir William Thornburgh, stands not far from the main road between Kendal and Shap, and near the road to Long Sleddale, and is an interesting example of fourteenth century domestic architecture. A most fascinating and informative little booklet called *Manners and Customs of Westmorland, by a Literary Antiquarian*, which was published in 1827, gives extracts from Dame Thomasine's account book, dated 1579, and headed by her 'The holle yeare waigs of Dame Thomasyne Lady Thornburgh of all her servants at Selsatt'. It appears she kept up some state after the death of her husband, but at such small expense that present-date housewives contending with high wages must needs sigh with envy. The *total* wages of her nine men-servants for the year was £10 1*s*. 4*d*., and of her eight women servants £4 8*s*. 8*d*. The highest-paid man-servant received only £2 a year, and four of the women servants only received 8*s*. a year each! Even allowing for the greater value of money in those days, they seem very low wages. There is a small monument bearing coats of arms and a long inscription to her memory in the Bellingham Chapel of Kendal church, which says that she 'Hence went heavenlye joyes to joye expected'.

Cunswick Hall, which stands in the deep woods below Underbarrow and Cunswick Scar three miles north-west of Kendal, although rebuilt, still retains its fifteenth century gatehouse and other traces of the original building. It became the chief seat of the Leyburnes in the fourteenth century, but their fortunes declined after the execution of James Leyburne in the reign of Elizabeth for maintaining the Pope's supremacy. George Leyburne, a Roman Catholic Divine who became chaplain to Henrietta Maria, was a member of this family, which ended in John Leyburne, who forfeited his estates for his share in the Rebellion of 1715. John Leyburne is buried in Kendal church with an epitaph giving a long catalogue of his virtues and recording that with his death 'that Ancient, Loyall and Religious Family is now extinct'. Fifteenth century Skelsmergh Hall, which lies a mile or two out of Kendal on the Shap road, also belonged to the Leyburnes.

Four and a half miles from Kendal on the high road to Windermere is Staveley, which was a market town in the time of Edward III, and is now a pleasant, busy little manufacturing town of grey stone houses scattered across the mouth of the Vale of Kentmere and along the banks of the river Gowan. Hollin Hall, a fourteenth century pele-tower, stands in Nether Staveley, and the fourteenth century tower of the old Chapel of St. Margaret, with its fragments of ancient glass, medieval font, and seventeenth century weather vane, survives in Over Staveley. It was as the result of a meeting of the local estatemen at Staveley in 1610 that they maintained their ancient rights and independence as tenants, which James I had tried to close down on account of the abandonment of Border fighting after the union of Scotland and England.

II

The Kentmere Valley runs into the hills from Staveley, a double line of trees marking the winding course of the Kent through its rich meadows. Only two modern guide books recommend the Kentmere Valley, but it is difficult to understand such a lack of enthusiasm; the only possible explanation is that the writers did not go far beyond Staveley, or that they walked *down* the valley, which is a mistake not only in the case of Kentmere, but in every Lakeland valley, all of which increase in beauty as they penetrate farther into the mountains.

Kentmere gains its name from a small lake which was drained about a century ago. Both Baddeley and Ward

Lock's guides see fit to bewail the 'detriment to the scenery', but Otley, who actually knew the lake, speaks of it in his guide as bordered by a morass and not possessed of any striking features, so that it is difficult to see why its loss should be lamented so deeply. Otley mentions Skeggles water in the same sentence as equally uninteresting, and as this tarn can still be seen on the way to Long Sleddale, those who are interested can judge for themselves—it is significant that neither of the modern guides think Skeggles Water worth mentioning at all. There is now a diatomite factory in Kentmere, hidden by woods from any viewpoint but its immediate entrance; the marshes are replaced by lush pasturelands and masses of wild flowers; and the modern reservoir is in far more impressive surroundings, higher up the valley, so that no one need be deterred from visiting Kentmere for lack of beauty, whilst the interest of the village is an attraction in itself, as there are not only several seventeenth and eighteenth century houses grouped round the grey church with the conspicuous saddle-backed tower, but there is the picturesque old Kentmere Hall in which the illustrious family of the Gilpins lived for over two hundred years.

The Kentmere estate was conferred by the Baron of Kendal on Richard Gilpin, in the time of King John. Richard Gilpin distinguished himself as a soldier and as a private gentleman, and is traditionally believed to have killed a ferocious boar which infested the valley, an exploit from which the boar's head of the Gilpin crest is supposed to have been derived. The killing of the boar is described in the 'Boatman's Story' in *Minstrells of Winandermere*, by the Rev. Charles Farish, whose mother was a Gilpin.

The most famous of the family was Bernard Gilpin, whose many acts of kindness are remembered when the warlike exploits of other members of the family have been forgotten by all but a few. The boy born at Kentmere in 1517 is still revered in the neighbourhood as 'The Apostle of the North' and innumerable stories are told which illustrate his integrity and charity. He was appointed to the living of Houghton and remained there for about thirty years, until his death in 1583, refusing all offers of preferment, including the bishopric of Carlisle, because he felt he could do the most good in his own parish and district.

The living was worth about £400, but by his personal frugality he was able to spend lavishly in hospitality and good works. Every day the poor people who called at his door could have as much broth as they wanted, and on Thursdays a large quantity of meat was especially prepared for them. Twenty-four of the poorest were his constant pensioners, and were invited to a special dinner four times a year, at which they received a quantity of corn and a sum of money, and at Christmas an ox was divided among them. Whenever he heard of any distress he relieved it, and would frequently bring home poor people and send them away clothed and fed, whilst it was his greatest pleasure to make good the losses of poorer neighbours. His generosity was as great in distant parishes as in his own, for an old manuscript records that when he began a journey he would have ten pounds in his purse and at his return would have spent that and ten pounds more which he had borrowed—the sum for which he was in debt always being repaid within a fortnight of his return home. He journeyed all through the North in his efforts to supply the wants of parishes neglected by their own clergy, or on his visits to jails which few, if any, other clergymen of his time thought it necessary to visit. He became so greatly revered that on one occasion a thief who had stolen his horses, on hearing to whom they belonged, returned them and declared that he believed the devil would have seized him directly had he carried them off *knowing* them to be Mr. Gilpin's.

He kept open hospitality for man and beast in his own rectory, whether he was in residence or not, and it was said that if a horse was turned loose in any part of the country, it would inmediately make its way to the Rectory of Houghton. The famous Lord Burghley, who called unexpectedly, was treated with his retinue in such a manner that he would afterwards say 'He could hardly have expected more at Lambeth', and on leaving said: 'There is the enjoyment of life indeed!—who can blame that man for not accepting of a bishopric! What doth he want to make him greater, or happier, or more useful to mankind?'

In addition to all his other generous charities, which were always given with a tact which made them truly acceptable, he built and endowed a grammar school which was an immediate success. Whenever he met a poor boy upon the road, he would question him, and if he found him intelligent, would provide for his education, and if he showed any special capacity, would send him to the University and maintain him there, whilst he would assist the other scholars to obtain work suited to their powers and inclinations. He watched over the careers of those whom he maintained at the University, corresponding with them and visiting them, and many of them became 'great ornaments of the church and very exemplary instances of piety'. Three of the best known were Henry Ayray, afterwards Provost of Queen's College, Oxford; George Carleton, Bishop of Chichester; and Hugh Broughton, who became famous as a man of letters, but whose character was such that he even tried to supplant his benefactor in the rectory of Houghton: almost the only one of those whom Gilpin had helped who proved himself unworthy of his kindness.

During the reign of Queen Mary, Gilpin's staunch adherence to the principles of the Reformation caused him to suffer considerable persecution and eventually led to his arrest, in connexion with which the best-known of all the incidents of his career is told. On the journey to London he broke his leg, and his guards, knowing his settled belief that nothing happens to us but what is for our good, mocked him, but he still maintained that he made no question that the accident was a blessing in disguise—and so it proved, for before he was able to travel the Queen was dead, and he was set at liberty.

Bernard Gilpin was the nephew of Cuthbert Tunstall, Bishop of Durham, and was probably related to the then Bishop of Worcester, and another uncle fought gallantly at the Battle of Bosworth Field, where he was killed, in the cause of Richard III, whose popularity as Governor of the North and personal bravery, drew many of the people of the Lake Counties into his train. George Gilpin, the elder brother of Bernard, was one of Queen Elizabeth's trusted ministers, and became her Ambassador to Holland. It was during the time of George's great-grandson, Captain George Gilpin, that Kentmere was lost to the Gilpin family, for the Captain took an active part in the Civil War on behalf of Charles I and was eventually compelled to take refuge abroad. His wife Catherine was the daughter of Robert Philipson of Hollin Hall and cousin of Sir Christopher Philipson, and when George Gilpin went abroad, he attempted to safeguard his lands by conveying them to two trustees—the Royalist Philipson, and the Parliamentarian Capt. Nicholson of Hawkshead. When Capt. Gilpin died abroad, the Parliamentarian held the estate until the Restoration, when he was ousted by Sir Christopher Philipson.

Among the descendants of the Kentmere Gilpins were Sawrey Gilpin, born at Carlisle in 1733, who became one of the best painters of horses this country has produced, and was elected President of the Royal Society of Artists in 1773. His brother was the Rev. William Gilpin, an educational reformer in advance of his time, who practised his ideas for several years in a school at Cheam. He wrote a number of books, including the *Life of Bernard Gilpin*, and a *Tour in the mountains and lakes of Cumberland and Westmorland*. Sawrey Gilpin's son, William Sawrey, born in 1762, was a water-colour painter and landscape gardener, and became first president of the Old Water-colour Society founded in 1804. He laid out several gardens in Ireland and the south of England. His cousin, John Bernard Gilpin, son of the Rev. William Gilpin, married and settled in Massachusetts, and his descendants have taken part in public affairs on both the eastern and western shores of the United States, and one of them was the first territorial Governor of the great State of Colorado. Catherine Gilpin, the Cumbrian poetess, born at Scalesby Castle in 1738, was also a collateral descendant of Bernard Gilpin. She was a close friend of Susanna Blamire with whom she often collaborated.

Kentmere Hall in the present day is used as a farm-house, and the fourteenth century pele-tower is falling into ruin. The house was reconstructed during the reign of Edward VI when, it is said, the workmen were aided by Hugh Hird, a boy from Troutbeck noted for his strength and gigantic size. He lifted a beam, thirty feet in length and thirteen inches by twelve and a half in thickness, into its place in the Hall.

Chapter III

WESTMORLAND'S WINDERMERE

I

THE most direct way to Windermere from Kendal runs through Staveley and Ings. The parish church at Ings was rebuilt in 1743, by Richard Bateman, a native of the village, who left as a poor boy, and made a fortune in London by his industry. He traded with Leghorn in Italy, from whence he sent the marble for the floor of the church. His story is alluded to in Wordsworth's poem, *Michael*, but his tragic end is not told. On his return to England with a valuable cargo he was poisoned by the captain, who seized the ship and cargo for himself. The seventeenth century Ings Hall, also known as Hugill Hall, was the home of Collinson, the naturalist and antiquary.

All the way along this main road the great peaks of Lakeland are arrayed against the northern horizon, and the shades of Dorothy and William Wordsworth, who tramped the road on foot over a hundred years ago, accompany the traveller and share in the delight of that wide-spreading and entrancing view of the great lake of Windermere which bursts so suddenly upon the sight when the road climbs over the shoulder of Orrest Head.

Everyone who comes to Windermere should be brimful of memories of Professor John Wilson of Elleray—the 'Christopher North' of *Blackwood's Magazine*—yet few of the visitors ever give him a thought; even the guide books either ignore him or dismiss him in a few words, which is rank ingratitude, for of all the 'literary giants' who helped to make the Lakes famous, he is probably the only one who would not have bitterly resented the excursionists who now flock to Windermere and Bowness all through the season. He had a gift for friendship which won him the love of all sorts and conditions of people, and was himself equally at home with the highest and the lowest. Harriet Martineau, in her biographical sketch of him, says: 'Such a presence is rarely seen; and more than one person has said that he reminded them of the first man, Adam, so full was that large frame of vitality, force and sentience. . . . He swept away all hearts, whithersoever he would.'

Wilson was a Scotsman, son of John Wilson, a wealthy manufacturer, and his wife, Margaret Sym, the latter of whom was descended from the Marquis of Montrose and from whom Wilson probably inherited his splendid presence and forceful character. He was captivated by Windermere whilst on a visit and bought the cottage of Elleray in 1806, when he was only twenty-one, and settled there immediately upon leaving the University. Two years afterwards he began building a larger house, but it never held the same place in his affections as his rose-bowered cottage. It was to the cottage he brought his young wife 'whose grace and gentle goodness could have found no lovelier or fitter home than Elleray', and their life there from that bright May day in 1811 when the young couple took up their life together, to the day in 1837 when she died, was filled with love and laughter, rich friendships, boundless hospitality, and simple joys. After her death, because she had loved Elleray, and its trees, he would not allow a twig of them to be cut, until the place became overgrown and he eventually parted with it.

It was at Elleray that, according to Harriet Martineau, 'He could collect as strange a set of oddities about him there as ever Johnson or Fielding did in their City lodgings; and he could wander alone for a week along the trout streams, and by the mountain tarns of Westmorland . . . and shed an intellectual sunshine as radiant as that which glittered upon Windermere.' It was here that De Quincey, Southey, Wordsworth, and Dorothy, Charles Lloyd and his wife, the Smiths of Tent Lodge, Blind John Gough from Kendal, and Dawson of Sedberg, Hartley Coleridge, full of devotion, Bishop Watson with his son and daughter, the Hardens of Brathay Hall, Will Ritson of Wastdale, or wrestlers and dalesmen from distant dales and fells would come for a 'crack' with the Professor who loved sports and high thinking equally well and excelled at both.

Four years after his marriage he lost the whole of his fortune—estimated at £50,000—through the dishonesty of an uncle who was managing his estate, and so far from sinking under the misfortune, turned readily to work, took up a Professorship at Edinburgh and commenced his contributions to *Blackwood's*, on which his fame now rests, heaping coals of fire upon the uncle by giving him financial assistance. 'Christopher North's' *Noctes Ambrosianæ* is now the best known of his works, and well reflects the complex richness of his character, whilst the only slightly less famous *Recreations of Christopher North* was pronounced by Hallam, whom Harriet Martineau calls 'the calmest of critics', to have an eloquence comparable to the rushing of mighty waters, and to bring the breezes of the moorland even into the sick chamber.

De Quincey in his *Reminiscences of the Lake Poets* speaks of his admiration for Professor Wilson's sisters, one of whom married the English Envoy to the Court of Teheran, and 'had a romantic life; has twice traversed with no attendants but her servants, the gloomy regions of the Caucasus; and once with a young child by her side'. Professor Wilson's younger brother, James, was a well-known zoologist, and a niece, Henrietta Wilson, wrote several books popular in their day.

Professor Wilson let Elleray to Thomas Hamilton, author of *Men and Manners in America*, published in 1833, a book so popular that in ten years it was translated once into French and twice into German. The house Wilson built at Elleray was pulled down in 1869, and the cottage, too, has disappeared, but the name of Elleray is perpetuated in a school on the site, and Orrest Head is now in the care of the National Trust, so that every visitor may see the view in which the Professor delighted, ranging over the length of Windermere Lake, the fells of Lakeland, and the distant sparkle of the sea in Morecambe Bay. The Professor wrote of this view: 'There is not such another splendid prospect in all England. The lake has much of the character of a river, without losing its own. The islands are seen almost all lying together in a cluster—below which all is loveliness and beauty—above, all majesty and grandeur. Bold or gentle promontories break all the banks into frequent bays, seldom without a cottage or cottages embowered in trees; and, whilst the whole landscape is of a sylvan kind, parts of it are so laden with woods that you see only here and there a wreath of smoke but no houses, and could almost believe that you were gazing on primeval forests.' It is a description which, apart from the fact that there are now many more houses, is substantially correct to-day.

II

When Wilson came to Elleray there was no village by the name of Windermere, for the small cluster of houses still bore the ancient name of Birth-waite, derived from Birch-clearing, and it was not until the arrival of the railway in 1847 that it took the name of Windermere. Harriet Martineau, in her *Guide to Windermere*, especially mentioned that all the houses in the village were new, and for the most part in a medieval style of architecture, owing to the fact that the vicar had a passion for ecclesiastical architecture and his parishioners followed his example. Windermere still has that look of newness, but it is not the crude newness of bricks, but the fresh and attractive newness of grey stone against a charming background of trees and flowers. Even the mile of main road between Windermere and Bowness has rather the air of a private park or garden, particularly on the side from which the lake is occasionally glimpsed through the trees, and there are byways down to Bowness which seem as though they are in the depths of the country.

Otley's guide of 1834 mentions that there are 'two inns' at Bowness, and the fact that to-day there is such a number to choose from proves that Bowness is largely modern, yet it has a most enchanting air of picturesque age, due in

part to the extreme irregularity with which it has been built, which has produced a curious jumble of tortuous little streets, or more accurately, passages, grouped round the ancient church. The greater part of the present church dates from 1483, and the building holds some special interest for every visitor. The antiquary is fascinated by the magnificent east window, filled with stained glass brought from Cartmel Priory and dating from the fourteenth century, with the exception of one light, representing the Virgin and Child, which dates back to 1260. It is said that before this window was restored in 1873 it was repaired in places with glazed tissue-paper stained with water-colours! There is a case of sixteenth century chained books and other relics; a seventeenth century carving of St. Martin sharing his cloak with the beggar; and other unusual features. The less learned visitor finds amusement in the quaintly-spelled texts painted on the pillars of the nave, and in the exceedingly curiously expressed inscriptions on some of the monuments; whilst every American visitor is attracted by the panels in the east window which show the arms of the Washington family.

In the graveyard outside there is a memorial dated 1822 to Rasselas Belfield, an Abyssinian slave who had found freedom in England. Another grave stone, to Thomas Ullock who died in 1791, is inscribed

'Poor Tom came here to lie
From Battles of Dettingen and Fontenoy in 1743 and 1745.'

The Rectory, originally built in 1416, and partly rebuilt in the seventeenth century, was described in 1770 as the 'only respectable building in the place'.

William Pearson of Winster, a close friend of Wordsworth's, was married in the church, with Wordsworth's son John as the officiating minister. In 1843 the poet Robert Percival Graves was curate there.

It was at Bowness that that curious character 'Poet Close' used to set up his little bookstall every summer, scattering fulsome compliments over those who patronized his stall and shrieking abuse after those who resisted his blandishments. There are still people alive who remember his queer methods of salesmanship, but those to whom his name means anything at all are few and far between—which would not have pleased him, for he had the highest opinion of his own powers and regarded even the mildest criticism as the work of fools or knaves—and as his verses were sheer doggerel, he naturally aroused plenty of adverse criticism, although he also achieved an extraordinary fame and patronage in his time. Born in Swaledale in 1816, the son of a butcher, he began issuing his little paper tracts of verse when he was only fourteen years of age, and in 1846 established himself as a printer in Kirkby Stephen. In the *Dictionary of National Biography*, which devotes a column to his career, of which he would have approved the length—but not the matter—it says: 'He had not a spark of literary talent of any kind, but his assiduity in be-rhyming his friends and neighbours, and more especially the gentlefolk of the district, won him patrons who in April, 1860, obtained for him a civil list pension of £50.' Not unnaturally, when it became known, the grant was the subject of questions in the House of Commons, and *Punch* led the way in ridicule until the pension was withdrawn. He received a grant of £100 in compensation but never lost his sense of grievance.'

Whilst one cannot but sympathize with the painful disappointment to a poor man resultant upon the withdrawal of the pension, a perusal of his works lessens the sympathy. Every issue of his annual *Grand Christmas Book* is prefaced by abusive references to people who had failed to order his works (although he had no possible claim upon them), and compliments to those who had given him presents in money or in kind. As an example of his flattery his account of one young lady's appearance at a concert at Smardale may be quoted: 'Miss Mary Fletcher . . . is a young Lady of remarkable Beauty—such Beauty as in this cold clime of ours is very rare, and reminds one of those enchanting Beauties made famous by the Immortal Muse of Byron; like the Spanish Dark-eyed Ladies, her Eyes are lustrous, dazzling as diamonds; of melting softness, whose silken fringes are like the curtains which hide the Treasures of an Empire; an Air and figure of pleasing deportment; with all, most enchantingly lovely, and what is the best of all—quite unconscious of such charms as would warm the coldest heart of Stoic or Philosopher, and grace the most lofty rank or station.' If the young lady was unconscious of her charms, it was apparently no fault of Poet Close! Possibly this young lady deserved his encomiums, but as he showers similar compliments on other ladies, and is equally fulsome to his male patrons, it is unlikely they were all such paragons, whilst it is scarcely possible that so many of the local landowners (always excepting the Lonsdales who were his patrons), could be quite such monsters as he pictures them, merely because they failed to order his poems when he circularized them. Poet Close figures in the Bab Ballad *Ferdinando and Elvira*. He died at Kirkby Stephen in 1891. His publications are now sought after as curiosities. Although the letterpress is of no value, they have many quaint woodcuts, and interesting plates of houses in the Lake District, including Eden Hall, and Professor Wilson's cottage at Elleray, and others which have since disappeared.

III

Although the Westmorland shore of Windermere only extends from a point slightly south of Storrs Hall to the mouth of the Brathay river at the head of the lake, by a curious provision the *bed* of the lake belongs to Westmorland, and the Islands are therefore in that county, which also has jurisdiction over the Lakeside Station, which is built out from the Lancashire shore on piles. Early cartographers were misled by the position of Belle Isle into believing that there was a bend in the lake opposite Bowness Bay, and up to about the middle of the seventeenth century all maps of the district embody this error. The lake has long been celebrated for its fishing. Defoe says of the charfish of Windermere: 'It is a curious fish, and as a Dainty, is potted and sent far and near by way of present. It must needs be a great rarity, since the quantity they take, even here, is but small. Mr. Camden's Continuator calls it very happily the Golden Alpine Trout.' Defoe does not, however, mention the fact noted by later writers that at the approach of the spawning season the char and trout of

Windermere swim up stream together until they reach the confluence of the Brathay and the Rothay, when all the char go up the former river and the trout up the latter, a curious arrangement that has been noted over at least a century.

The Islands of Windermere have been described frequently, and their charms sung by Wordsworth in *The Prelude*. Several of them are especially rich in wild flowers, including the lily-of-the-valley. Lady Holme once had a hospital founded in 1256 by one of the de Lindesay family, and later a chantry dedicated to the Virgin Mary, which fell into ruin in the time of Henry VIII. It was still standing in Wordsworth's time, and was referred to by him in *The Prelude*, but has since completely disappeared. The De Lindesays, who were of Scottish extraction, were the first known owners of the largest Island, then called The Holme. Walter de Lindesay, who in his early days had been one of the ambassadors from the Scottish King to Henry III, was the first of this family there, and died in 1272. Since their time a succession of people have owned it, including the Philipsons of Calgarth, one of whom was the hero of the exploit in Kendal church—if it ever took place—who composed the curious epitaph for his own tomb in Bowness church.

The present house on the island was built some time before 1770 by a Mr. English, and about the end of the same century it was re-named 'Bel Isle', an abbreviation of the name of Isabel Curwen, heiress of Workington Hall, who bought the island for £14,000 prior to her marriage with her cousin John Christian of Unerigg, who in 1790 took the name of Curwen in addition to his own. Bel Isle, or Curwen's Isle, has remained the property of the Curwen family ever since.

Some modern guides perpetuate the old idea that the Curwens were directly descended from Ivo de Taillebois, but John Hodgson Hinde, in his Introduction to the Pipe Rolls of Cumberland and Westmorland, showed that the monks of St. Mary's Abbey at York had falsified some early notes of benefactions into a statement that Ivo was the ancestor of the family. They were, however, a family of very ancient and distinguished descent. The Island is usually called 'Belle Isle' in the present day, and is the only one of the Windermere Islands which is not open to the public.

Rampholm, south of the ferry, was called Rogerholm in the thirteenth century, and formed part of the estate of William de Lancaster. His daughter granted the Abbot of Furness right to use two boats on the lake, one for carrying goods and the other for fishing. Its present name is derived from the garlic or 'ramp' growing there, and it is part of the Levens Hall estate. The grant to the Abbot of Furness may have been the origin of the present day ferry, which was certainly in existence in the seventeenth century, as Richard Braithwaite of Burneside composed a poem on the great accident which took place in October, 1635, when forty-seven people were drowned. There is a copy of the poem in the Bodleian Library at Oxford.

IV

Storrs Hall, now an hotel, attained its greatest distinction in 1825, when Sir Walter Scott, Canning, and Lockhart were staying at the Hall as guests of the Boltons. A dinner party was given in their honour at which Wordsworth and Professor Wilson were present. Neither Scott nor Lockhart appears to have enjoyed himself very much, as both have left on record rather unkind criticisms of Wordsworth and Canning, the Home Secretary—the late Canon Rawnsley has suggested they had not got over the effects of their voyage from Ireland. Certain it is that the next day, the 22nd August, when a Regatta was held in Scott's honour, appeared to meet with their full approval, although attended by the same guests. The Regatta was arranged by Professor Wilson, and his wife in a 'grand turban and flying streamers', presided over the Elleray boat containing their relatives. The Regatta was the greatest success from everyone's point of view, the weather being beautifully calm and sunny. The last owner of Storrs Hall before it was turned into an hotel was the Rev. Thomas Staniforth, who rowed stroke for Oxford in the first Oxford and Cambridge boat race in 1829, when both crews wore top-hats, and Oxford 'won easily'.

Another famous man who wrote enthusiastically of the beauty of Windermere was Benjamin Disraeli, who stayed with the Earl and Countess of Bradford at their Lakeland home, St. Catherine's, Windermere, in August, 1874.

On Scott's earlier visit to Windermere, in 1805, he had stayed at Calgarth as the guest of Bishop Watson of Llandaff, of whom De Quincey wrote that he was a 'joyous jovial and cordial host', but at the time of Scott's second visit the Bishop was dead, and the poet visited his grave in Bowness church. The Bishop was the son of a Master of Heversham Grammar School, and his aptitude for mathematics secured him an entry at Cambridge, where he was appointed to the Chair of Chemistry and later given a professorship of Divinity, and after several further preferments was appointed to the See of Llandaff. According to the account of A. G. Bradley in *Highways and Byways in the Lake District* the Bishop was a most unconscionable shirker of all his duties and only visited his See once in the thirty years he was Bishop of the diocese, preferring to spend all his time enjoying life at Calgarth. Other accounts give a better report of him, for he was indefatigable in writing pamphlets on various subjects which gained him at various times the Fellowship of the Royal Society, a premium from the Society of Arts, and a gold medal from the Board of Agriculture. His *Apology for the Bible* published in 1796 in answer to some of the works of Thomas Paine, was eagerly read in this country and America, and was also translated into French, and it was presumably as a result of this work that he was offered and accepted Membership of the Massachusetts Historical Society in 1807. There is no gainsaying the fact that he spent the greater part of his time at Calgarth, where he planted the now glorious woods, but he usually visited his diocese triennially, which if not particularly zealous, was at least better than once in thirty years!

Calgarth Hall has a fourteenth or fifteenth century doorway surviving from an earlier building, the remainder of the house being of sixteenth or seventeenth century work.

It belonged to the Philipson family down to the early part of the eighteenth century and is remarkable for its plaster decorations. There is a tradition that Myles Philipson coveted some land belonging to Dorothy and Kraster Cook, and by bearing false witness against them secured it for himself, but Dorothy stood up in the Court House and cursed him, telling him to beware, for that small piece of ground should be the dearest he ever bought. While Calgarth walls should stand she and her husband would haunt it night and day, and time would be when no Philipson should own an acre. The Philipsons have long gone, and the tradition persisted of two skulls which returned to the hall in spite of every effort to get rid of them by throwing them into the lake or burning, but all such memories have been banished in these days, for by the generosity of voluntary subscribers, the old Hall has been turned into a Children's Hospital, and everyone knows that true charity can overcome the most ancient evil.

Rayrigg Hall, which lies about half-way between Calgarth and Windermere, bears the date 1702, in which year it was probably built. It formerly belonged to the Flemings of Rayrigg. At the end of the eighteenth century William Wilberforce spent several years there, and wrote in 1788, during the last year of his residence: 'I never enjoyed the country more than during this visit, when, in the early morning, I used to row out alone and find an oratory under one of the woody islands in the middle of the lake.'

The grassy hill, crowned by a flagstaff, which lies between Rayrigg and Bowness has been known as 'Queen Adelaide's Hill' since the Queen—the only English sovereign who has ever visited the Lakes—admired the delightful view from its summit.

During a few weeks in the summer Bowness is as crowded as the most gregarious could wish; as many as 6,000 excursionists flock in by railway from Windermere Station, or by steamer from Lakeside, in one day, and the camp-chair man at Bowness Bay does such a brisk trade that the chairs are set out in many rows, practically touching each other, whilst the boatmen and the steamers reap a welcome harvest and add to the bustle. Those who have a horror of such wholesale enjoyment will do well to avoid Bowness Bay in summer. For them the ideal time to see the very real beauty of the bay is during spring or early summer, with all its exquisite accompaniment of myriads of wild flowers and the varied green of trees bursting into leaf; or in autumn, when the woods which cover the shores and the islands so thickly are a brilliant frame of red and gold for the shining steel-colour of the water. Even a rainy day of late autumn has a magic of its own, when the grey haze gives an illusion that the hills on the farther shore are merely a group of islands in an illimitable sea.

Those who are compelled to take their holidays during the height of the season should not be deterred from seeing Bowness, however great their dislike for crowds, for it can be seen at its best by a visit in the morning before the arrival of the first excursionists, when the heat mists are still rising, and the whole lake is as nebulous and delicate in its enchantment as any dream; or after the excursionists have gone, when twilight enfolds the lake, lights twinkle out on the shores, and the moon begins to rise above the fells.

Chapter IV

TWO ROADS FROM WINDERMERE

I

ALTHOUGH Windermere and Bowness can count on their thousands of visitors every summer, there are places within two or three miles whose beauty has unaccountably been overlooked by all but a few visitors, and of these not the least lovely is the Winster Vale, reached by a road which gives a splendid backward panorama of the great lake of Windermere and its surrounding mountains, and an enchanting view forward across Cartmel Fells to the shimmer of the sea in Morecambe Bay, before dropping down from the summit of Winster Hill into the secluded vale with its air of inviolable peace.

Nowhere in Lakeland to-day can the spirit of Wordsworth's times be recaptured more successfully than at Winster, which has quietly acquiesced in its neglect by tourists, and placidly continues to cultivate its rich fields and wide-spreading orchards of damson and apple trees. It is all the more delightful that time has apparently stood still in Winster Vale when it is remembered that William Pearson the naturalist and poet who was a valued friend of Wordsworth's, was born in 1780 at the Yews, Crosthwaite, lived in Borderside, the house he built on the lane from Winster to Bowland Bridge. William Pearson's father was a studious farmer, and his mother told the boy many tales of fairies and folk-lore as she sat at her spinning wheel. After a short time at school in the neighbouring village of Crosthwaite, and later at Underbarrow, he became a teacher at the little school in his native village, but soon left to become a grocer's assistant at Kendal, where in his stay of only a year he made the acquaintance of Gough, the blind botanist, and did a prodigious amount of study. A short spell in London, followed by seventeen years as a bank-clerk at Manchester, and the homesick Pearson returned to Winster finally in 1820, and two years later bought the Borderside estate near Crosthwaite—a seventeenth century house now in disrepair. He farmed and wrote his poems, and pursued his studies in Natural History, contributing many interesting papers to the Kendal Natural History Society, and came into closer contact with Wordsworth, whose works had given him his chief pleasure in the frugal years at Manchester. Many glimpses of his intimacy with the Wordsworths are given in Dorothy Wordsworth's letters and journals, and in after years Pearson wrote more than once in defence of the poet's memory. Hartley Coleridge was also a friend of Pearson's and wrote a sonnet to him when he married. The Pearsons lived at Low House in Crosthwaite after their marriage until Pearson built a house in the village, which was described in a poem by Percival Graves in 1862 and in one of Pearson's letters to Wordsworth.

Pearson was a keen fisherman and wrote an interesting paper on Walton and Cotton's *The Compleat Angler*.

Among the most valuable of his papers are his notes on changes in the Lake district, and *Sketches of existing and recent Superstitions of Westmorland*, in which among many other observations he tells that Winster dalesfolk lit Beltane, or Need fires as late as 1840, and that he actually saw them drive their cattle through the smoke as a cure for a then prevalent cattle-disease. His poetry had all the charm of a deep understanding of, and love for, nature, and especially of the scenery of his native valley. One of his first poems, published in the *Lonsdale Magazine* in July, 1821, was inspired by the river Winster:

'Though small thy stream, and all unknown to fame,
To me more dear than those of prouder name—

. . . .

I indeed
Must praise thee gentle river for the meed
Of many gifts; but chiefly for the sense
Of rural pleasures, and the influence
Of natural beauty on the mind and heart.'

Nearly all the little white-washed, slate-roofed cottages of Winster and the scattered farms which make such an attractive picture against the background of orchards, and the rich green of the pasturelands and wooded hills, date back to the seventeenth and eighteenth centuries, and the church, although rebuilt in 1875, has a seventeenth century table and bell, and a medieval font. It was in one of Winster's old houses that Jonas Barber made his famous clocks nearly three hundred years ago, and was succeeded in the work by 'Philipson of Winster'.

Southward from Winster village, the river marks the boundary between Westmorland and Lancashire, and all east of the river is in the former county, and all west is in Lancashire. On the Westmorland side are Crosthwaite —not to be confused with Crosthwaite in Cumberland— Crook, and the mansions of Cowmire Hall, Poolbank, Flodder Hall, Nether Hall, and Witherslack, whilst over in Lancashire is the interesting chapel of Cartmell Fell and beautiful Gummer's How. Crosthwaite lies in the delightful valley of the river Gilpin. The ancient church of

Crosthwaite and Lyth was rebuilt in the nineteenth century but retains a sixteenth century cup and cover paten and the octagonal bowl of a fifteenth or early sixteenth century font in the churchyard. There are also some attractive old houses and amusing memories of John Audland and Jamie Muckelt, rustic rhymsters who were the life and soul of gatherings at the local inn and be-rhymed every incident. Among the rhymes still remembered is the one which resulted from a quarrel between Audland and an Ulverston lawyer:

> God Meäd men, and men meäd money;
> God Meäd bees, and bees meäd honey.
> Bit the Divil himself meäd lawyers and 'tornies,
> And pleäced them i' U'ston and Dalton i' Forness.

Eastward of Crosthwaite is the attractive village of Crook. Sir Daniel le Fleming, in his description of the County of Westmorland in 1671, speaks of 'Crooke Hall, heretofore called Twatterden Hall (which) has for several descents belonged to the Philipsons, and is now possessed by Chr. Philipson, Esq.'. The hall was rebuilt about the beginning of the eighteenth century, and only the seventeenth century tower of the old church is left, the rest having been pulled down when the new church was built about a quarter of a mile away. A fourteenth century bell with an inscription and a crowned shield of old France quartering England was transferred to the new church. Crook is at the head of a wide valley sheltered on the east by the limestone height of Underbarrow, and Scout Scar, and beautified by damson orchards and woods in which the wild lily of the valley grows in profusion.

South of Crosthwaite and Winster lies a group of fine old manor-houses. The seventeenth century mansion of Cowmire Hall was probably built by Richard Fleming, and incorporates a sixteenth century pele-tower built by the Briggs family who were the original owners. South House, Pool Bank is a picturesque seventeenth century house; Flodder Hall, although largely rebuilt in the seventeenth century, incorporates part of an earlier building on the site, and Nether Hall was probably built early in the sixteenth century.

Witherslack Hall has twice been forfeited by its owners, once by the Harringtons after the battle of Bosworth field, and within two or three years by its new owner, Sir Thomas Broughton of Broughton Tower, who had taken part in Lambert Simnel's rebellion. It is said that after the failure of the rebellion Sir Thomas lived for many years concealed in a cave in Witherslack woods. Faithful tenants carried food and other necessities to him, and after his death, buried him in the woods, where the site of his grave was known up to 200 years ago, but is now entirely lost. The confiscated Hall and lands were granted to the first Earl of Derby, and it is still a seat of that family, although Sir Daniel Fleming mentions the Hall as the seat of Thomas Leyburn, who had derived the manor from the Earls of Derby.

Witherslack church was originally founded as a chapel of Beetham in 1664, by a provision in the will of John Barwick, a native of Witherslack who became Dean of St. Paul's. Although much altered in the eighteenth century, it is of great interest, and has the original glass; a monument to the founder; and hatchments of the Dean and his brother Peter. These two boys were selected from the family of five sons to be 'bred scholars', and both justified the choice. John entered the church and Peter the medical profession, and both threw themselves heart and soul into the Royalist cause. John was eventually arrested and committed to the Tower at a time when his state of health was so poor that he was not expected to live. He resisted all threats of torture and offers of rewards to betray the Royalist cause and remained in prison for over two years, winning the hearts of all the officials by his charm of manner and Christian fortitude. On his release he continued working for the Royalist cause, and when appointed Royal chaplain was unselfishly urgent in the interests of his friends whilst declining preferment for himself. His great services to the cause led to offers of the Bishoprics of Mann and of Carlisle, both of which he refused, but he eventually accepted the Deanery of Durham and later that of St. Paul's.

Peter Barwick, who married a kinswoman of Archbishop Laud, had an equally distinguished career. He became Physician in Ordinary to Charles II and was one of the most enlightened doctors of the period. His treatise in support of Harvey's discovery of the circulation of the blood is said to be the best written in his day, and he was one of the few physicians who stuck to his post during the plague in London. Dr. Hodges particularly mentions his great services, and his energy in persuading those of the clergy who were inclined to desert to remain and bring comfort to the sick and dying.

The whole of the district which lies east of the Winster is rich in seventeenth and eighteenth century cottages and farmhouses, for which the natural scenery of hills and river valleys, orchards, woods and innumerable little tarns, makes a captivating setting.

II

The challenge of the road which climbs so steeply over the Kirkstone pass on its way to Ullswater is invariably accepted by every visitor to Windermere and Bowness, for there is rich reward for any effort involved, in the magnificent and ever-changing panorama of mountains and lakes, the intimate fascination of Troutbeck in its deep valley, and the triumph of achieving the summit of the pass and the inn which was until comparatively recently claimed to be the 'highest in England', from whence there is the steep rough road down into Ambleside, and the road hemmed in by bleak mountains which leads to the final beauty of Brotherswater and Ullswater.

Cumberland also has a Troutbeck, but it is undeniably less attractive than Westmorland's Troutbeck, which has been acclaimed by every writer, and has been an acknowledged beauty spot since the days when Professor Wilson wrote so enthusiastically of its enchantingly lovely situation. Troutbeck has been known by that name since the thirteenth century at least, and Miss Martineau in her guide to Windermere painted a thrilling picture of the Britons of the district taking refuge there from the Romans whilst the invaders were making their great road from Kendal, and of 'the soldiers with their armour and weapons gleaming in the sun, while the trembling natives cowered in the forest below'. The route of the Roman road to Ambleside has been traced in recent years by Mr. S. O'Dwyer. There are traces of prehistoric stone circles, cairns, and foundations of buildings in Troutbeck Park; and a three-hundred-year-old bridge over the Trout Beck, about three-quarters of a mile north of the Park, lies on the ancient trackway.

Many tales are told of the Troutbeck Giant, although his name is given variously as Hugh Hird and Hugh Gilpin. The majority of writers say he lived in the time of Edward VI, but the late Canon Rawnsley gives it as the reign of Henry IV. His nickname of the 'Cork Lad of Kentmere', given because of his feat at the building of Kentmere Hall, would fit either date, as the Hall was built in the earlier reign and enlarged in the later one.

The Cork Lad was said to be the son of a monk at Furness, and in the course of begging and wandering he and his mother came to Troutbeck valley, and made their home in a house belonging to the Crown. When Hugh was twenty the King conferred the house and land on one of his retainers, but the young giant strenuously prevented his taking possession, as a result of which Hugh was summoned to London. All accounts agree that he walked the whole way, meeting with many strange adventures, and on arrival, joined in the wrestling matches which were then in progress. He attracted the King's notice by his astonishing prowess, and on being asked who and what he was, he said he did not know his own name, but that folk 'commonly called him the Cork Lad of Kentmere'. He further told the King that he took for food 'Thick poddish (porridge) an' milk that a mouse might walk on dry-shod, to my breakfast; an' the sunny side of a wedder (a whole sheep) to my dinner, when I can get it'. The King took the hint and ordered a whole sheep to be roasted, and the young giant ate it there and then! Asked what he would like as reward for gaining the wrestling championship, he asked for the house in which he lived at Troutbeck, the land adjacent to get peat off, and wood from Troutbeck Park for fire, which was granted him. He remained in

LANGDALE VALLEY

possession for the next twenty-two years but then injured himself in attempting to pull up a tree by the roots. As he left no children nor will, the estate reverted to the Crown. It was granted by Charles I to Hudleston Philipson of Calgarth.

The medieval chapel of Troutbeck was rebuilt in the sixteenth century and enlarged in 1736, when the west tower was rebuilt. Among the fittings are two collecting shovels inscribed 'Remember the poor. 1692. W.B., I.E.', and the East window is the work of Burne-Jones.

Town End, a delightfully picturesque house with yew trees standing sentinel each side of the gateway, was built in the seventeenth century. The famous Mortal Man Inn incorporates the remains of a seventeenth century building. It gained its name from a sign painted by Julius Cæsar Ibbotson, about 1800, depicting a lean man one side and a fat man the other—portraits of natives of Troutbeck—and the rhyme

> 'O mortal Man, that liv'st on bread
> How comes thy nose to be so red?
> Thou silly ass that looks so pale
> It is by drinking Sarah Birkett's ale.'

The sign lives on in memory, although it disappeared over a hundred years ago; Black's guide, published in 1841, in mentioning the sign says 'which a few years ago decorated the sign board'. Troutbeck men love their little joke—they have made the fact that the parish is divided into three hundreds the basis for a joke that 'Troutbeck had three hundred bridges, three hundred constables and three hundred bulls'.

Troutbeck has yet another claim to fame as the home of Thomas Hogarth, frequently referred to as the father of William Hogarth the famous painter, but in actual fact his uncle. 'Auld Hoggart of Troutbeck' was a poet whose works were as satirical and cynical as the art of his nephew. Adam Walker, who was born in Troutbeck in 1727—about seventeen years after 'Auld Hoggart' died, acted as a child in an open-air play called *The Destruction of Troy*, which was given at Bowness in memory of Thomas Hogarth, and later wrote an article on the old poet which attracted Dr. Craig Gibson to collect and publish specimens of Hogarth's rhymes. Dr. Gibson also interviewed Mr. Birkett of Town End, Troutbeck, then in his eighty-seventh year, who told him that Auld Hoggart was as noted for his rollicking good fellowship as for his habit of rhyming, play-writing and producing dramatic entertainments. Many of his plays would not pass the censor in the present day, but he also had an extensive acquaintance with the classics which he turned into homely rhymes. One of his songs is headed 'The Play Song made for the Play "The Lascivious Quean" as it was acted on St. James' Day, 1693, upon a scaffold at the Moss Gap in Troutbeck'. All the plays appear to have been acted at Moss Gap. A number of the verses were included by the late Canon Rawnsley in his book *Round the Lake Country*, and show a surprising command of language and feeling for rhythm, whilst the subject matter reflects most interestingly the old poet's insight into the lives and characters of his neighbours, particularly in his 'epitaphs'.

III

The road over the Kirkstone Pass was one of the very few in the district in existence when Clarke drew his maps in 1785, but it must have been little more than a cart-track, for two years later William Gilpin speaks of it as a 'tolerable road; but I mean only for horses. It has not the quartering and commodious width of a carriage road'; and it was not until the nineteenth century that there is any mention of the Kirkstone Inn, a guide of 1841 speaking of it as 'lately erected'. On the strength of a pronouncement of the Ordnance Surveyors the Inn displayed a board over the porch announcing that it was the 'Highest Inhabited House in England', and was so known for many years, but it has long lost its priority and is now about fifth on the list of inns.

The rock whose church-like shape gives the Kirkstone Pass its name lies on the Patterdale side of the summit, where the road runs through scenery in complete contrast with the wooded Troutbeck Valley. Although there are glens in the Highlands of Scotland and of Donegal more desolate, the bleak hills on either side, particularly in a mist or at dusk on a wet day, can give a very vivid impression of utter solitude, and even in the summer with the many cars, buses, chars-a-bancs and pedestrians struggling up or down the steep road these screes and rocky peaks seem withdrawn and remote until Brotherswater is sighted with its flowery meadows and woodlands.

In the meadows south of Brotherswater is Sykeside Farm, the home for forty years of 'Old Charlie Dixon', who died there in 1936 at the age of eighty-three. Although he never left the Lake District, he was world-famous, for he was the original of some of the most famous photographs ever taken—'The Shepherd and the Lost Sheep', 'A Westmorland Shepherd', 'When He hath found it'; and other camera studies which have penetrated to all parts of the world. He was born at Ambleside, and when reminiscing, once said with a twinkle: 'Ay, me and —— at Ambleside were 'tonly yans in oor class that t'maister could mak' nowt on.' Among those who called upon Charlie, and his sister Grace who kept house for him, was Mr. John Finley, the then Minister of Education in New York State; Sir Herbert Barker; and Mr. Kellaway, the former Postmaster-General. Dixon's Obituary in the *Cumberland Herald* tells that in speaking of Mr. Kellaway's visit, Grace Dixon said: 'I've fergettin' his name, but he was summat in t' Post Office. He was a nice homely man, and he handed acid drops around.'

About a quarter of a mile to the west of Sykeside is Hartsop Hall, at the mouth of the Dovedale Valley. The Hall dates from the sixteenth century, and was extended in the following century, when it was held by the de Lancasters. It passed to the Sir John Lowther who afterwards became the first Lord Lonsdale, about the end of the seventeenth century. An extension on the south in the eighteenth century was built over a bridle path which ran close to that side of the hall, with the result that a public right of way through that part of the house was created. It is said that during the nineteenth century one of the local dalesmen used to make a special journey annually in order to maintain this right.

Beyond Brotherswater, on the east of the main road as it crosses Pasture Beck, is the village of Low Hartsop, which has an unusually large proportion of seventeenth century houses, including Low House and Thorn House, both of which have their original open spinning galleries. There is also a building of very unusual design, said to have been a drying kiln for grain, which probably dates from the sixteenth century; and the ruins of an old watermill. Footpaths climb the fells beyond the village to run across the lonely heights to Hayes Water, High Street, Mardale, north to Martindale Common and Bampton Common, and south to Kentmere, Troutbeck and a network of tracks over the Shap Fells, which are neglected by all but the knowledgeable, and are a refuge for the seeker after solitude in the tourist season.

As the road runs through the valley watered by the Goldrill Beck, the scenery grows more friendly, with woodlands and meadows, a fleeting backward glimpse up the Deepdale valley as the Deepdale Beck is crossed, and a scattered group of cottages and farms announcing the approach to Patterdale, which in spite of its church dedicated to St. Patrick and its St. Patrick's Well, was almost certainly never visited by the Irish Saint, but derived its name from a former owner. The church is modern, rebuilt on the site of an Elizabethan foundation and preserving a seventeenth century Bible and plate from the earlier church, and also a font which grows younger as it grows upward, from a fourteenth century base, as it has a thirteenth century stem, and an eighteenth century bowl with a modern upper part. When Gilpin visited Patterdale the clergyman, Mattison by name, had just died, at the age of ninety. Mattison had been minister of Patterdale for sixty years, and during the early part of his life his benefice brought him in only £12 a year, afterwards increased to £18, which it never exceeded. On this income he married, brought up four children, educated a son at college, lived comfortably, and left upwards of £1,000 at his death—a tale to rival that of the more celebrated 'Wonderful

Walker' of Seathwaite whose stipend although only £5 to begin with, rose to £50, which would doubtless have seemed riches to his Patterdale counterpart. Gilpin, needless to say, seized upon this anecdote as an opportunity for several pages of moralizing on the responsibility of travellers 'whose casual intercourse with this innocent and simple people tends to corrupt them'.

Patterdale Hall, which lies about a quarter of a mile from the church, dates from the seventeenth century, but has extensive modern alterations, but there is a doorway in the south-west range bearing the initials and date I and D.M., 1677, evoking memories of the days when it was known as the 'Palace' of Patterdale, the home of the Mounseys, acknowledged kings of Patterdale from the day when their ancestor had led the dalesmen in defence of their homes against Scottish raiders. The traditional site of the encounter was a ledge on Stybarrow Crag. Gilpin duly records seeing the 'king' of that day and reports 'I could not help thinking that if I were inclined to envy the situation of any potentate in Europe, it would be that of the King of Patterdale'. The 'dynasty' lasted until 1824, when the Marshall family came to the Hall.

Both Patterdale Hall and Patterdale churchyard are filled with memories of the love story of William Henry Smith, the poet and mystic, and Lucy Cumming, the poetess, who spent the summer of 1858 wandering together in the neighbouring valleys. The story of this happy wooing and the happy married life that followed has been charmingly told by Lucy Smith in *The Story of William and Lucy Smith*.

The old inn at Patterdale saw all the famous company of the Lake Poets at one time or another, and it was from there that Scott, Wordsworth and Sir Humphry Davy climbed up to the Red Tarn in 1803 to see the place where Gough's body was watched over for three long months by his faithful dog—a story known far and wide as a result of the poems the two poets wrote after their visit to the site.

Patterdale is an altogether enchanting place—delightful in itself and delightful as a centre for a group of lovely valleys and fells which are never overrun, even in the height of the season. The track up Grisedale to Helvellyn with its incomparable views, or the track by Grisedale Tarn and the shoulder of Dollywaggon Pike to Grasmere are, of course, popular with good walkers, but there are others less frequented, each with its own appeal, whilst the head of Ullswater with its grand array of mountains, its flowery meadows, its glory of daffodils in spring, and in early summer its masses of yellow iris fringing the lake and its great bushes starred with dog-roses, has a beauty beyond words.

Glenridding, where the steamer pier juts into the lake, is now practically a continuation of Patterdale. The echoes hereabouts are said to be the finest in the Lake District, although cannon are no longer fired at the pleasure of each visitor, as they appear to have been when Gilpin stayed there. He records that the sound of a cannon is distinctly reverberated six or seven times, and that the Duke of Portland, who had property in the neighbourhood, had a vessel on the lake with brass guns for the 'purpose of exciting echoes'.

Broadbrow, the seventeenth century cottage which Wordsworth acquired with the help of Lord Lonsdale, although the poet never lived there, can be seen on Place Fell, across the lake from Stybarrow Crag.

Like all the Lakeland villagers, the men of Patterdale were addicted to cockfighting, and there is an oval depression by the side of the Glenridding beck, nearly a mile north-east of the church, which tradition points out as the local cockpit. Goat-hunting was another favourite sport, and productive of more excitement than one would imagine. Clarke describes various efforts made to catch these goats, which were so extremely wild and difficult to take that a butcher who bought four at the price of two guineas, spent 'thirty shillings for catching them, and the takers even then had reason to complain of their bargain'. On another occasion Mr. Mounsey having given Clarke a goat on condition that he caught it for himself, he set out with eleven companions provided with guns, hounds, and other dogs in quest of it—and although they saw twenty, the only result was that one of the dogs was killed by a goat it attacked! The next day 'being so fatigued myself that I was unable to attend', Clarke sent ten men armed and provided as before, but they only succeeded in bringing home a kid, taken with the greatest difficulty.

In the present day Patterdale has an annual Sports Day of sheep-dog trials and athletic events in friendly rivalry with the Sports Day at Pooley Bridge, but the chief sport of the district is fox-hunting. The Ullswater pack was the outcome of an amalgamation of the Bald How, Matterdale, pack and the Patterdale pack, in 1873, and an article which appeared in *The Field* in March, 1878, gave the interesting information that although the Patterdale hounds had been in existence longest and dated back to a very remote period, each of the packs partook largely 'of the blood of the renowned John Peel's hounds'. The Blencathra Pack also claims to represent the John Peel pack, and to hunt the fells in the true 'John Peel' style of following the hounds on foot. Most of the Lake District hunting is done on foot owing to the nature of the ground covered, so that a day's run is far more strenuous than any known to those who hunt on horseback, although it has its compensation for enthusiasts in the added sense of personal endeavour and triumph for those in at the death.

The Ullswater pack also rejoiced in a huntsman who had achieved a fame among fox-hunters only second to that of John Peel, and is said to have been responsible for the death of even more foxes than his famous predecessor. Joe Bowman retired in 1922, having been officially elected Huntsman to the pack forty years before, and his Reminiscences have since been written up by Mr. W. C. Skelton in a book which also includes the songs popular with the Ullswater Hunt, not the least of which is 'Joe Bowman', written by Dr. Walker of Southport.

The Ullswater hounds are so noted that they have been sent to places as far distant as India and Chile for breeding purposes. The district hunted by the pack includes the deer forests of Martindale and Gowbarrow, and the hounds have been carefully trained to ignore the deer trails.

In the olden days every tenant in the district was bound to render the service known as 'boon day', once a year, when the bailiff called upon them to stand with their dogs during the lord's hunt, to prevent the deer escaping to the mountains. Each tenant received his dinner and a quart of ale, and it was also a custom that the first person who seized the hunted deer should have its head for the trouble.

Beyond Glenridding the Glencoin Woods, now in the care of the National Trust, cover the hillside and reach down to the shore of the lake, stretching nearly the whole way to the county boundary at Glencoin Dale, where the Glencoin river flows into Ullswater beyond House Holme. The boundary between the two counties runs down the middle of the lake to Pooley Bridge, where it follows the course of the River Eamont, all the eastern shore of Ullswater being in Westmorland, and the western shore, beyond Glencoin, in Cumberland.

The grand Westmorland fells rise so steeply along the eastern shore of Ullswater that there are few places where it is possible to land, and the only road in the whole of this wild and lonely region is that from Pooley Bridge to Martindale. This road runs through the tiny hamlet of Howtown, where there is a steamer pier, and at Martindale branches into three 'dead ends', one of which runs to the head of Bannerdale, the second to the head of Boardale, and the third to the hamlet of Sandwich, at the mouth of Scale How Beck.

Martindale parish church stands on How Grain, about a thousand feet above sea level, and is one of the most remote and inaccessible churches in Britain—yet even here Dorothy and William Wordsworth found their way, and recorded their impressions, proving how well they knew Lakeland. Dorothy wrote an enthralling description of their mountain ramble in Boardale, and Wordsworth, in the second book of *The Excursion*, gave a touching description of the old peat gatherer who sheltered from the storm in the roofless chapel. Martindale church was mentioned in the early thirteenth century. It was rebuilt in 1633, and has an unusual amount of seventeenth century woodwork. Martindale also had an example of frugality in Richard Birkett, who was parson there for sixty-seven years. He brought up a family and died worth £1,200, on a stipend of £20 a year.

No less than four beautiful, lonely valleys converge on Martindale—Fusedale, Rampsgill, Bannerdale and Boardale, and on the fells above is the deer forest of Martindale, the Roman High Street, Angle Tarn with its little islands, and the more distant Hayeswater, an attractive tarn nearly 1,400 ft. above sea level, which is used as a Reservoir by Penrith.

Pooley Bridge lies partly in Cumberland and partly in Westmorland, and is chiefly of interest as the starting point of the Ullswater steamers. Within a short distance on the Westmorland side of Ullswater is Eusemere, once the home of Thomas Clarkson, who began the discussion which resulted in the abolition of the slave trade—a man whom Southey honoured and whose untiring labours in the cause he had at heart were described by Samuel Smiles in *Self Help*. Both Clarkson and his wife Catherine, were friends of all the Lake poets, who often visited them whilst they were living at Eusemere.

Chapter V

WINDERMERE TO AMBLESIDE AND THE LANGDALES

I

THE road from Windermere to Ambleside, one of the most frequented in Lakeland, retains much of its old charm, thanks to the storm of protest, headed by Wordsworth with two sonnets and letters to the *Morning Post*, which greeted the suggestion that the railway should be extended from Windermere to Ambleside—a proposal which would have involved laying the track side by side with the road the whole way.

Soon after passing Ecclerigg, where Richard Luther Watson, a relative of Bishop Watson, lived for some years, there is a by-road to Troutbeck, from which can be seen the Briery, a house which was in 1850 the home of Sir James Kay-Shuttleworth, the founder of the English system of popular education, and father of the first Baron Shuttleworth. It was as his guest in that house that Charlotte Brontë first met her future biographer, Mrs. Gaskell, and made her first acquaintance with the country of the Lake poets. Her impressions of the immediate neighbourhood of Briery, and her intense pleasure in the natural beauty of its surroundings, have been recounted by Mrs. Gaskell.

On the west of Ecclerigg Farm is White Cross Bay, which takes its name from a little cross set up to the memory of two young men who were drowned there during last century. In the private grounds of Crag Wood, on the shore of the bay, there are some large flat rocks which were most beautifully inscribed by John Longmire of Troutbeck, an engraver who became mentally deranged, and occupied all his time with this work for several years, walking down every day from Troutbeck. Two of the rocks are dated 1835 and 1836 respectively, and the inscriptions consist of the names of famous heroes and poets of the past or of his day. and short sentences. One runs 'National Debt £8,000,000. O Save my Country, Heaven'. What would the poor man have thought of our present National Debt, one wonders? A guide to Windermere, published in 1843, speaks of him as still working at his self-imposed task, and quotes a poem on the subject, which runs:

'The oddest sure of all odd men
Has work'd for years upon his knees,
The gazing public eye to please.
A writer of no common kind,
For sentiments the most refined;
And mottoes which from age to age
Have pleas'd the senate and the sage
By him are written not with ink
Or simple quill as you may think;
But on the rock with iron pen,
He has engrav'd the deeds of men. . . .'

The rocks have become rather overgrown with weeds, and some have been broken in quarrying for stone used to build Wray Castle on the opposite shore, but a great deal of the work is still perfectly readable.

Following along the main road from Ecclerigg, the beck near Dove Nest is passed, beside which Dorothy and William Wordsworth, then in the hey-day of their youth, sat to rest during their walk from Kendal to Grasmere in the Spring of 1794. They retained such happy recollections of the charming scene that years after the poet referred affectionately to the 'little unpretending rill' in one of his sonnets. Nearby is the Low Wood Inn, backed by the height of Wansfell. One of the landlords of the inn befriended Hartley Coleridge on many occasions, and Hartley wrote a poem to his memory when he died. The inn also figures in Stanley Weyman's *Starvecrow Farm*, the farm itself being on the hill-side above.

Here, too, is Dove Nest, the house in which Mrs. Hemans spent the summer of 1830 and made friends with Wordsworth and the other Lake poets. The house has since been improved by the Rev. Robert Percival Graves, who lived there after her departure, and was himself a poet. Mrs. Hemans wrote an enthusiastic description of the beautiful situation of Dove Nest, in which she said: 'I am so delighted with the spot that I scarcely know how I shall leave it.' When circumstances compelled her to move, she fully intended to return later, but never found the opportunity to do so.

The little pier at Low Wood is for the use of hotel visitors, and the place of call for the Ambleside steamers is a mile farther along the road, at Waterhead. Ambleside originally stood about a mile away from the lake, but is gradually extending towards the group of houses and hotels clustering round the Waterhead pier.

II

Ambleside has two great claims upon the interest of visitors—its rich memories of the Lake poets, who were so often entertained there, and its central position for exploring the Lake District, which inspired James Payn, the novelist, to describe it as 'The axle at the wheel of beauty'.

Although Ambleside has grown considerably since those days it has still many quaint nooks and corners in the older part of the town, and the Stock Ghyll Force still tumbles in a 76 foot drop over a rocky ledge of Wansfell in the woods behind the Salutation Hotel. Miss Martineau wrote of the fall: 'It is the fashion to speak lightly of this waterfall—it being within half a mile of the inn, and so easily reached; but it is, in our opinion, a very remarkable fall (from the symmetry of its parts) and one of the most graceful that can be seen'—remarks that apply equally well to-day.

On the other hand, Miss Martineau had some very harsh things to say about the then newly erected church designed by Sir Gilbert Scott. Fortunately this has now mellowed a little, and is also much more closely invested with houses than in her day. The memorial window to Wordsworth in the church was presented by subscriptions from English and American admirers of the poet. The old church, still to be seen on the hillside, was rebuilt in 1812, but in a style which did not arouse such violent criticism as the newer building in the valley.

Ambleside had its first charter for a market in 1650, and another, in 1688, confirmed its right to a market and gave power to collect tolls for the benefit of the poor. Fairs are still held there in Whit-week and October for the sale of the famous Herdwick sheep, but the old buildings have disappeared from the market place. The Salutation Inn of which Gray complained so bitterly has been rebuilt in a dignified style and offers the comforts which the older building lacked, and the only survival of the ancient market place is the shaft of a medieval cross. Julius Cæsar Ibbotson, who lived near Ambleside for some years and married Bella Thompson of Windermere, painted a view of Ambleside Market Place with the old buildings as they stood in 1801. Another artist who lived in Ambleside for a while and gave drawing lessons there was 'Old' Crome. One of the pictures he painted there now hangs in the National Gallery.

Cornelius Nicholson, author of the *Annals of Kendal* and other informative books on the Lake District, was born in a house which stood on the site now occupied by the Market Hall, which was later the lodging of Owen

Lloyd, the composer of the Rushbearing Hymn. Gale House was the home of Miss Fenwick, the helper, and adviser of Wordsworth in later years, and the annotator of his poems.

The Rushbearing Festival is held at Ambleside during the last week-end in July, and rivals the Rushbearing at Grasmere in antiquity and interest, although it has not now the final charm of the village setting. Wordsworth and his family attended the Rushbearing at Ambleside as assiduously as that in their beloved Grasmere, sitting in the little front room of the old post office in the market place, now Brown's Coach Office. The Rev. Owen Lloyd, Hartley Coleridge, and Faber entered so thoroughly into the joyous occasion that they usually joined in the procession here, as Wordsworth and his family joined in the one at Grasmere.

The building in Ambleside which excites the most interest, and is most frequently photographed, is the curious Bridge House, which probably dates from the late seventeenth century, and is said to have been built as a garden house. It occupies the whole of a narrow bridge across the Stock Beck, beside the road to Rydal, and although so very small, is complete with an outside staircase to the first floor, an oven on the ground floor, and a low chimney. The quaint little building is now in the care of the National Trust. Nearly opposite is the picturesque old water-mill, and a little higher up the Stock Ghyll is the bobbin mill which attracted the attention of Dickens on his visit in 1857.

Those who intend to visit the site of the Roman fort excavated by Professor R. G. Collingwood in Borrans Field, between Ambleside and the head of the Lake, would do well to see first the really beautiful models in the Armitt Museum, which show reconstructions of the first fort on the site, probably built during Agricola's northern campaign in A.D. 79, and of the second century fort which overlies the greater part of the earlier fort.

Ranged round the walls of the room are the finds made on the site, together with careful drawings showing their original appearance, and notes giving interesting details—the whole comprising the most intelligently arranged museum of the period on a small scale that could be desired—so understandingly arranged, in fact, that it is calculated to rouse interest in those who have been unmoved by larger collections.

Without a study of the models and relics in the museum, and a gift of imagination, Borrans Field should be visited with no higher aspiration than to see the magnificent view, commanding the whole length of the Lake and bounded by a vast amphitheatre of mountains. More than one sight-seer has come away from Borrans Field saying that there was 'nothing to see'—apparently having expected a fort complete with soldiery!—but in actual fact the foundations are easily traceable and clearly marked with name-posts corresponding to the plan displayed on the site, and the size of the fort—270 feet by 395 feet—is realized by pacing along the line of the outer walls.

III

All along the road which runs from Ambleside to Rydal there are memories of the celebrities who have loved this district. Within a few yards of the Bridge House is the easily overlooked entrance which leads to The Knoll, the house which Harriet Martineau built in 1845 with money earned by her writings, and in which she lived until her death in 1876. During the thirty-one years in which she made her home at Ambleside she had long spells of illness, and occasional absences from the district, but this did not prevent her taking a very real interest in the poorer people of Ambleside, by whom she was greatly beloved. James Payn in his *Literary Recollections* speaks warmly of her kindly 'motherly' ways and of her strong good sense—characteristics which impressed everyone who came into contact with this lovable woman. It was in very great part due to the influence of her writings that peace was maintained between England and the United States during the American Civil War. Among the many guests who stayed with her at the Knoll were Charlotte Brontë, George Eliot and, for two days in March, 1848, Emerson, the great American essayist. John Bright, the great statesman, also stayed there, and on one occasion was found on his knees

LEVENS HALL

measuring the rooms for carpets as a surprise gift for his hostess.

Opposite the Knoll, which is hidden from the road by a dilapidated building originally a chapel and now used by the local Territorials, is Green Bank, once the home of Mrs. Benson Harrison, the niece of Wordsworth, by whom she was brought up. She came to Green Bank with her husband and family in 1827 when the Wordsworths were still living at Rydal Mount, and lived there until 1890, the last of the Rydal Dorothys. Her funeral procession was attended by the late Canon Rawnsley, and was touchingly described by him in *A Rambler's Notebook*, in which he also paid tribute to her beauty and goodness.

Green Bank also has memories of the Rev. F. W. Faber, who came as tutor to the Harrison boys in the days before his conversion to Roman Catholicism. He acted as assistant curate to the old church at Ambleside, and trained a little choir to sing there. He was a poet of no small merit, and his earlier poems on Westmorland, especially *Loughrigg* and the *Brathay Sonnets* are still remembered. His sonnets *To a little Boy; Richard's Tree;* and *On my Pupil's Portrait*, were also written here, inspired by his affection for his pupils. It was as a hymn writer that he achieved his greatest fame, and among those in *Hymns Ancient and Modern* which he wrote are the well-known 'Hark! Hark, my soul! Angelic songs are swelling'; 'My God, how wonderful Thou art'; 'Paradise! O Paradise'; and 'Souls of Men, why will ye Scatter?' His departure from Ambleside was regretted by everyone there, for as an old man who had known him said: 'Faber loved the people, and the people loved him.' He became a Roman Catholic in 1845, and was appointed Head of the London Oratory established in King Street, and remained in charge when it was transferred to Brompton Oratory, until his death in 1863.

On the hill-side above is Eller How, at the entrance to the Scandale Vale, where Anne Jemima Clough, the first principal of Newnham College lived from 1852 to 1862, and ran a school in Ambleside. She wrote an article on Girls' Schools for *Macmillan's Magazine* in 1866.

At Lesketh How, on the Rydal road beyond Green

Bank, lived Dr. Davy, brother of Sir Humphry, and away under Loughrigg is Fox How, where the great Dr. Arnold of Rugby lived during his holidays with his wife and family, including his grand-daughter, later Mrs. Humphry Ward the novelist, and his son Matthew Arnold, who continued to visit his mother and sister there after the death of his father. Fox How was built by Dr. Arnold, and the date 1833 is recorded on the gable.

The house in which Gordon Wordsworth, the last surviving grandson of the poet, lived until his death and burial in Grasmere Churchyard in 1935, is opposite the famous Stepping Stones across the Rothay, whilst Fox Ghyll was the home of the Rt. Hon. W. E. Forster, Irish Secretary; Loughrigg Holme, where Dora Wordsworth and her husband Edward Quillinan lived for a short while, and Loughrigg Brow, home of the late Canon Bell, vicar of Ambleside and Lakeland poet, are also ranged between the hill and the river Rothay.

IV

There are many excursions to be made from Ambleside. One which appeals only to walkers and is often overlooked even by them, is up the Scandale Valley with its low stone bridges of High Sweden and Low Sweden, hopefully said locally to be 'probably pre-Roman', but more soberly judged by the Royal Commission to be about three hundred years old.

The road up to Kirkstone Pass, known as 'the struggle' with good reason, is a very popular walk giving fine views and passing many fields and banks massed with wild flowers. The local guide issued by the Ambleside authorities includes a chapter on the wild flowers of this district, one of the most easily available sources of information on this subject, although J. G. Baker's *A Flora of the English Lake District*, Hodgson's *Flora of Cumberland* and Albert Wilson's *Flora of Westmorland* are, of course, more comprehensive.

Apart from the almost obligatory visits southward to Windermere and northward to Rydal, Grasmere and Keswick, probably the most popular excursions from Ambleside are to Hawkshead and Coniston in Lancashire, and to the Westmorland Langdales, both excursions involving a visit to the cluster of houses known as Clappersgate, which although scarcely seeming big enough to warrant being called a village, has its memories of the Lake poets, for here is the house in which Derwent and Hartley Coleridge lodged when they went to school at Miller Bridge, run by Parson Dawes, who came to Ambleside from Dublin in 1805, and had among his pupils not only the Coleridge boys, but four of the young Lloyds, and the sons of Wordsworth, Prof. Wilson, the Hardens, and others who afterwards achieved distinction.

The Croft, when it was the home of Mr. Branker, was very often the scene of happy gatherings of the Lake poets, and so too were those neighbouring houses, just over the Lancashire boundary, Low or Old Brathay under the Lloyds and High Brathay, or Brathay Hall, under the Hardens.

In Clappersgate, too, was the home of Mrs. Millar and Miss Cullen, the two Scottish ladies of whom De Quincey tells us in his *Reminiscences of the Lake Poets.* Daughters of Dr. Cullen, a well-known Edinburgh physician, they were left in very straightened circumstances on his death, but managed to maintain their independence and to offer hospitality to their friends. Among those whom they entertained at Clappersgate was a M. Louis Simond, a Frenchman who had lived twenty years in Charleston, South Carolina, and had befriended Mrs. Millar on the death of her husband in that town. M. Simond was accompanied by his wife, who was a niece of the great John Wilkes, and his wife's niece, who shortly afterwards married Lord Jeffrey. M. Simond wrote an interesting account of his travels in England during the years 1810 and 1811, but especially mentions in the preface that 'private anecdotes' have been excluded as much as possible, and so unfortunately gives none of his impressions of Wordsworth or De Quincey, both of whom he met.

In the present day the greatest attraction of Clappersgate is the wonderful rock garden of White Craggs, which is open to the public. Created by the late Charles Henry

Hough and his family out of a wooded hill-side about the beginning of this century, it has flowers brought from all parts of the world, including rare plants from China and Tibet collected by Reginald Farrer, and William Purdom on the expedition described by the former in *The Eaves of the World*, and its sequel, *The Rainbow Bridge*. The paths lead up to a seat on the summit of the garden commanding a glorious view of the Brathay River flowing to join the Rothay on its way to the lake, which stretches away to the horizon. This private garden, the result of years of loving care, was opened to the public in 1919, and has given joy to thousands of visitors since then. No charge is made, but two collecting boxes are placed there on behalf of the South London Church Fund, a cause in which Mr. Hough was interested by his brother the late William W. Hough, Bishop of Woolwich, and to which so many visitors have willingly contributed that the boxes have yielded an average of £50 a year to the fund, and one year the amount totalled over £100. The story of the making of the garden and an account of all the rare plants to be found there, beautifully illustrated, is told in a little booklet *A Westmorland Rock Garden* by the late owner, whose daughter now maintains the garden he loved. All the profits from this booklet are also devoted to the fund.

The River Brathay marks the boundary between Lancashire and Westmorland, and the road to Little Langdale crosses into Lancashire at Skelwith Bridge, and back again into Westmorland a mile farther along at Colwith Bridge. There are 'forces' near both these bridges—the Skelwith Force, which has the greatest volume of water of any in the Lake District, but is only about 20 feet high, and the Colwith Force, one of the most charming and undeservedly neglected of Lakeland falls. The Colwith Force lies in a narrow, tree-filled glen more like those of the Isle of Man than most of the valleys of the Lake District, and the water falls over 90 feet in two leaps, the upper fall being split into five by rocks.

This district is the background for the fascinating story of the Norse Settlers of the Lake District, told by W. G. Collingwood in *The Bondwomen*, the chief scenes taking place in a homestead above Skelwith Force, and another at Colwith.

Little Langdale, though far less often visited than Great Langdale, has the beauty of fields so rich in flowers that they are a veritable garden, rich woodlands, and prosperous-looking farms, with the rocky crests of the mountains at the head of the valley by way of contrast. Beyond the reedy Little Langdale Tarn is Fell Foot Farm, immediately behind which is a terraced mound which, Mr. Swainson Cowper suggested, in a paper read before the Cumberland and Westmorland Archæological Society, was a 'Law Ling', or mound, used by the Norse of Lakeland for their open-air assemblies for the promulgation of laws, in the same way as the famous Tynwald Mount of the Isle of Man.

At the head of Little Langdale the road divides, the left hand track climbing over Wrynose past the Three Shires Stone which marks the meeting of Cumberland, Westmorland and Lancashire, and the right hand track climbing over into Great Langdale, past Blea Tarn and the farm where Wordsworth's 'Solitary' lived. The seeker of solitude would have to go much farther afield in the summer months now, for Blea Tarn is a favourite haunt of picnic parties, and there is usually a group of cars parked there during the season, although it is deserted enough at other times during the year.

Great Langdale and the Dungeon Ghyll Force have received their due meed of attention from every guide-book writer since the days when Wordsworth and Coleridge wrote about this curious and very attractive fall. A guide published in the days before 'hikers' were known, quoting from Wordsworth's description of the bridge made over the waterfall by a fall of rock adds: 'Over the bridge thus formed ladies have been known, like Wordsworth's Idle Shepherd Boy, to possess the intrepidity to pass.' Nowadays ladies have the 'intrepidity' to climb all the crags of the Langdales, once the sole haunt of cragsmen, and summer visitors with any pretensions to be walkers take it as a matter of course to climb up above Dungeon Ghyll or Mill Ghyll and cross the almost trackless fells past Stickle

Tarn to Easedale, whilst a considerable number take the more strenuous and difficult track over Crinkle Crags to Eskdale, or the pass to Borrowdale, or Wastwater, either of which opens up some of the wildest and grandest scenery of the Lake District, the greater part of which is, fortunately, in the care of the National Trust.

At the foot of Great Langdale, near the village of Chapel Stile, is the slate quarry of Thrang Crag, which Otley mentions rather ambiguously, as far back as 1834, as 'excavated in an awful manner'. Langdale church, at Chapel Stile, was rebuilt on a new site in 1857, but has some ancient plate from the previous church, which is remembered for its associations with the Rev. Owen Lloyd of Old Brathay, who was incumbent for nearly 12 years. The tombstone which marks his grave in the churchyard has an epitaph written by Wordsworth.

Eltermere House, originally called Elterwater Hall, which stands at the head of the series of lakes which make up Elterwater, was built in the sixteenth century, and enlarged in the seventeenth, and there are other seventeenth and eighteenth century farms and houses in the villages of Chapel Stile and Elterwater. Either of these villages can be made a starting point for Loughrigg Tarn, which lies cradled in low grassy hills backed by the peaks of Lakeland, and figured in a poem by Professor Wilson. Otley's guide urged the traveller to walk to the top of Ivy Crag, above the tarn, where 'he will have an instantaneous burst upon a most extraordinary assemblage of landscape beauties'. Although Loughrigg Fell is only 1,100 feet in height, few mountains give such glorious views, and it was from a spot half-way up its northern side that the Pastor and his companions, in the ninth book of Wordsworth's *Excursion*, sat quietly admiring the view.

Chapter VI

GRASMERE AND RYDAL

I

ALTHOUGH Grasmere and Rydal are 2½ miles apart, the spirit of the Wordsworth family so informs them that they seem closely allied, and even the visitor who is determined to resist the Wordsworth cult cannot resist it long. It is not merely a cult to attract tourists—rather does it seem to have flourished in spite of the tourists. The most humble of the countryfolk round have their personal memories of the poet and his family, handed down from parents and grandparents—tales of kindliness and sympathy in time of trouble; of cheerful gatherings of friends and relations at Dove Cottage; the Grasmere Rectory—where Wordsworth lived for a year; Allan Bank, where he also lived for a while; and finally at Rydal Mount. Many are the intimate details of the happy family life there, not to mention anecdotes to match the well-known one of Scott's stay at Dove Cottage, when he 'stepped down' to the Swan Inn daily for his glass of whisky rather than display his tastes to his water-drinking host, only to be confounded one morning when setting out on an excursion with the Wordsworth family by the host of the inn greeting him with: 'Ye've comed seun for ya glass to-daäy.'

So much has been written about the lives of Wordsworth and every member of his family that it is unnecessary to dwell upon it here, but as a counterblast to the 'revelations' of De Quincey's *Reminiscences*, which have given rise to a very general impression that Wordsworth was unsociable, and rude to strangers, it is interesting to read in a guide by James Gibson of Ambleside, published in 1843: 'On returning from the (Rydal) falls, visit Rydal-mount, the sweet retreat of Mr. Wordsworth, who most kindly invites all strangers to walk through his grounds. . . . The person who shows the water-fall will ask permission for the visitor, and the poet never refuses: on the contrary, he is always pleased to see strangers on his ground, and frequently walks round with them himself.'

Rydal Mount is, of course, in private possession, and the present owners do not emulate the poet in admitting visitors, but Dora's Field is in the care of the National Trust, and the terrace Wordsworth had constructed in the garden at Rydal Mount can be seen from there, whilst any deprivation is compensated by the intimate appeal of Dove Cottage, where in spite of the thousands of visitors who pass through every summer's day, the custodian has lost not a jot of her enthusiasm, and loves to speak of the memories which crowd the little cottage and its garden.

No similar 'pilgrim's shrine' could have a greater appeal or a more real sense of the living presence of those who have gone, for there is the room which Dorothy and William papered themselves with newspaper in the days of their poverty; the door they made into the garden; the mosses they collected and pressed, the steps they made in the garden, the lawn they tended, and the ground where William dug and planted his vegetables to eke out their slender housekeeping funds, and the kitchen in which Dorothy cooked their meals. Many were the little shifts by which Wordsworth and his wife and his sister contrived to keep their expenditure within bounds and still have enough to entertain their friends. Some of the books they bound with fragments from their old dresses are still preserved at Allan Bank, and Dorothy's Journals mention many other devices, all most cheerfully carried out, rather than get into debt as so many of their contemporaries did.

The recently opened Museum, just opposite Dove Cottage, also has the greatest interest, although as yet neglected in comparison with the cottage. It contains many interesting autograph letters of the Wordsworth family and their friends, including one written by Hartley Coleridge when a boy of eight, telling his mother that 'they were all very fond of me at Penrith' and hoping that when he returns home she will think him a good boy. In another room is an extremely fine reconstruction of a Westmorland farmhouse kitchen with its great fireplace, two lifelike wooden figures of the inmates, and all the furniture and utensils.

De Quincey lived at Dove Cottage for twenty-six years after the Wordsworths left, and he afterwards went to live at the Nab, the house looking over Rydal Lake. Poor De Quincey! In those days he was so full of eager friendship, so welcome at all the gatherings of the poets and their friends for his powers both as conversationalist and listener. He was full of charm and enthusiasm, and delighted in children who, in turn, adored him, and his love of books was such that he crammed Dove Cottage so full with them he lent 500 at a time to Coleridge at Allan Bank—yet in his later years at Edinburgh, he was so changed that he could write those ungenerous *Reminiscences* of the Grasmere friends by whom he had been beloved and whom he had loved in return! Those years at the Lakes with his friends, and with his young wife Peggy Simpson and their children, seem to have been the happiest and most normal of his life.

Most people know that Hartley Coleridge lived at the Nab for the last years of his life, from 1838 to 1849, but few people seem to know that the attractive Rose Cottage on the corner of the turning down to Dove Cottage, was his home for some time, and that although it has been enlarged since then, the original part is much the same as in his day. Lil' Hartley, beloved by everyone with whom he came into contact, has left behind him countless anecdotes of his wit, his kindliness, his affection for children, his rare gifts and unfortunate failings, and of his extremely queer appearance as he scurried along the lanes to have a 'crack' with a neighbour, or returned more slowly and unsteadily, but still witty and enjoying a laugh at his own expense.

Grasmere and Rydal are so full of memories, it is hard to tear oneself away, or to think of anything else but these people so long dead, and yet still so vividly alive that it would never seem strange to meet Dorothy and her beloved William walking over the hills or along the roads. Anyone who visits Grasmere and Rydal without having read Dorothy's Journals and William's poems has lost more than he can dream, for they re-create not only the life of their day, but point the way to a far closer observation and keener appreciation of the natural beauties of the district which they knew so intimately.

II

Apart from its literary associations, Rydal has an attraction for holiday-makers in its famous Sheep Dog Trials, held annually in August. They rank as the most important Sheep Dog Trials in Westmorland and rival the most famous Cumbrian events. The trials are held in the beautiful park of Rydal Hall, which has been the seat of the Fleming family since the early fifteenth century. The old Hall stood where a clump of fir trees crowns a knoll on the left of the main road from Ambleside, and it is traditionally said that the site was abandoned because it was most disturbingly haunted, so that when Sir Michael le Fleming built his new Hall in the sixteenth century he chose the present site. The Hall was enlarged in the seventeenth century and has extensive modern additions, but the central portion of the north-east wing, and the west range, represent the original building. Near one of the Rydal falls is a seventeenth century stone summer-house panelled in contemporary woodwork, and there are several seventeenth century outhouses in the grounds.

The Flemings trace their descent back to Sir Michael le Fleming, who was living at Beckermet in 1126, but modern research traces their origin to Reiner le Fleming, Seneschal of William de Meschines, First Lord of Egremont, early in the twelfth century. They came to Rydal when Sir Thomas le Fleming, then living at Coniston, married one of the joint-heiresses of Sir John de Lancaster. The best known of the Flemings of Rydal was Sir Daniel, the antiquary, who was born in 1633, and many of whose letters are preserved in the Record Office. His descriptions of Cumberland and Westmorland, which he drew up in 1671, have been reprinted by the Cumberland and Westmorland Antiquarian and Archæological Society. Sir Daniel was a Sheriff of Cumberland, and a Member of Parliament for Cockermouth, and was a strong supporter of the Church of England, to the disadvantage of Dissenters and Roman Catholics, and had a particular dislike for Quakers, of whom he was always prepared to believe the worst. He was succeeded by his eldest son, William, who was created a baronet, and Sir William was succeeded by his brother George, Bishop of Carlisle.

The story of the Flemings, with fascinating details of the dress and customs of Westmorland and Cumberland gathered from their accounts and papers, is to be found in the late Miss M. L. Armitt's book, *Rydal*, which also gives a considerable amount of space to the early history of the district, and to the life of De Quincey and Hartley Coleridge at the Nab, and a chapter on the birds of the district and other interesting points. Miss Armitt, who also wrote a book on Grasmere Church, was an authority on the history of Rydal and Grasmere, and had a wide knowledge of the bird and plant life of the neighbourhood. Her garden at Rydal Cottage is still aglow with flowers, and it was the joint collection of the books and furniture of Miss Armitt and her sister, together with a monetary bequest, which was the origin of the Armitt library in Ambleside.

Another association, of especial interest to the many American visitors who pass through Rydal every year, is with the late President Wilson, who, when Principal of Princeton University, rented Loughrigg Cottage for three months in 1906. He visited the district again two years later, when he stayed at the Rothay Hotel in Grasmere. He walked and cycled to all the famous beauty spots, and those who knew him there have pleasant memories of his sensitive response to the scenery of the lakes, and of his personal charm, and powers as a raconteur. It was during one of his visits that Fred Yates, who lived at Rydal, painted the President's portrait. Woodrow Wilson was one of those who gathered at Gowbarrow Fell in 1906, when it was handed over to the keeping of the National Trust.

III

Grasmere has three outstanding annual events—the Rushbearing, held on the Saturday following 5th August; the

Grasmere Sports, held on the Thursday nearest the 20th August; and the Dialect Plays, held in February.

It is typical of the endearing simplicity of Grasmere that the influx of so many tourists has not affected the 'Rushbearing Festival' in the slightest. The children gather together for half-an-hour before the event, and sit or stand on the broad stone wall of the churchyard, with their bright 'bearings', of fresh flowers and rushes in every conceivable design, making a delightful picture against the grey stone tower of the church. Not until the procession is actually wending its way down the village street is the traffic stopped, and the whole occasion is one of the most charming informality. After walking round the village with the local band at their head, the children troop into the church to lay their bearings on every ledge, and the sight-seers follow until the church is literally 'filled to the brim' for the rushbearing service in honour of St. Oswald, when the rushbearing hymn composed by Owen Lloyd is sung, together with a hymn, specially composed for the occasion, by the late Canon Rawnsley.

Each child taking part in the procession is given a new penny and a 'ginger-bread ticket', which on being presented at the School-house after the service entitles them to a large piece of St. Oswald ginger-bread. On the following Monday all the children are entertained to tea and sports in the school playground. One of the most attractive features of the whole idea is that it is a true village festival, with children of every denomination taking part to carry on the tradition in which their parents and grandparents once took their part. The festival dates back to at least the sixteenth century, and probably much earlier, being a survival of the days when rushes were strewed on the earth floor of the church in place of a carpet. Many of the bearings show the greatest ingenuity and beauty of design—the 'snake uplifted in the wilderness', in rushes, competing with an arrangement of water-lilies from the lake, and the deep blue of bog gentians contrasting with the golden flowers which form the cross heading the procession. The Rushbearing Picture painted by the late Frank Bramley, R.A., who lived at Tongue Ghyll, hangs in the Hall at Grasmere, and is now in the care of the National Trust.

The Grasmere Sports attract an average of 30,000 spectators annually, and are not only a social occasion, but far better arranged than many such events, as there are no waits between the various items, and enthusiasm is kept at a high pitch throughout, although it rises to its greatest intensity during the hound trails and the guides race—both of which no visitor to the Lakes should miss. Those who have themselves toiled up to Butter Crags cannot but marvel at men who race up and down that steep slope in less than a quarter of an hour, whilst the excitement roused by the hound trails is marvellously infectious, particularly when the waiting owners catch sight of the hounds as they return over the Crags, and pandemonium seems to break loose as each owner strives to call or whistle louder than his neighbour. The Westmorland and Cumberland style of wrestling, too, is so completely different that it catches the interest even of those who dislike such contests, and usually yields some amusing 'holds' in addition to the thrills—the positively affectionate embraces of the opponents before coming to grips, in particular, appealing to those who lack the expert knowledge to appreciate the finer points. The heavyweight championship of the Grasmere Sports carries with it the title of World Champion in this form of the sport. The Dialect Plays, although less widely attended owing to the season in which they are held, are deservedly famous.

Grasmere and Rydal have been so minutely dealt with by Baddeley and other guides, and so incomparaby described by Wordsworth and his circle, that their beauty has been acknowledged not only by visitors but by many who have only seen it through the eyes of the poets. Most of the visitors to the Lakes make every excursion around Grasmere, however much they neglect the rest of the Lake District, but it is worth pointing out to the hundreds who go up the Easedale Valley that in the little off-shoot, Blind Tarn Ghyll, is the house in which Jane Green waited in vain for the return of her parents who had been lost in the snow, and mothered her younger brothers and sisters until the snows cleared sufficiently for her to reach her distant neighbours—a story which has been told and re-told by Wordsworth, De Quincey and many others, and has also been re-edited by Mr. E. de Selincourt. Incidentally, the house in which she lived was the last place in the district to make use of a handloom for home weaving, and the first, apart from the inns, to 'take in lodgers'.

There are few who do not undertake the walk up to Easedale Tarn from Grasmere, although there is nothing but the tarn itself as an object, as the lost-looking pool is shut in by bleak mountains, yet the far more rewarding walk to Alcock Tarn is frequently neglected. The best way up is through Greenhead Ghyll, in which is the sheep-fold of Wordsworth's *Michael.* The path zigzags up the hill-side to the tarn, an old reservoir which is now a miniature lake cradled in a horse-shoe of fells on all sides but the south, where is the nebulous, cloudlike outline of the distant peaks ringing Windermere. The view from the crags on the west of the tarn is superb, particularly on a day when the sky is overcast but the atmosphere clear, when Easedale Tarn and Grasmere Lake are a sullen slate-grey and distant Windermere and Coniston a steel colour bright only in comparison with the nearer waters, whilst the fells are dark and threatening unless there is a break in the clouds, when their peaks seem luminous as though fires are glowing from their heart.

At one point of the path along the tarn there is a curious optical illusion that Lake Windermere—so distant and so far below—is a continuation of the tarn, which heralds the marvellous view of lakes and valleys opened out from the southern end of the tarn. The return journey by a path dropping down behind Dove Cottage gives a view across the Grasmere Valley, with the village laid like a giant's sickle across the fields, and the lake with its island looking more than usually like a child's toy with trees stuck on by hand, rather than actually rooted there.

Another delightful walk, even more neglected, is by way of Wordsworth Terrace, which runs through the wooded grounds of Lancrigg House to Easedale, but is open to the public. A stone inscribed in Latin commemorates the fact that Dorothy Wordsworth took down some of her brother's poems on that spot.

LAKE WINDERMERE

Lancrigg House was the home of the 'beautiful Mrs. Fletcher' from 1839 to her death in 1858. She and her family were intimate with the Lake poets, and one of her daughters married Sir John Richardson, the Arctic explorer and naturalist, who is buried in Grasmere churchyard, and another married Dr. Davy of Ambleside. Mrs. Fletcher's *Autobiography* is one of the many sources of information about the society of the Lakes in that period, and after her death Lancrigg was the home of Sir John Richardson and his wife. His writings during his seven years' residence at Lancrigg included articles for the *Encyclopædia Britannica*, and valuable papers on the Polar Regions and natural history.

Among the many celebrities whose connexion with Grasmere and Rydal has been overshadowed by the greater fame of the Wordsworths, Coleridges and De Quincey, are Sir Humphry Davy, Charles Lamb, and other friends of the poets who visited Dove Cottage or Rydal Mount. Jemima Clough's brother, Arthur Hugh Clough, the English poet who lived in America for many years, and was the friend of Emerson and other eminent Americans, spent many holidays at the old Grasmere post office, and his name is inscribed on his mother's monument in Grasmere churchyard, although he is buried in Florence. It was his death that inspired Matthew Arnold to write *Thyrsis*.

The Rev. G. Butler, Canon of Winchester Cathedral, and James Anthony Froude, the historian, stayed at Grasmere in 1844, and an account of their visit was written by the former for *Longman's Magazine* in 1888. Edward Thring, the poet, who rivalled Dr. Arnold as one of the most notable headmasters of the nineteenth century, and raised Uppingham from an obscure school to its present fame, spent his holidays at Greenhead Ghyll for many years. His books on the principles of education are still read in England and America, and his poetry on the Lake District has great charm. Some thirty years later his godchild, the late Canon Rawnsley, after his long association with Crosthwaite, Keswick, came to spend the last years of his life at Allan Bank, with all its memories of the poets he loved and wrote about so well.

Chapter VII

SHAP AND THE FELLS OF THE EASTERN BORDER

I

SHAP, alone of Lakeland towns, is not set in a valley, but high on the breezy Shap Fells, which stretch for miles in every direction. It is pre-eminently for the enthusiastic walker, for there are few roads, but many footpaths through the valleys and across the fells to the more populous centres of the Lake District, yet those who prefer its breezy climate to that of the sheltered Lakeland towns but cannot, for one reason or another, undertake long walks, need not be debarred from making it a centre. It is on the main road between Penrith and Kendal, to which it is linked by motor-bus services and the railway, and all the important centres of the Lake District can, of course, be reached from these towns. In addition, motorists will find a superb road from Shap Quarries direct to Burn Banks, constructed by the Manchester Corporation in connexion with their Waterworks at Haweswater. It is a boon to motorists which it is only fair to acknowledge in view of the amount of abuse that has been showered on the Corporation—although there are many who would add this to their list of 'crimes'.

Shap consists of a double row of houses, many of them bearing seventeenth century dates, strung out for a mile or more along the main road to the north. The town was originally called Heppe, and must have been in existence from an early date. W. G. Collingwood is of opinion that it was the place where the Norse held their Parliament. Shap church was founded in the twelfth century although the only part of the fabric surviving from the original church is a beast-head corbel. The south arcade of the nave dates from early in the thirteenth century, but the remainder of the building has been extended and altered several times since that date. The seventeenth century communion table, communion rails, church plate, and a chest, have been preserved, together with some medieval coffin lids and other survivals from the earlier church.

Some woodwork in the nave bearing the initials and date 'P.L.W. 1674' apparently refers to the fourth Baron Wharton, a former Lord of the Manor of Shap, who fought against the Royalists at Edgehill. Bibles and prayer books are still distributed annually to Shap children who have learnt the catechism and seven psalms specified by a deed he made in 1662, which provided for 1,050 Bibles and as many catechisms to be given yearly in the towns and villages of his estates in Buckingham, York, Westmorland and Cumberland. Shap came to the Wharton family at the Dissolution of Shap Abbey, and was sold to the Lonsdales by the last Wharton—that Duke of Wharton who was lampooned by Pope for his inordinate love of praise.

Shap's charter to hold a market was granted in 1687, and it was probably soon after that date that the Market Hall was built—a quaint little place with a range of three round-headed arches on two sides, partly blocked by stonework and partly by windows with diamond-leaded panes, the whole covered by a pyramidal roof. It was at one time used as a school, and is now the parish room.

The once famous 'Shap Stones' or 'Karl Lofts', described by all the earlier writers on Shap, have practically disappeared. This megalithic monument consisted of two stone circles and an avenue of stones about a mile long. Practically the whole of the avenue has disappeared, but a drawing made by Lady Lowther in 1774 preserves knowledge of its form, and there are a few surviving stones, of which the Thunder Stone, and the Goggleby Stone, are the most important. There are other prehistoric stone circles at Bampton, Crosby Ravensworth, Gunnerkeld and other places in the neighbourhood.

Prince Charles Edward stayed at West Farm, Shap, on the night of 17th December, 1745, on his journey south, and recorded in his household book that his landlady was a 'sad wife for imposing'—as well he might, for she charged him £4 17*s.* for 'ale, wine and other provisions' and two guineas for 'use of the house'. If all the places where the

Scottish army stayed charged at this rate the Highlanders might well be excused for any foraging they did on the way! Shap was also slightingly noticed in Anthony Trollope's novel, *Can you forgive her?* for he mentions that the coach passengers stopped just long enough at Shap 'to thank Heaven they had not been born Shappites', a reflection with which no Shappite would agree, for they stoutly maintain that anyone who has once tasted Shap bread and Shap water will long to return again.

Shap had the only abbey in Westmorland, and the ruins lie a mile to the west of the town, beyond the tiny hamlet of Keld which has a disused sixteenth century chantry chapel in good condition. The ruins of the abbey stand beside the Lowther, here a pretty streamlet, in a quiet pastoral valley which seems to have been made for meditation and is still enfolded in its ancient peace. Originally founded by Thomas Gospatrick at Preston Patrick in 1191, as a convent for Premonstratensian Canons, it was removed to Shap in 1199, the church being begun soon after that date, and the other buildings gradually rising as the rich endowments added to the fame of the abbey. The West tower was not added until early in the sixteenth century, and by 1540 the abbey had surrendered and the building began to fall into ruin. The site was excavated in 1886, when most of the worked stones were removed, but the tower is still standing, and although the remainder of the walls only vary from ground level to a few feet in height, the whole makes an interesting example of monastic planning in the eyes of the antiquary, and the charm of the setting rewards the less expert visitor. The ruins are now a part of Shap Abbey Farm, which, with its 6,500 acres, claims to be the largest in Westmorland and Cumberland. The modern farm house stands beside the tower and is built partly over the site of the Abbot's Hall. It has a seventeenth century block of stabling at the south end incorporating material from the abbey, and two carved stone heads are built into the wall of the farm itself. Sir Daniel le Fleming mentions that not far from Shap Abbey was a 'well or fountain which after the manner of Euripus, ebbeth and floweth many times in a day'.

Shap Spa lies four miles south of Shap, in a hollow of the

hills well away from the main road, and consists chiefly of the Hydropathic built for the use of visitors who come to take the waters, and also popular with those wishing to explore the district. The waters are said to be similar to those of Leamington Spa.

The famous Shap summit, where the railway line climbs a thousand feet, is between Shap Wells and Shap. It was on Shap Fell that the first sod of the Lancaster and Carlisle Railway was cut in 1844. The no less famous granite quarries are beside the main road and should be eyed indulgently by the majority of visitors, at least, as the source of many familiar sights, among which are the Thames Embankment, Temple Bar Memorial, and Albert Memorial in London; the Town Hall, Royal Exchange and Owens College at Manchester; St. George's Hall, Liverpool; the New University Buildings at Glasgow; the Leighton Buzzard Monolith, and the pedestal of the monument to Lord Lawrence in India.

II

West of the main road the fells are piled higher and higher as they reach away to the lakes, and the valleys by which they are penetrated are among the loneliest in the Lake District. Even the farm houses are few and far between, and tourists seldom find their way up Bannisdale, or Wet Sleddale with its seventeenth century hall and grange, nor, in spite of the fact that they are 'recommended routes' for those walking to Haweswater from Windermere, Kendal or Shap, are Long Sleddale or Swindale, much more frequented.

Long Sleddale is a narrow valley penetrating into the hills for six miles or more to the foot of the dominating crags of Goat Scar and Buckbarrow. The church stands in the midst of the valley, and although rebuilt has some fittings surviving from the earlier church on the site. Ubarrow Hall, about a quarter of a mile lower down the valley, has a ruined medieval pele-tower with a neat, whitewashed, seventeenth century house attached rather incongruously. John Wilson, who was born in Long Sleddale in humble circumstances, became a famous botanist, and published in 1744 a *Synopsis of British Plants in Mr. Ray's Method . . . together with a Botanical Dictionary*, which was the first systematic account of British plants in English. He died at Kendal in 1751. On the fells between Long Sleddale and Kentmere is Skeggleswater, which it may be remembered Otley likened to the now vanished lake in the vale of Kentmere.

Long Sleddale and Bannisdale figure in Mrs. Humphry Ward's *Robert Elsmere* under the name of Long Whindale and Marrisdale. Mrs. Ward describes some of the old beliefs and customs which survived in these remote dales long after they were forgotten or fallen into disuse in the more populous valleys. The little pamphlet on *Manners and Customs of Westmorland*, written by 'A Literary Antiquarian' in 1827, gives still more fully some idea of the primitive life of the dales at a time when the rest of England was beginning to have the modern standard of living. Agriculture and gardening were so neglected that there was little variety of food, and oaten bread, dressed barley and a few onions constituted the chief part of the vegetable diet of the dalesmen during winter, whilst the art of fattening cattle in winter was not much practised until the beginning of the nineteenth century, the animals being killed off and salted or dried in smoke. The briny liquor in which the beef had been cooked, thickened with a little meal, was taken as broth, and this meal was helped down with pickled red cabbage.

Fresh provisions in winter were confined to eggs, poultry, geese, and badly-fed veal, but salmon was sold at a penny or twopence a pound, and was so abundant that at least one charity school in Westmorland had a special clause in the indentures of boys apprenticed by them to the effect that they should not be given fish more than three times a week, and a similar clause was included in the indentures of servants and possibly of agricultural labourers. Agues were so common on account of this food that they were regarded as necessary evils. It was not until about 1730 that potatoes were used, and then only sparingly, and it was about the same time that tea became a favourite beverage with the women, although its use was not universal, and one old lady who received a pound of tea from her son in London smoked it under the impression it was tobacco, and said it was not so good as tobacco from Virginia!

III

Although the fells which shut in Swindale are not so mountainous as those in some of the more westerly dales, the loneliness of the valley and ruggedness of these fells make it strangely impressive, and extremely characteristic of the Lake District. With its few scattered farms, its quaint little church, its babbling brook and its wild flowers blooming in their season from early spring to mid-autumn, and the heather and bracken which make a glory of the fells, Swindale has a rare beauty which makes the thought of its danger of flooding as a supplementary reservoir to that at Haweswater most unwelcome. Swindale has never been a populous valley, but it has had one native who achieved fame: the Rev. John Hodgson, the historian of Northumberland, who was born there in 1780. On the strength of the removal of the Hodgson family to the neighbouring village of Rosgill soon after his birth, Rosgill has claimed him for a native, but John Hodgson himself, in a chapter on Westmorland contributed to *The Beauties of England and Wales*, mentions that he was born at Swindale. He was educated at Bampton School and began his career as master of the village school in Matterdale at a salary of £11 a year. Among many other works, Hodgson wrote an interesting account of the old system of coal-mining, and was for several years employed in making experiments to prevent accidents in coal mines. Sir Humphry Davy acknowledged that Hodgson helped him to complete his invention of the safety lamp, and Hodgson was one of the first to venture into a mine with the new lamp and explain its principle to the colliers.

Swindale chapel is a little grey stone building near the head of the dale, with a tiny schoolroom at the west end. The church was probably built in the seventeenth century, and in one of the windows is some fifteenth century stained glass, said to have come from Clifton church. The screen incorporates some early eighteenth century balusters. The school was founded in 1703, and the little schoolroom was presumably built in that year. It had an average attendance of three scholars, and at the beginning of this century the master had a salary of £30 a year, but the school has since been abandoned.

The Rev. J. Whiteside, in a paper on Swindale, recounts some amusing stories of the old vicars. Stephen Walker, who became curate in 1816 and vicar in 1833, found the parsonage so dilapidated that he stayed with each of his parishioners in turn. He kept his sermons in a box, and took one from the top of the pile each Sunday, and whilst he was staying with Mrs. Sewell of Swindale Head, the outspoken old lady told him to 'Stir up that box; they 's beginning to come verra' thick'. It was during Walker's time that a dispute arose in the chapel on one occasion as to whether it was really Sunday, until at last one old man ended the discussion by saying definitely: 'The Parson's reet; gang on.' On another occasion the bottle of wine for communion being accidently broken, the vicar used rum instead, regarding it as a practical expedient and not realizing in the least that anyone would think the matter unusual in any way. Thomas Sewell, another vicar, was one of a band of brothers who were men of note in their day. He was buried at Shap in 1870 at the age of seventy-three.

Mardale is now a place of memories. No one who walked up the valley in 1936 and saw the fields carpeted with wild flowers and the hedges in a glory of bloom, and the great rhododendron bushes clustering round the Dun Bull Inn, could fail to regret that it was their last flowering before the water began to flood in during the following winter. The picturesque old church stood ruined, and forlorn, Measand Hall, too, had been shattered by explosions, the farms were nearly all evacuated, and the walls of the new Dun Bull rising beside the new road, so high above the then level of the lake, were a reminder that the old Dun Bull, which had seen so many jolly gatherings at Sheep Fairs, Sports Meetings and Hunts, would soon be deserted, and later drowned fathoms deep. The oldest part of the Dun Bull dated back to the seventeenth century.

The date of the foundation of Mardale church is uncertain. It was formerly a chapel of Shap, and the Royal Commission on the Ancient Monuments of Westmorland considered that the chancel and nave were probably of medieval date, with a late medieval roof. Up to 1729 the dead of Mardale were strapped to the backs of horses and taken up the Corpse Road over Mardale Common and Swindale, for burial at Shap. Hall Caine, although he laid the scene of the *Shadow of a Crime* in Thirlmere, wove his story round an incident which traditionally occurred in Mardale, when the corpse of a Mardalian who had died with an undivulged crime on his conscience was taken over the fells, but during a dreadful thunderstorm the horse bolted and was not captured until the secret came to light three months later. Various fittings from the church are being preserved at Shap and Borrowdale, and the bones of those buried in Mardale churchyard have been transferred to a special corner of the mother church at Shap.

Mardale, like Patterdale, had its 'Kings', who originated in Hugh Holme, who fled north in 1209, after the discovery of a plot against King John in which he was implicated. He took refuge in a cave in the wildest part of Riggindale, known as Hugh's Cave to this day, and after the death of King John had made it safe for him to return to his home, still lingered in Mardale, where he founded the long line of the 'Kings' of Mardale, which lasted 700 years, and only ended with the death of Hugh Parker Holme, the last male in the direct line, in 1885. One of the Holmes is said to have founded an oratory at Mardale in the fourteenth century. Such a long and unbroken connexion with the valley makes it seem providential that the direct line did not live to see the destruction of their ancient home. An early branch of the family was settled at Riggindale, a seventeenth century house also at the head of the Mardale valley, and a sixteenth century branch at Bowderthwaite close by, but both houses are now flooded.

The inscription on Measand School, which was founded in 1711, and stood on the western shore of the lake, is being preserved by the Manchester Corporation, together with other inscribed stones. Measand Hall, which has shared the fate of the buildings on Mardale Green, was the home of the Blands, and had many associations with Jacob Thompson, the famous Penrith artist who received his first commission from a former Earl of Lonsdale. His pictures of Haweswater, which include 'Drawing the Net', and 'Pleasure Party on Haweswater', and others portraying the last King of Mardale and his brother, have an added interest now the valley is so altered, and it is equally fortunate that the Westmorland volume of the Royal Commission on Historical Monuments has been completed before it was too late to see and describe the old buildings of Mardale, whilst the little booklet, *A Backwater in Lakeland*, by Isaac Hinchcliffe, with its many illustrations, will be invaluable as a picture of the life in the dale where there was much good cheer of a homely and delightful kind, although it was said that the sun never penetrated from Martinmas to Candlemas, so encompassed is it with great mountains.

Although it is impossible not to regret the changes at Haweswater and Mardale, which can never have the perfection of beauty which was originally theirs and was compact of the relation between the high fells and the low-lying lake, and the gentler beauty of the meadows and signs of centuries of human occupation of the valley, the Manchester Corporation deserve the greatest praise for the way in which they have carried out their work. It is impossible to deny that the road they have constructed along the east side of the lake has a far better surface than the old road, and there are many of the most enthusiastic lovers of the district who have admitted that the new foot-path on the north-western side provides better views than those afforded by the old road. The trees of the deer-forest of Naddle hide much of the stonework of the low wall bounding the motor-road, and the Corporation even had the forethought to plant trees and bushes round the workmen's settlement at Burn Banks, so that the scars made by the removal of the houses on the completion of the work would be hidden.

The prehistoric fort on Castle Crag at the head of Mardale remains above the water level, and at the Burn Banks end of the lake the beautiful Thornthwaite Force and the Elizabethan Thornthwaite Hall still give interest to the district. Naddle House, which dates from the sixteenth and seventeenth centuries, also survives.

The present Thornthwaite Hall was probably built when it was in the possession of the Curwen family. Sir Daniel le

Fleming mentions that Thornthwaite 'was the antientest land belonging to ye Curwens of Workington in Cumberland, it being possessed by that family from the Conquest until Sr. Hugh de Curwen Knt. sold the same unto ye. Lord William Howard of Naworth Castle in Cumberland, who gave it to Sr. Francis Howard, his younger son, whose son and heir Francis Howard of Corby Castle in Cumberland, doth now enjoy it'. The Lord William Howard mentioned by Sir Daniel was the original of Sir Walter Scott's 'Belted Will', in *The Lay of the Last Minstrel*, although he was never Warden of the Western Marches, and most of the exploits ascribed to him by Scott were those of the Dacre family. It is traditionally believed that Lord William died at Thornthwaite, as it is on record that he was there two days before his death. Thornthwaite Hall was used by Anthony Trollope for the setting of *Can You Forgive Her?*

Hugh's Laithes Pike, which dominates the Burn Banks end of Haweswater, is crowned by a stone which is said to mark the last resting place of Jimmie Lowther, who after a riotous life, came to a bad end by breaking his neck through steeple-chasing whilst he was drunk, and having died too suddenly to allow him a death-bed repentance, could not rest quietly in his grave. He haunted the villagers in spite of all the efforts of the parson of Lowther to 'lay' his ghost, until at last his body was dug up and re-buried on the highest point of Naddle Forest, where he could trouble them no longer.

The neighbouring Walla Crag—cheerfully rendered here, as elsewhere in the Lake District as 'Wallow' Crag on the Ordnance Survey—was once a favourite haunt of eagles, and it is said that when the nest of an eagle on this crag was robbed on one occasion, thirty-five fishes, seven lambs, and other provisions for the eaglets were found. Bleawater Crag with its tarn, which lies at the head of Mardale, also has its story, for in 1761 a man named Dixon of Kentmere, when following a hard run fox, slipped and fell down the sheer precipice of three hundred feet, striking the rocks as he fell, but was still able to call out to those who came to his rescue 'Lads! lads! t'fox is gane oot at t'hee end! Lig t'dogs on, an' I'll cum seun!' before becoming insensible. Although terribly battered, not one of his bones were broken, and he ultimately recovered. The rocks have since been known locally as 'Dixon's three jumps'.

The great Roman road of High Street runs on the crest of the mountains to the west of Haweswater, and there are numerous prehistoric remains on the surrounding peaks. Wrestling, jumping, horse races and other sports were held annually on High Street for many years—an extremely breezy and awkward situation to reach, as it is over 2,718 feet above sea level, but the gathering originated in the shepherds' meeting for the identification of stray sheep. The High Street meetings were discontinued about the beginning of the nineteenth century, and the sports and wrestlings were held on Whit-Mondays at the Dun Bull and in November at the Kirkstone Inn—liquid refreshment being a great feature of the occasion.

Chapter VIII

FROM HAWESWATER TO THE BANKS OF THE EAMONT

IMMEDIATELY north of Haweswater the character of the scenery changes with all the swiftness and completeness of a transformation scene. Gone are the great crags and precipices characteristic of the wilder valleys of the Lake District, and in their place are widespreading meadows and low rolling hills and woodlands—yet this countryside, too, has its place in any tour of the Lakes, for this was the route the invading Scots frequently took in their descents on England, and the great pele-towers which cluster round Penrith defended this route as well as that over the Shap Fells.

Bampton, a scattered village which is the centre of a large parish, has produced several notabilities, and its grammar school, founded in 1623, achieved such fame that one master alone, the Rev. J. Bowstead, who flourished there in the early part of the nineteenth century, educated over 200 priests, and it was said that 'they drove the plough in Latin at Bampton'. A free library was established in the village as early as 1710. Richard Hogarth, father of the celebrated eighteenth century engraver and painter, was born at Bampton, migrating to London as a young man after an unsuccessful attempt to run a school in his native county. A letter he wrote in London is preserved in the British Museum, and a dictionary he compiled in Latin and English is still in existence.

Two Bamptonians who achieved fame were Hugh Curwen, successively Archbishop of Dublin and Bishop of Oxford, and John Mill, Principal of St. Edmund Hall, Oxford. Both had consciences which allowed them to change their opinions to suit circumstances. Hugh Curwen managed to keep in high favour with Henry VIII, Edward VI, Mary Tudor and Elizabeth, which involved a good deal of change in his religious 'convictions', whilst John Mill gained himself the nickname of 'Johnny Wind-mill' by his political vacillations. Mill's chief claim to fame is his compilation of the New Testament in Greek, which has been designated 'a masterpiece of scholarship and critical insight'. Richard Bancroft, Archbishop of Canterbury, was a great-nephew of Hugh Curwen, and was educated at his expense.

The Gibsons, a very old Bampton family, with a record dating back to the time of Henry VIII, also produced some notable men, and these had the additional virtue of strict integrity in their opinions. Thomas Gibson, the author of *The Anatomy of Humane Bodies epitomized*, married as his second wife Anne, sixth daughter of Richard Cromwell, and was appointed physician-general to the army in 1718. His nephew and heir, Edmund Gibson, became successively Bishop of Lincoln and of London. He was a most able churchman, not afraid to denounce prevalent evils, and compiled the *Codex Juris Ecclesiae Anglicanae*, a monumental work which is still the highest authority on church law. His brother, John Gibson, was provost of Queen's College, Oxford, for thirteen years.

Bampton church was rebuilt in 1726 and restored in 1884, but contains numerous seventeenth century fittings.

Bampton Hall has a square pigeon house with a gabled roof, dating from the sixteenth century, and Knipe Hall dates chiefly from the same century.

Beyond Bampton the road passes the foot of the slope on which the village of Helton is set—a village which is most attractive when seen from the higher road which passes in front of the houses, but is undistinguished from the 'back view' it turns to the highway.

About a mile beyond Helton is Askham, which claims with good reason to be the prettiest village in the district. Its seventeenth century houses border two long village greens shaded with gigantic trees, with the dignified Hall and parish church standing a little apart, close to the river Lowther. Robert Southey's son Charles was Vicar of Askham until his death in 1888. Askham Hall belonged to the Sandford family from 1375 until 1680, and the pele-tower and part of the house appear to date from the fourteenth century. Much rebuilding was done from 1575 onwards, and a panel on the west wing bears an achievement of the Sandford arms, with the initials T.S. and A.S.—Thomas Sandford and his wife Anne—with the inscription: 'Thomas Sandford Esquyr for this payd meat and hyr The year of our Savyore xv hundredth seventy-four.'

The church was entirely rebuilt in 1832 but retains the seventeenth century communion table, pews, font and monuments, whilst a medieval carved corbel has been reset in one of the walls. In Setterah Park, south of the village, is an earthwork which was probably a homestead moat, but is marked on the Ordnance Survey as a Roman camp, Roman relics having been found there. There are other earthworks on Askham Fell and Moor Divoc, and village settlements can be traced on Skirsgill Hill.

At Askham the road from Mardale branches into two, one branch making direct for Penrith and the other running through Lowther Park. It is well worth the slight detour involved to take the road through Lowther Park, whether the traveller's destination be Penrith or Pooley Bridge, for the more direct roads have no features of special interest, whilst the drive through the park runs close to the great castle, once the pride of the North, but now deserted, with its gardens

ASHNESS BRIDGE, NEAR KESWICK

and park relapsing into wildness since it was abandoned by Lord Lonsdale.

The original building on the site, occupied by the Lowthers from the reign of Henry II, was pulled down by Sir John Lowther in 1685, and rebuilt on a large scale. Defoe speaks of this mansion as 'a very noble and ancient seat . . . the house was beautiful, but the Stables were the Wonder of England, being esteemed the largest and finest that any Nobleman or Gentleman in Britain is Master of: and his Lordship breeds as good running horses and hunters, as most in England. But the house was of late unfortunately burnt down and all its fine pictures and Furniture consumed, and is not yet rebuilt'. Gilpin speaks of the family in 1787 as inhabiting a temporary mansion whilst the materials were being gathered for the present enormous building, which was designed by Sir Robert Smirke, and commenced about 1806.

Sir John Lowther, who died in 1700, was the first Viscount Lonsdale, and James Lowther, who succeeded the third Viscount Lonsdale, was created the first Earl of Lonsdale in 1784. He was succeeded by Sir William Lowther of Swillington, as he left no son, and it was Sir William who, as second Earl, became the good friend of Wordsworth, and, as a contemporary guide said, 'as beloved by all as his predecessor had been hated'.

St. Michael's Church, Lowther, dates in part from the twelfth century, although alterations and extensions were made in later centuries. Its monuments to the Lowthers are of much interest, and the pre-Conquest stones in the churchyard, consisting of three hog-backed stones and two tomb-stones, all richly carved, attract antiquaries.

Hackthorpe Hall, which is near the south-eastern entrance to the great park of Lowther, was built by Sir Christopher Lowther early in the seventeenth century, and was the birthplace of the first Viscount Lonsdale. Like so many of the ancient Halls of the neighbourhood, it is now a farm house.

Northward from Lowther is the village of Clifton, and the old pele-tower of the Wybergs, who were seated there from the fourteenth to the nineteenth century. It is of particular interest, as the remainder of the house has been demolished, and the fifteenth century tower stands in solitary defiance, as all the pele-towers stood before they were almost hidden by later extensions. The neighbouring farm house, although modern, has a Roman slab with carved figures and an inscription inset into its walls, and the rectory garage has a fifteenth century window which is said to have come from the Hall.

The nave of the parish church of Clifton dates from the twelfth century, and various extensions made in the thirteenth and fourteenth centuries survived the restoration of 1846, when the chancel was rebuilt with old material. There is a medieval cross with a later sundial on top in the churchyard, and numerous medieval and seventeenth century fittings and monuments in the church. The registers contain several entries recording the burial of those killed in the clash between the Highlanders and Royalist forces on December 18th, 1745, which is frequently referred to as the last 'battle' on English soil, but is more properly the last 'skirmish' on English soil.

The Highlanders laid an ambuscade round the Town End, the house of Thomas Savage, a Quaker, which is still in existence. During the ensuing skirmish the Quaker and his daughter apparently shut themselves up in their house, but this did not prevent Savage from writing an account of the fight. A full account is given by James Ray, a volunteer of Whitehaven, who served in the Royalist army, and published a *Compleat History of the Rebellion* dedicated to the Duke of Cumberland. Ray says that 'we pushed them (the Highlanders) with such intrepidity that in about an Hour they quitted the Field and the neighbouring Villages, and fled to Penrith. It was so late before the Affair was over, and the Country so covered, that it was impossible to follow them with any Probability of Success; so that his Royal Highness took up his Quarters at Thomas Savage's House, who rejoiced much in the Spirit that such a Guest was come under his Roof'. Savage described the Duke who was so soon to earn for himself the name of "Butcher' as 'pleasant agreeable company . . . a man of parts, very friendly, and no pride in him'.

Beyond the railway line which cuts across the scene of the

skirmish are the pele-towers of Cliburn and Newbiggin, and northward along the main road to Penrith is the turning for Brougham Hall and Castle.

Brougham Castle is most picturesquely situated in meadows beside the river Eamont, and there are extensive remains of the twelfth century Keep and additions of later periods, which are built partly over the site of the Roman fort of Brocavum. The castle was finally added to and repaired by the Countess of Pembroke in the seventeenth century, and is now in the care of the Commissioners of Works.

By far the most notable person associated with the castle is the Lady Anne Clifford, more generally known as the Countess of Pembroke, who had such an important influence not only on the fortunes of Brougham but of other castles and wide estates that the Report of the Royal Commission on the Historical Monuments of Westmorland has a special chapter dealing with her life and character—the only person in the history of the County so honoured.

Lady Anne was born in 1590 and was the daughter and heiress of George, third Earl of Cumberland. She married first Richard, third Earl of Dorset, with whom she lived at Knowle in Kent, and secondly Philip, fourth Earl of Pembroke, and she was related by birth and marriage to an extraordinary number of powerful families. Her mother was the daughter of the Earl of Bedford and her aunt was the Countess of Warwick, and among other families to whom she was kin were the Percys, Howards, Sydneys, Talbots, Scropes, Stanleys, Devereux, Russells, Whartons, Cecils, Dudleys, Lowthers, Coniers, and Bouchiers. Her eldest daughter and heiress married the Earl of Thanet, and her second daughter was wife to the Earl of Coventry, and a granddaughter married Christopher Lord Hatton.

By the will of her father the vast estates in the north passed through the male Clifford line before reverting to the Countess, and it was not until the deaths of her uncle and cousin, the fourth and fifth Earls of Cumberland, that she entered into her inheritance. During the time when the fourth Earl was living at Brougham Castle, he and his son entertained King James I for three days in 1617, and Sayer's

History of Westmorland, published in 1848, mentioned that a book was still extant entitled 'the airs sung in Brougham Castle before King James'.

The Countess was nearly sixty before she took possession of her lands, but she soon showed herself a most remarkable old lady. She restored her castles of Appleby, Brougham, Brough, Pendragon, Skipton and Barden, restored or rebuilt all the churches on her property, founded the almshouses of St. Anne at Appleby, and assisted many of her retainers or poorer tenants in building and restoring their property.

The Countess had never submitted to the ruling of King James over her inheritance, and was equally defiant of Cromwell's power, whilst she ignored Charles II's expressed wish for a male holder of the office of Sheriff of Westmorland, which was hereditary in the family of Clifford. She assumed all the duties and responsibilities of the office to the end of her life, and as a last defiance had inscribed on her coffin 'High Sheriffess by inheritance of ye County of Westmoreland'. She was the most just and generous of women, but sturdily resisted the least infringement of her rights. She entered into law suits on the slightest provocation. and once spent £200 in proving her right to a 'boon hen' from one of her tenants—and then invited her opponent to an elaborate dinner at which the fowl was served up as the first course.

There appears to be no documentary evidence that she ever wrote the often quoted letter to Sir Joseph Williamson, who had dared to nominate a candidate to stand for election as member of Parliament for Appleby: 'I have been bullied by a usurper; I have neen neglected by a court, but I will not be dictated to by a subject. Your man shan't stand. Anne, Dorset, Pembroke and Montgomery.' The letter is, however, completely in character and the anecdote deserves to be true!

The full story of the life of Lady Anne Clifford has been written by Dr. G. C. Williamson, and Hartley Coleridge included her in his *Lives of the Northern Worthies*, but the most fascinating source of information is her own diary, which commences in 1653 and is prefaced by autobiographical memories of her early life. She describes her early beauties of face and figure with great complacency, and in her diary is uniformly satisfied with her own behaviour, but there is much information and many 'human touches' which make it most readable. She records on one occasion that she paid Mr. Robert Williamson of Penrith for a runlet of sack, but thought it too dear, and was very angry with him 'and then he slipt away from me in a good hurry'.

Under the date 1658 she mentions that some mischievous people took down the famous Hartshorns placed on a tree in the park in 1333 to commemorate the occasion when Edward Baliol, King of the Scots, came by permission of the English King to a great stag hunt in the forest of Lord Clifford. The Countess took the greatest pride in her ancestry and had the history of the Clifford family carefully recorded. She died in 1675 and is buried in a splendid tomb in the church of St. Lawrence of Appleby, near the tomb of her mother, whom she had most tendeerly loved.

Bishop Rainbow said of her: 'she was not ignorant of knowledge in any kind which might make her conversation not only useful and grave but also pleasant and delightful; which, that she might better do, she would frequently bring out of the rich storehouse of her memory, things new and old, sentences, or sayings of remark, which she had read or learned out of authors, and with these her walls, her bed, her hangings and furniture must be adorned, causing her servants to write them in papers, and her maids to pin them up that she or they in the time of their dressing, or as occasion served, might remember and make their descants upon them. So that, though she had not many books in her chamber, yet it was dressed up with the flowers of a library'.

Brougham Hall was the seat of a family called Bird, from the time of Henry VI to the eighteenth century, and was locally known as 'Bird's Nest'. The last of the family was James Bird, who was an eminent lawyer and antiquary, and was for many years law agent and manor steward to the Countess of Pembroke. He died without male heirs, and the estate was sold by his grand-daughters in 1726 to John Brougham of Scales, who was succeeded by his nephew Henry, grandfather of the first Lord Brougham and Vaux, the most famous of that family, who supported the cause of

Queen Caroline against George IV, and became Chancellor of the Exchequer in 1830. It was during his Chancellorship that he drove about in the carriage specially built for him, which was the forerunner of the closed carriages which bore his name.

The seventeenth century Brougham Hall was largely rebuilt by the first Lord Brougham, but was demolished in 1924, and now only the first floor walls are standing of the splendid mansion which was once famous as the 'Windsor of the North'. A bridge across the road connects the Hall with the beautiful little chapel of St. Wilfred, which was entirely rebuilt by the Countess of Pembroke, and thoroughly restored in the middle of the nineteenth century by Lord Brougham, who fitted it with rich woodwork and wall decorations. Both this church and the old parish church of St. Ninian, which lies in a lonely situation on the Westmorland bank of the River Eamont, are still used for services. St. Ninian's, which was formerly called Ninekirks, was rebuilt by the Countess in 1660, and remains an interesting example of seventeenth century work.

The main road between Appleby and Penrith runs close under the walls of Brougham Castle, passing by the Countess Pillar, erected in 1654 by the Countess of Pembroke to commemorate her last parting with her beloved mother in 1616. There is a long inscription on the pillar recording her wish that an annuity of four pounds be distributed every second day of April to the poor of Brougham 'for ever upon ye stone table here hard by'. The stone table still stands about three yards east of the pillar, and although the village of Brougham has long vanished, the money is still distributed to the most needy people in the parish of Brougham.

The Kendal highway to Penrith is the one which runs direct from Clifton and crosses over the River Eamont into Cumberland at the village of Eamont Bridge. Up to the beginning of this century there was a gigantic sign at Eamont Bridge, showing a huge Highlander shaking hands with a small man, and the legend 'Welcome to Cumberland'. The road for Pooley Bridge strikes off from the main road on the Westmorland side of the river, and on the corner is the great earthwork known as King Arthur's

Round Table, which was the first Ancient Monument in Westmorland to be placed under the protection of the Commissioners of Works. It consists of a prehistoric earthwork, roughly circular in area and 150 feet by 160 feet in diameter, bounded by a ditch with a bank on the outside, and although the Pooley Bridge road cuts across the northern bank, is otherwise in very good condition. The origin of the earthwork is unknown, but the old ballad whose first line Shakespeare puts into the mouth of Sir John Falstaff, 'When Arthur first at court began, and was approved king', describes a terrible single combat between Sir Lancelot du Lac, and the robber chieftain Torquin, a man of gigantic stature who lived in a den on the Cumberland bank of the Eamont—still known as the Giant's Cave—and had imprisoned many knights of Arthur's Court. The ballad ends the description of Sir Lancelot's victory:

'Forthwith he strucke his necke in two;
And, when hee had soe done,
From prison threescore knights and four
Delivered everye one.'

King Arthur's Round Table was at one time used as an amphitheatre for sports, and Stukeley records that the Scots Army which accompanied Charles II to Worcester camped for some time on the site.

A quarter of a mile away is the great earthwork of Mayburgh, which occupies a slight knoll. The ramparts are now largely covered with turf and planted with trees, and a single stone in the enclosure standing nine feet above the level of the soil is the only survivor of eight stones which stood there up to the eighteenth century.

On the Westmorland bank of the river Eamont, about a mile from Eamont Bridge, is Yanwath Hall, guarding a ford over the river. The pele-tower is said to have been built by John de Sutton in 1322, and part of the house probably dates from the same period, but it was largely rebuilt and extended in the early fifteenth century, when it came into the possession of the Threlkelds, and again in the sixteenth century when it passed to the Dudleys by marriage. It came into the possession of the Lowther family in 1671 and is now used as a farm house, but is an exceptionally interesting example of the development of a pele-tower into a manor house. It has figured in several technical works on the subject of fortified manor houses.

Sir Lancelot Threlkeld of Yanwath, who also owned the manors of Crosby Ravensworth and Threlkeld, was the second husband of Lady Clifford, and helped her to conceal her young son from his enemies—a romantic tale that has been told in full by Wordsworth and many others. The boy was the son of 'Black' Clifford, who killed the young Earl of Rutland at the Battle of Wakefield and was himself killed shortly afterwards. The Clifford family was attainted for nearly a quarter of a century, during which time the young heir was brought up by shepherds on the estates of his step-father. The 'Shepherd Lord' was restored to his titles and vast possessions on the accession of Henry VII, but his long years on the fells made him disinclined for Court life, and he lived chiefly on his estates, immersed in his books, and especially devoting himself to the study of astronomy. His descendant, the famous Countess Anne, gave many details of his life in her history of the Clifford family.

Within a short distance of Yanwath Hall is the Grotto, once the home of Thomas Wilkinson, the beloved friend of Wordsworth. When Dorothy and William Wordsworth and Coleridge went on their Highland tour in 1803 they borrowed Wilkinson's account of his tour and followed his route, and it was a sentence in Wilkinson's journal which inspired Wordsworth to write *The Solitary Highland Reaper*. Wordsworth wrote a sonnet to the spade used by Wilkinson, and mentioned him in other poems. Wilkinson delighted in landscape gardening, and designed the rock path in Lowther Park which lies beside the river, and helped to plan the grounds at Tent Lodge, Coniston. Many famous people visited Wilkinson at the Grotto, and all were charmed by his simple, lovable character. He was a staunch Quaker, and helped Clarkson in his work for the abolition of slavery. He was buried in the graveyard of the little Quaker Meeting House at Tirril, where John Slee, a noted mathematician of his day and Charles Gough, who died on Helvellyn, are also buried.

Within a short distance of Tirril is the village of Sockbridge, and the Hall, which formerly belonged to the de Lancasters, and passed to the Lowthers early in the seventeenth century. The pele-tower was destroyed about 1830, but the main block, which dates back to the seventeenth century, or earlier, survives. Richard Wordsworth, Receiver-General of Westmorland, and grandfather of the poet Wordsworth, lived for many years at Sockbridge. He was buried in the churchyard of the nearby church of Barton. This church dates in part from the twelfth century, with various extensions made in succeeding centuries, including the adding of stabling north of the tower in the seventeenth century, which was used until comparatively recent years. There are some ornamental medieval coffin lids, monuments and other fittings in the church. The neighbouring Barton Church Farm dates back to the sixteenth century, and the main block of Winder Hall, about a mile to the south, is dated 1612.

PART II

CUMBERLAND

Chapter IX

IN AND AROUND PENRITH

I

PENRITH deserves considerably more attention from visitors to the Lakes than it usually receives, for not only are there interesting buildings and antiquities in the town and its immediate neighbourhood, but it is an excellent centre for north-eastern Lakeland.

The history of Kendal was stormy enough, but that of Penrith was far stormier, and it has known many different lords. The greater part of Penrith's early history is like a concentrated account of Cumberland as a whole, with its settlement by the Celtic tribe of the Brigantes, its invasions by Romans, by Danes from the east, and by Norsemen from the Isle of Man. After the defeat of the Norse king of Cumberland, Dunmail, in 945, Penrith, in common with the rest of Cumberland, fell under Scottish rule up to 1032, when King Canute exchanged Cumbria for Lothian, and drew for the first time the line which afterwards became the Border.

With the coming of the Normans, although nominally under their rule, Cumberland became a battleground seldom free from warfare up to 1237, when the kings of Scotland and England came to an arrangement, and it was ceded finally to England. Less than fifty years later, however, the Scots dynasty ended, and the consequent changes caused the Scots to claim their old territory in Cumberland. Their raids recommenced with all the added enthusiasm engendered by a feeling that justice was on their side, and continued up to the time of the Union between Scotland and England in 1610.

Penrith, so temptingly near the Border, and so entirely without natural defences, bore the brunt of these attacks.

In addition to countless unrecorded raids from 1311 onwards, it was burned down in 1314, and there was the devastating occasion when Black Douglas descended on the town in 1347, with 30,000 Scots who not only laid Penrith waste, but took prisoner all the able-bodied inhabitants whom they did not kill. Thirty-five years later the town was again burned down.

How Penrith ever survived its misfortunes is known only to the sturdy Cumbrian townspeople who so doggedly rebuilt and defended their town after each major raid, but a court-leet and view of frank pledge were held there from time immemorial, and as early as 1222 it had been of sufficient importance to receive a charter for a weekly market and a yearly fair extending from the eve of Whitsun to the Monday after Trinity.

The early history of Penrith's principal buildings is extremely difficult to trace satisfactorily, and several writers on the subject have made conflicting statements without any attempt to reconcile them. William Strickland, Bishop of Carlisle, who died in 1419, is credited with having built an earlier fortress on the site of Penrith Castle, but the licence to crenellate "quandam cameram suam in ville de Penreth" was not granted him until 1397, and was confirmed in 1399. It is also said the castle had been granted to Ralph Neville, first Earl of Westmorland, in 1397, and he is credited with the construction of the earliest part of the present castle. Strickland's property in Penrith was inherited by his daughter Margaret, who married Robert de Lowther, and the Two Lions Hotel at Penrith was originally the house of Gerald Lowther, one of her descendants. The building dates back to 1585, but the magnificent panelling and plaster-work of the interior is believed to be still older, indicating an earlier house on the site which might well be the building fortified by the Bishop.

Again, the Gloucester Arms Hotel displays the arms of Richard, Duke of Gloucester, and was almost certainly used by Richard as a place of residence—probably whilst he was extending the castle—yet one guide gives the date of the house as 1580—nearly a hundred years later than Richard's death on Bosworth field!

It seems certain that Bishop Strickland built a chantry at Penrith—perhaps on the site of an earlier foundation, and the town undoubtedly owes to him the water supply brought from the River Petteril, a tributary of the Eamont, by means of the Thacka Beck, a water course which has been built over in modern times, with the exception of a short reach behind Robinson's School in Middlegate. A Grammar School was attached to Bishop Strickland's fourteenth century chantry, and was refounded by Queen Elizabeth in 1564. The Tudor building is still in existence near the church, although now only occasionally used.

Presumably it was Strickland's chantry which was rebuilt by Richard Neville, Earl of Warwick—the famous 'King-maker'—and when the church was again rebuilt in the eighteenth century the tower of Warwick's building was retained, with its pinnacles showing the Warwick badge of a bear climbing a ragged staff.

Visitors to Penrith should disabuse their minds of the traditional figure of Richard III created by Shakespeare and others who wrote with one eye on Henry VIII or Queen Elizabeth, immediate descendants of the man who had caused Richard's death and ascended his throne with very inadequate claims to the dignity. It was not until Richard came south on the death of his brother Edward IV, to whom he had always given unswerving loyalty, that circumstances conspired to make him so mad with ambition and ruthlessness. There are some in the north who accept the conventional idea of Richard as a hunchback without one redeeming quality, but he is more generally remembered there as the gallant young Duke of Gloucester who, from the time he was eighteen until the death of Edward IV, thirteen years later, held various offices in the north, including that of Warden of the West Marches, and whose personal courage and brilliant leadership in his campaigns against the Scots resulted in a cessation of invasions for the time being.

The princely state he kept at Penrith Castle and his other seats in the north, and his many admirable qualities, won him ardent friends and loyal followers in all parts of Westmorland, Cumberland and Yorkshire, whose allegiance never wavered until his death on Bosworth Field. Incidentally, his feats of swordsmanship and exploits on the field of battle prove that any deformity must have been extremely slight.

Richard's mother was the celebrated 'Proud Cis of Raby', who married Richard Plantagenet, Duke of York, and paid for the distinction of having two of her sons crowned kings of England, by the deaths of her husband, and her second son, the Earl of Rutland, at the Battle of Wakefield; her third son, the Duke of Clarence, being put to death in 1478, and other relatives meeting with violent deaths in battle or by execution. It is not surprising that she eventually sought refuge in the nunnery of Berkhampstead, where she spent the last years of her life. A stained glass window in Penrith church is said to be a contemporary portrait of Cecily and her ill-fated husband.

Penrith, like Kendal, adopted the system of 'yards' as an added defence against the Scots raiders, and a number of these yards survive in the town although, as its population never equalled that of Kendal, the number of yards is correspondingly smaller, and has been further reduced by the clearing away of considerable portions of the old town to make room for modern buildings. The house of Grey Friars, founded at the end of the thirteenth century, was dissolved within a hundred years, the site now being occupied by the modern houses of Abbot Bank and the Friarage. The town jail, built in 1547 with stone from Penrith castle, was used as a lodging for Mary, Queen of Scots, on her fateful journey south. Only a fragment of stone wall remains in Scotland Road to mark the site.

Nevertheless, Penrith has some notable old buildings surviving. It is impossible for those who arrive by train, or even pass through by rail, *not* to see the castle ruins, unless they are exceptionally unobservant, for they stand directly opposite the station and by daylight are undeniably disappointing. The best time to see the ruins is in the gloaming, when the public garden in which they stand is deserted, and the red sandstone walls are etched blackly against a flaming sunset sky. At such a time there is a magic and beauty in the crumbling walls, and it is possible to dream of the days of its greatness when the powerful Nevilles held their state there and Richard III was still a gallant stripling.

From the castle it is but a step or two downhill to the old Dockwray Hall, now the Gloucester Arms Hotel where many visitors ask to sleep in 'Richard's Room'. In the open space of Great Dockwray and at Sandgate the crowds used to gather for the bull and bear baitings, where as many as five bulls have been baited in one day. Both Penrith and the neighbouring village of Stainton were noted for bull-dogs of a pure and courageous breed.

Among the ancient inns surviving in the town are the Blue Bell, dated 1668, and the old George and Dragon Inn, which has been reconstructed as the George Hotel, and now includes the house where Prince Charles Edward stayed with his officers in 1745. The old Golden Fleece inn, with its oak ceilings, staircases and floors, is now used as a warehouse, and another ancient building in Rowcliffe Lane is said to have once been the principal inn of Penrith and also used as a letter office in the seventeenth century. A building in the Corn Market, dated 1624, was formerly the Black Lion Inn. As compensation for these inns turned to other uses there are Gerald Lowther's House, Dockwray Hall, and a house in King Street which although reconstructed in 1904, bears the date 1669 on the original entrance door, all three of which are now inns.

The churchyard of Penrith is nearly circular, and outside its railings is a foot-path edged by dignified old houses, giving it all the quiet charm of a cathedral Close. The 'Roger Bertram' House bears the date 1563, and another of the buildings is the Elizabethan Grammar School. Apart from the interest of the church itself, there is the famous 'Giant's Grave', variously explained in local traditions as the last resting place of the giant Torquin killed by Sir Lancelot du Lac at King Arthur's Round Table, Eamont Bridge; and as a Knight of gigantic stature called Owen Cæsarius. The stories of Owen Cæsarius vary considerably, some do not even agree upon his name—sometimes he is a pagan, at other times a Christian knight; sometimes it is he who killed the giant in the Giant's Caves above the River Eamont; and at other times he is said to have rid the great Inglewood Forest, which stretched north of Penrith, of its wild boars. Antiquarians dismiss all the stories and suggest

GRANGE IN BORROWDALE

they are a re-arranged group of pre-Norman grave monuments, consisting of two crosses and four hog-backed stones, all originally carved, but so worn by the weather that the design is difficult to distinguish. Sir Walter Scott was so fascinated by the problem of their origin that he never passed through Penrith without stopping to look at them and ponder over them, and even on his last journey south, when enfeebled by illness, his family could not persuade him to forgo his customary visit as they drove through the town, although he had seen them 'dozens of times'. There is also a pre-Norman wheel cross known as the Giant's Thumb, in the churchyard, and in the church is the Plague Stone recording the death of 2,260 people in the parish during the Plague Year. One of the earliest victims was Lancelot Musgrave of the house in Middlegate now known as the Long Front. In recent times it was the home of the Countess Ossalinsky, who was one of the Jacksons of Thirlmere before her marriage.

The feeling of security following on the Union of Scotland and England was evidently followed by a fever for building on the part of the townspeople. Bowerbank Hall has an inscription over the door-head, 'John Matthews, 1612', and the worthy man had ventured to build his house well away from the north gate, on a site which must have been quite isolated in those days, although the Hall is now surrounded by the houses of Penrith's newest development schemes. Sandgate Hall was built in 1646, by the Fletchers of Hutton-in-the-Forest, and survives as three dwelling houses. In Benson Row is the Hutton Spout, provided by a member of the family about two centuries ago for the watering of cattle and horses, and in the same road is Hutton Hall, where the last Hutton died in 1746. The Duke of Cumberland was entertained there in 1745 after the skirmish at Clifton. Williamson's Yard has a stone at the entrance showing a pair of shears and the initials and date R. L. E. 1697, probably denoting the home or warehouse of a wool-stapler. The old weigh-bridge for weighing wool brought to Penrith market is still standing in Great Dockwray.

Robinson's School also dates from this period, having been founded by William Robinson, a London merchant who left £55 for ever to the town in his will. It is said he was born and brought up in Penrith.

A *Description of England and Wales* published in 1749 describes Penrith as a town of considerable note, carrying on a great trade, and also says it 'is accounted the second town in the County for Wealth and Trade'. The increasing prosperity of the town was again reflected in its building activities. The little tower on Beacon Hill was built in 1719, replacing an earlier one, and the beacon flamed its last warning for the Rebellion of the '45, when the worst that Penrith suffered seems to have been the loss of a steaming hot-pot seized by Highlanders in the Three Crowns Yard as it was being carried from one of the public bakehouses. The Penrith people saw some fighting, however, as a band of the townsmen routed out a company of Highlanders who had taken possession of Lowther Hall. James Ray's account of the action says that about thirty young men of Penrith, under the leadership of one of Lord Lonsdale's Stewards, were engaged, and only one was slightly hurt.

The Duke of Portland, who was at that time lord of the manor, presented the townsmen with fifty guineas in appreciation of their 'defence of the government and town of Penrith against the rebels in 1745', and two large gilt candelabra, duly inscribed, were purchased and hung in the church, where they remain to this day.

The two houses which have been reconstructed to form Penrith's handsome Town Hall are reputed to have been built originally in the eighteenth century by the celebrated architect, Robert Adams; and the New Crown Hotel was built in the same century.

It is from the eighteenth century that Penrith's chief associations with William and Dorothy Wordsworth date. Their mother, Ann Cookson, was one of a Penrith family. The parish register records her baptism in 1748, her marriage, eighteen years later, to John Wordsworth of Cockermouth, and, only twelve years afterwards, her burial. Unfortunately her home in Penrith and her grave in the churchyard cannot be identified, although there are local memories of her parents and relations, and of her father in particular, who 'hedn't a bit of po'try in him'.

All memory of the early home of Mary Hutchinson, who afterwards became the wife of William Wordsworth, has also been lost, but the grave of her mother can be identified near the north-east corner of the church tower, and the Penrith parish registers give details which prove them Penrith people, and incidentally disprove De Quincey's statement that Mary Hutchinson and William Wordsworth were cousins.

It was in Burrowgate, in a house now rebuilt, that the young poet saw his mother for the last time, and in which he and his brothers and sister lived with their grandfather after the death of their father in 1783—a time of much unhappiness for the orphans. Wordsworth and the little girl whom he called a 'phantom of delight', and his scarcely less beloved sister Dorothy, attended the school of Dame Birkett in Penrith. Although Wordsworth only remained at the school for a year, he paid tribute in after life to the excellent grounding the Dame had given him, and his association with Penrith did not cease, for he spent his long vacations from Hawkshead and later, from Cambridge, with his sister and Mary Hutchinson at Penrith, and in 1795 nursed his dying friend, Raisley Calvert, there.

In this century James Clarke, who kept the Old Swan Inn, which has been demolished since, published his *Survey of the Lakes*, which is full of interesting local history and has the first important maps and plans of the district. At the beginning of the eighteenth century, too, the Quakers built their first Meeting House in Penrith, and at the end of the century John Wesley paid a visit to the town and preached to the people. Dr. Joseph Hodgson, who was born at Penrith in 1788, took a prominent part in founding the Birmingham Eye Infirmary in 1824, and became a President of the College of Surgeons.

The nineteenth century also has interesting associations. In 1800 many chapbooks were printed in the town by Ann Bell and Anthony Soulby, and twelve years later a Penrith printer came to Coleridge's rescue with an offer to print his paper *The Friend*. In 1806 Jacob Thompson, the painter, was born in a cottage in Langton Street, the son of a Quaker who had so little sympathy with his aspirations that he apprenticed him to a house-painter. The boy attracted the attention of Lord Lonsdale, and after carrying out some commissions for him, was sent to London in 1829 with an introduction to Sir Thomas Lawrence. Many of Thompson's pictures were exhibited at the Royal Academy, and two of his paintings can be seen in Penrith parish church.

Dr. Michael Waistell Taylor, who died in 1892, lived at Penrith for many years, and wrote the standard work on the *Old Manorial Halls of Westmoreland and Cumberland*. He is buried in Christ Church burial ground at Penrith. Another famous man who had associations with Penrith, although not a native, was Samuel Plimsoll, 'The Sailor's Friend', whose parents removed to Penrith when he was a small boy. He was educated in the town and Page Hall, the house in which he lived, can be seen north of Town Head, near one of the few houses surviving in Penrith which have a flight of stone steps outside leading to the upper storey.

Other local celebrities of this period were Samuel Jameson, a cartwright, who became famous as a wrestler, and his son William Jameson, an even greater champion. George Dennison, although a champion wrestler in his youth, became more famous at his trade of bone-setting. He succeeded Benjamin Taylor, a well-known bone-setter, whose service he entered as a servant, but soon proved so observant that he rapidly outdistanced Taylor's pupil, a dull youth to whom Taylor used to say: 'Thoo blind divel! thoo can see nowte—nowte at aw; an' theer 'tudder chap actually larnin' faster than I larn't mysel'! I can keep nowte frae *him*!'

His most notable cure was the setting of a badly-broken thigh bone for an eleven-year-old boy, Richard Chapman, who in after years became a famous wrestler. Dennison would watch Chapman's strenuous feats, exclaiming delightedly: 'Leuk, lads, leuk! Theer yan ov my cures of a brokken thie!'

Dennison died in May, 1840, at the age of fifty-five.

Louis Simond visited Penrith in 1810, and mentions in his journal that most of the houses had long boxes of mignonette in their windows and that his inn was quite perfumed with its scent—a charming touch which has unhappily vanished from present-day Penrith. One wonders whether Wordsworth's Penrith home had this delightful decoration, and whether they were still there to delight Prince Leopold, the widower of Princess Charlotte of Wales, who stayed at the New Crown Hotel in 1819.

II

The widespread view from Penrith Beacon is an indication of the charm of the town's surroundings. West and south is a magnificent panorama of Lakeland peaks and valleys. Northward is the countryside which was once the famous Inglewood Forest, scene of the exploits of the popular outlaws Adam Bell and Clym of the Clough, who so daringly rescued their companion William of Cloudesley when he was under sentence of death in Carlisle —a tale that is told in an ancient ballad. Carlisle itself, with its castle, cathedral and Bishop's palace, and its close associations with the Lake District, lies only eighteen miles away, close to the Border and the Roman Wall.

Eastward from the Beacon is the valley of the Eden, so captivatingly lovely that it is claimed locally it was the setting for the famous picture 'The Plains of Heaven', by John Martin, the Northumbrian historical painter. The same claim is, however, made for Scout Scar near Kendal, and for the view from Dreemlang in the Isle of Man.

In the Eden valley is Eden Hall, for centuries the seat of the Musgraves, but recently demolished. The 'Luck of Eden Hall', probably the most famous 'Luck' of the many in the British Isles, was kept in the hall from the fifteenth century and is now preserved at the Bank of England. It is an enamelled goblet in a leathern case, and was for long supposed to be of Venetian work, but has more recently been identified as of rare oriental workmanship. The story has been celebrated in ballads by the Duke of Wharton and by the German poet Uhland, whose poem was translated by Longfellow. North of Eden Hall is the great stone circle known as 'Long Meg and her daughters', ranking fourth in importance of all those in England. A service was instituted by the late vicar of Little Salkeld some years ago, and is held in the circle annually during June, attracting large crowds of people.

Chapter X

PENRITH TO KESWICK

I

THERE are two main roads westward into Lakeland from Penrith, the direct road to Keswick which skirts, but does not touch, Lakeland scenery until it reaches the foot of Souther Fell, the outlier of Saddleback; and the road to Ullswater which plunges into Lakeland scenery from the moment Pooley Bridge is reached. In the countryside which lies between or to the north of these two roads are some of the most interesting and neglected pele-towers, manor-houses and villages of Lakeland, for this is a district of which Gilpin said in his guide: 'No part of Cumberland is more inhabited by the genteeler families of the country than this.'

South of Penrith, near Eamont Bridge, is Carleton Hall, which was a seat of the Carleton family from the twelfth to the seventeenth century. George Carleton, the protégé of Bernard Gilpin who became Bishop of Chichester, was a member of this family, being born in Northumberland when his father, Guy Carleton, was warden of Norham Castle.

Among the manors to the west of Penrith are three which are closely associated in their history, although differing in their ultimate fate—Dalemain, bought by the Hasells in 1665—Dacre which the Hasells bought in 1715, and Greystoke, which came to the Howards by marriage with the heiress of the Dacres.

Dalemain is still the seat of the Hasells. Elizabeth Julia Hasell, who was born there in 1830, contributed articles to the *Quarterly Review*, *Blackwood's* and the *Athenaeum*, and wrote the studies of Calderon and Tasso which are two of the most scholarly volumes in the series of 'Foreign Classics for English Readers'. She also wrote several books on Theology.

Dacre, although now a farm house, is well worth a visit, not only for its intrinsic interest, but for the charm of its setting. Only the keep and some earthworks remain of the fortress of the Dacres, but it is an interesting example of a fourteenth century pele-tower only slightly altered in the seventeenth century. The solar above the hall once had a wooden minstrel gallery, and is still known as the King's Chamber, from a local tradition that it was the meeting place of the three kings, Athelstan of England, Constantine of Scotland, and Owain of Cumberland, father of Dunmail, in 926. The fact that the tower was not built until four hundred years after the meeting is light-heartedly ignored. There is little reason to doubt, however, that the meeting, which is recorded by William of Malmesbury, and in the Anglo-Saxon Chronicle, actually took place somewhere in the neighbourhood—possibly in the Abbey of Dacre mentioned by Bede, who tells the story of a wonderful cure performed there in the year 698. Ancient cross-shafts in the church of Dacre prove that there were important pre-Norman graves there, and in 1931 an ancient drain was found in the churchyard, which probably came from a pre-Norman building on the site. The quaint carvings of the four bears in the churchyard are of unknown origin.

The Dacres originally took their name from the place, but gained far wider lands by two famous elopements, the first in the time of Edward II when Ranulph de Dacre carried off the heiress of Gilsland, the betrothed of the Earl of Warwick; and the second when the Lord Dacre who fought at Flodden Field carried off the heiress of Greystoke from Brougham Castle in 1506. The Dacres continued in possession of the baronies of Dacre, Gilsland and Greystoke until 1569, when the three Dacre co-heiresses were married to the three sons of their guardian, the Duke of Norfolk. Anne Dacre, who received Greystoke as her portion, was betrothed to the Duke's eldest son, Philip Howard, afterwards the first Earl of Arundel, when neither of them were more than twelve years of age. Greystoke has been a seat of the Howard family since that date.

Greystoke was originally the seat of an ancient barony which included all Cumberland between Inglewood, Penrith and Castlerigg (Keswick), which was granted by Ranulph de Meschines to Lyulph some time before 1120. During the

Civil War Greystoke Castle was garrisoned for the King, but was besieged and taken in 1648 by a detachment of the troops occupying Penrith. It was at Greystoke Castle that Shelley and his young bride were entertained by the Duke of Norfolk, an old friend of the Shelley family, and first met the Calverts of Windy Brow. The present building is a splendid modern mansion in an immense park.

Greystoke village is a small place with a very large and beautiful church of ancient foundation. There are traces of Norman and Early English work in the fabric, but the present building is chiefly Perpendicular. It has some ancient bells, stained glass, and eighteen stalls with carved misericords. There is a brass to Richard Newport, dated 1451, and some interesting monuments. The village was the birthplace of the Cumbrian martyr of Reformation times, Elizabeth Foster, who was burned at the stake at Smithfield in 1556, 'for not coming to church'.

The Greystoke Pillar, which stands beside the main road a mile and a half west of Penrith, was erected to mark the boundary between the manors of the Dukes of Norfolk and those of the Earls of Lonsdale, and bears the arms of the old barons of Greystoke. In the immediate neighbourhood are the house known as Bunker's Hill, which derived its name from the Battle of Bunker's Hill in America in which one of the Howard family took an active part; and Greenthwaite Hall, the ancient manor house which was built about 1650 by Dorothy Halton, the last of the Halton family who had been seated there from the time of Richard II. This lady was famous for her poaching proclivities, and made a practice of feeding her servants with deer poached from the Greystoke preserves. When summoned to the assizes at Cockermouth to answer for her misdeeds the counsel for the prosecution was one of the Fletchers, who had achieved wealth through trade and was unwary enough to say in her hearing: 'Here comes Madame Halton with her traps and gins', to which the witty lady retorted: 'There sits Counsellor Fletcher with his packs and pins'.

South of Greystoke is Hutton John, which must not be confused with the magnificent mansion of Hutton-in-the-Forest, which lies rather far north for the Lakeland visitor.

Hutton John was held by the Huttons from the fourteenth century until the reign of Queen Elizabeth, when Mary Hutton married Andrew of Hudleston of Farington Hall near Preston in Lancashire. One of her sons, Richard, born in 1583 became a Benedictine monk, and his nephew John Hudleston, born 1608, was the Benedictine monk who followed Charles II after the Battle of Worcester, and became his private chaplain. It was John Hudleston of whom the Duke of York said to Charles as he lay on his death-bed: 'Sir, this good man once saved your life. He now comes to save your soul.' Another of the Hudlestons, Andrew, together with Sir John Lowther, began hostilities against James II in 1688 by capturing a royal ship at Workington and handing it over to the Prince of Orange. The mansion was built at various periods round a pele-tower and is still inhabited by the Hudlestons.

II

It is no longer possible to find at Pooley Bridge the Earl of Surrey's barge, described in Clarke's *Survey of the Lakes* as adapted for eight rowers and mounting twelve brass swivel guns for the purpose of trying the echoes—a lordly conveyance which was open to all visitors to use at a small charge. To-day one must take the steamer and do without the discharge of cannon, but there is no more enchanting way of approaching Patterdale than this journey by the little steam yacht, with the three reaches of Ullswater gradually opening up, and the scenery changing from the quiet pastoral charm of Pooley Bridge to the grandeur of the peaks which hem in the head of the lake, topped by mighty Helvellyn and softened by the woods of Glencoin and Gowbarrow. The return journey, though beautiful, cannot be compared with the magic of the journey from Pooley Bridge.

On the Cumberland side of Pooley Bridge is the low, wooded hill of Dunmallet, crowned by double ramparts which may be of early medieval construction. It was climbed by the poet Gray, who doubtless thought he had done something very strenuous when he had reached the top. His nervous fears of the Lakeland mountains make curious reading in the present day, but the lower end of Ullswater had a gentler turn than Borrowdale, and he could look on it without trembling. His account of the foot of Ullswater can scarcely be bettered, but he did not venture up to Patterdale, doubtless being intimidated by the grandeur of the mountains round the head of the lake.

About two miles beyond Pooley Bridge is Watermillock where Dr. John Brown, a Provost of Queen's College, Oxford, was born in 1700. The old church is on the lake shore, at Hallsteads. The "new" church was consecrated by Bishop Oglethorpe in 1558, when he was on his way to the coronation of Elizabeth. Hallsteads House is a seat of the Marshalls, and was the home of Carlyle's friend John Marshall, whose wife was Dorothy Wordsworth's school friend, Jane Pollard.

Beyond Hallsteads the road comes right down to the lake shore to skirt the splendid Gowbarrow Fell with its deer forest. It was along this shore that Dorothy Wordsworth saw the daffodils which 'seemed as if they verily laughed with the wind', as she records in her journal—the same host of daffodils which gave her brother the idea for his famous, often-quoted, and at one time much-abused poem.

Daffodils still dance and flutter beside the lake and in the woods of Gowbarrow every spring-time, for nowhere in England do wild flowers grow in richer profusion than in the Lake District, which from earliest spring to late in the autumn has a gay and gracious procession of flowering bushes and meadows. Every field, and every wood, is tinted with their beauty; gorse, heather and bracken fling their swathes of colour across the fells; and water-lilies and graceful yellow irises invade the shallows of nearly all the lakes, to come as a joyful surprise to those on their first visit to the Lakes who have imagined that because the Lake District is a mountainous northern region it is cold, bleak and flowerless.

Lyulph's Tower, which comes into sight just before Aira Force is reached, heralds the most impressive scenery of Ullswater. The tower is modern, but traditionally stands on the site of an ancient pele-tower around which many legends grew up. It is said to take its name from Lyulph, the first lord of the district, and an old tale tells how he visited the Bishop of Durham in 1080, and by his high sense of honour aroused the jealous envy of the Bishop's chaplain by whose means he was done to death, his innocent host, the Bishop, being killed at the altar in revenge.

Aira Force is, of course, linked with the name of Wordsworth for ever through his ballad of the *Somnambulist* which is founded, with considerable poetic licence, on a local incident. Clarke, in his *Survey*, grows positively lyrical about the beauty of the falls, but devotes even more attention to the riddle of how the fish got into the stream above the fall, which he concludes must have been by way of a pail carried up from the lake! Beyond Gowbarrow Fell and Aira Force, which are now in the care of the National Trust, the Glencoine Park stretches to the Westmorland boundary at Glencoine Beck, but the road to Keswick runs north through the attractive little village of Dockwray, which lies nearly a thousand feet above sea level, and Matterdale, whose church was built in 1685, and restored about 1846.

There is a glorious retrospective view of Ullswater from the Dockwray road, but beyond Matterdale bleak moors stretch away to the Cumbrian Troutbeck, which consists chiefly of the tiny station and an hotel, with a few cottages nearly a mile away beside the beck.

The main road from Penrith to Keswick is joined near the foot of Souther Fell, once famous for the curious mirage first seen on Midsummer Eve, 1735, when troops appeared to be exercising on the top of the fell. In 1743 a Mr. Wilton of Wilton Hall, and his servant, saw a man and a dog on the mountain, pursuing some horses over precipices where it was impossible for human beings to tread, and on Midsummer Eve, 1745, a large number of people saw an army with carriages on the top of the fell where no carriages could possibly go, and on examining the fell-side the next day could find no footprints or carriage tracks. The full story of these eye-witnesses was told in the *Lonsdale Magazine*, together with the information that on the occasion in 1745 when the 'army' was seen it had been ascertained that Scottish troops were exercising many miles away. It was suggested that the apparitions were in each case a form of mirage, and no other explanation has ever been found.

Threlkeld is a scattered village under Saddleback which has extensive granite quarries. Threlkeld Hall, once owned by the stepfather of the 'Shepherd Lord' Clifford, is now a farmhouse. The church was rebuilt in 1777, but has two medieval bells. In the churchyard is a unique cenotaph to the memory of notable local hunters 'who in their generation were noted veterans of the chase'. There is a long list of names and the verse:

> 'The forest music is to hear the hounds
> Rend the thin air, and with lusty cry
> Awake the drowsy echoes and confound
> Their perfect language in a mingled cry.'

Saddleback is the modern name of Blencathra. On its heights is lonely Scales Tarn, which lies deep in precipitous cliffs. Tradition asserts that two immortal fish live in the tarn—a tale which might have its origin in the *Arabian Nights*—and travellers of old asserted that the sun never shone on it, and the stars of heaven might be seen at noonday. Scott mentions the tradition in his *Bridal of Triermain;* in the earlier editions he called the mountain 'Glaramara' but altered it later to 'stern Blencathra'. The tradition has also been attributed to Bowscale Tarn on Bowscale Fell. Sir Hugh Walpole's novel *A Prayer for My Son* has a house on the slopes of Blencathra for its background.

At Threlkeld a road branches south to run through the Vale of St. John to Thirlmere, but the main road continues on to Keswick, roughly parallel with the course of the Greta, which grows gradually nearer and nearer, until they run side by side into Keswick at the foot of Skiddaw.

Chapter XI

KESWICK, CROSTHWAITE AND SKIDDAW

I

KESWICK is the only town in the district which has two lakes, and there are many who claim that its setting is the loveliest in Lakeland. It lies in an open valley on the banks of the river Greta, with some of the grandest heights of the Lake District around, between the contrasting beauty of the mountain-cradled Derwentwater and the more pastoral Bassenthwaite.

The written records of Keswick do not begin until the thirteenth century, but prehistoric relics have been found at Portinscale and there is a magnificent stone circle on the hill-side east of the town. Traces of the Romans and the Norsemen have been found on the shores of Bassenthwaite, and traditions associate the foundation of Keswick's parish church at Crosthwaite with the sixth century saint Kentigern, whilst St. Herbert's Isle, according to the Venerable Bede, was the home of the saintly hermit of that name who was a friend of St. Cuthbert, and prayed with him that they might both die on the same day—a prayer that was granted in 687.

It has been claimed for the family of de Derwentwater that they were settled in the district long before the coming of the Normans, but the *Chronicle of Cumbria* says they were given their lands of Castlerigg and the forest between the Greta and the Calder early in the twelfth century.

Edward I gave Keswick its charter for a market on the representations of Thomas de Derwentwater, and from that date onwards there are continual references to the town. Leland, speaking of Keswick in the reign of Henry VIII, described it as a 'poor lytle market town' but its condition became greatly improved in the time of Elizabeth. It is a strange thought that this improvement, and the most accurate and detailed account of life in Elizabethan Keswick, was due to a German firm. According to Mr. John Postlethwaite's interesting book on *Mines and Mining*, mining has been actively carried on in the neighbourhood of Keswick for about two thousand years, but it was due to Bavarian enterprise that the most ambitious and prosperous of Keswick's mining enterprises was developed.

In 1561 a German company with its headquarters at Augsburg financed an enterprise to exploit the mines in the Keswick district, with Queen Elizabeth as their patron and Lord Burghley as one of their chief shareholders, and in 1562 Daniel Hechstetter and Thomas Thurland had a warrant from the Queen to bring over 300 or 400 foreign workmen. It was the detailed accounts of this company, preserved at Augsburg, that W. G. Collingwood translated and edited, with interesting explanatory notes and extracts from the Crosthwaite registers, in his monograph on *Elizabethan Keswick.* A summary of this was written in his characteristically delightful style by Canon Rawnsley in his *Past and Present at the English Lakes*, which also includes a description of the Canon's visit to Schwaz in the Tyrol, in a fruitless search for further details.

Two years after the arrival of the foreign workmen the dalesmen 'ill-treated' them, it is said because they feared the strangers would 'take the bread out of their mouths' —a quite unfounded fear, as the Germans spent lavishly and brought prosperity to Keswick. It may be suspected that the ill-treatment was partly due to jealousy, as Crosthwaite registers show that in the two years following the arrival of the Germans no less than sixteen of them had married girls of the neighbourhood—a fact which might well cause consternation among the young dalesmen, in view of the scanty population of the district at that time.

The account books of the company were extremely carefully kept and are full of fascinating little details, not only of the great business enterprise, but of the daily life of the Germans and their families. It is strange to think that whilst the Border wars were still in progress and Mary Queen of Scots was gambling for her throne, and even whilst she stayed in Cockermouth, these foreigners were quietly carrying on their business and periodically taking holidays in their homeland in the Tyrol as a matter of course. The accounts cover the period from 1569 until 1577 when the business passed into other hands, but although some of the Germans returned to the Tyrol, taking their Cumbrian wives, a number of them remained in the district, or migrated to the Welsh mining areas. Joachim Gans, who came to Keswick in 1581 to demonstrate a better method of smelting, and Ulrich Frass, or Franz, who made further improvements in the smelting of copper, had their ideas adopted at Neath in South Wales, and their methods have never been entirely superseded there.

A number of the dalesfolk in and around Keswick to-day can trace their descent back to the marriage of these Germans with daleswomen, and it is said that William and Raisley Calvert, the friends of Wordsworth, Coleridge, Southey and Shelley, could trace the descent of both their parents to the Bavarians. Daniel Hechstetter, the manager of the mines, had several notable descendants. His daughter Susanna married Allan Nicholson of Hawkshead Hall; his grand-daughter Thomazine married George Tullye of Carlisle and was the mother of a Dean of Ripon and grandmother of a Dean of Carlisle; another grand-daughter was the wife of Thomas Rawlinson, of Grisedale Hall and became the mother of Daniel Rawlinson the friend of Samuel Pepys, and grandmother of Sir Thomas Rawlinson, Lord Mayor of London; and a grandson married the sister of Sir John Bankes, Lord Chief Justice, a native of Keswick.

The mines were worked, chiefly by the German miners, until the destruction of the smelthouses during the Civil War, generally said to have been perpetrated in 1651 by Cromwell's army, then on the way from Edinburgh to Worcester, but more probably in 1648 when Penrith and Cockermouth were occupied by the Parliamentarians.

After the destruction of the mining equipment Keswick must have bitterly regretted the loss of the mining industry which, so far from impoverishing the district, had brought a prosperity which was not maintained by the woollen trade and pencil-making industry. A writer of 1749 described the town as 'greatly decayed and much inferior to what it was formerly'. Several writers of the eighteenth century refer to the fact that the poorer inhabitants lived chiefly by stealing the valuable black lead or 'wad' of the Borrowdale mines and selling it to itinerant Jews, and an Act of Parliament was passed in the reign of George II making it a felony to steal the wad.

The pencil-making industry still flourishes in Keswick, although the lead is no longer obtained locally and the tedious process of making pencils by hand has been superseded by machinery. Fortunately the modern factory is far from being a drawback to the town, and the local shops, displaying a marvellous assortment of pencils and penholders, on any of which the name of the purchaser is printed in gilt lettering, free of charge, are thronged with visitors during the season.

Although there are many literary associations at Keswick, particularly with Coleridge and Southey at Greta Hall, it has never been the 'literary shrine' that Grasmere has become, and local recollections of the poets are not so universal. Nevertheless, it would be a poor sort of coach-driver who did not point with pride to Greta Hall where Southey learned to lose his longing for Portugal and the Welsh mountains in his growing love for the Lake District. He lived there from 1803 until his death forty years later, working unremittingly to support not only his own dearly-loved wife and children, but those of Coleridge, who after nine years at Greta Hall, left his family, never to return. Life at Greta Hall has been described by Sara Coleridge, who was born there, and in the life and letters of Southey and of his sister-in-law, Mrs. Coleridge, and many have paid tribute to the charm and innate goodness of Southey.

Among those who visited Southey at Greta Hall were Samuel Rogers, the banker-poet, Hazlitt, De Quincey, Wordsworth, Shelley, and many another celebrity of that day. Gentle Charles Lamb and his sister Mary spent three weeks there, and became captivated by the two-year-old Derwent Coleridge in the little yellow jacket which gave rise to his nickname of the 'Stumpy Canary'. The little boy always called the 'striped opossum' a 'Pipos' and Lamb never forgot his 'friend Pipos' in after years.

Among the many relics of the Lake poets in the Keswick Museum are the clogs which Southey used to wear on his

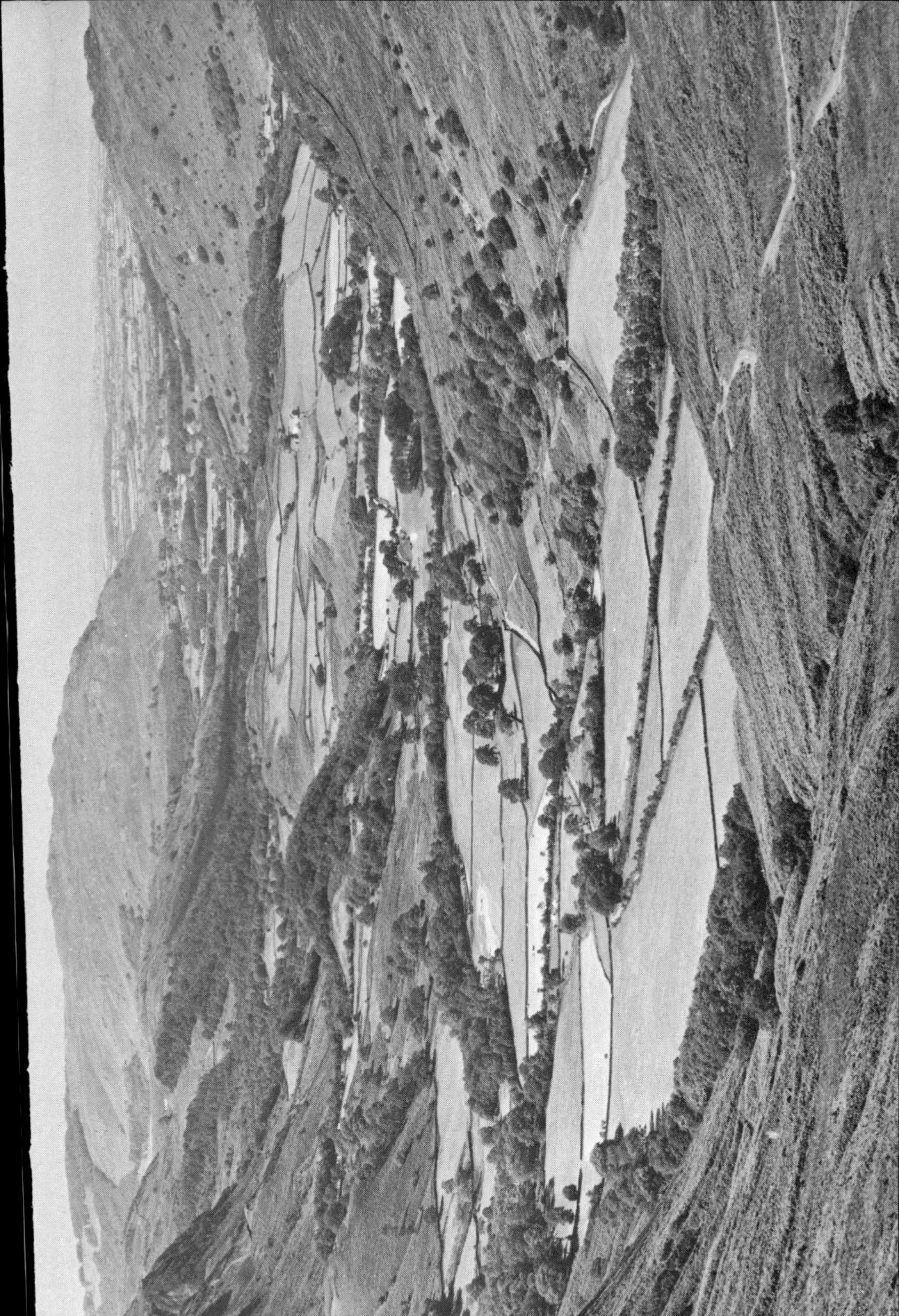

daily walks. Clogs were universally worn outdoors in the Lake District until a late period, and in order to prevent them from wearing holes in their stockings the dalesfolk used to smear the heels of new stockings with melted pitch and dip them into the ashes of the turf fires. The glutinous mixture incorporated with the woollen and formed a compound which was both hard and flexible and well adapted to resist friction of the clogs. Doubtless Mrs. Southey followed the local recipe for the stockings of her husband and family.

Shelley, barely nineteen, came to the cottage on Chestnut Hill with his still younger bride and his sister-in-law Eliza Westbrook, in 1811, and was befriended by the Calverts and by Southey, although Shelley in his youthful intolerance chose to dislike Southey for his opinions, and left for Ireland without troubling to say farewell. Windy Brow under the Calverts (whose ancestral home was Greta Bank Farm), was a great resort of the famous people of their day, and in after years the daughter of the house, who married Joshua Stanger, returned to Keswick in the year Southey died, and lived at Fieldside, entertaining those who still lived of the famous literary circle known and loved by her parents.

Among the celebrities who visited Keswick without actually living there, the first to write up the charms of the town was John Dalton, Canon of Worcester—not to be confused with John Dalton the chemist. The Canon wrote a poem on Keswick in 1758. Nine years later Dr. John Brown wrote to explain why he liked Keswick so much better then Dovedale, describing its scenery as 'Beauty in the lap of Horror'. In the same year, Gray visited the district, and his descriptions drew many in his wake, although he never went farther up Borrowdale than Grange, and his exquisite descriptions of the scenery are combined with shudderings at the horror of the mountain precipices. After Gray, celebrities, guide-book writers, and holiday-makers came in ever-increasing numbers, and even those who never visited the Lakes became well acquainted with the general opinion of their natural beauty. Jane Austen made her heroine Elizabeth Bennet 'excessively disappointed' when her proposed tour of the Lakes was abandoned in favour of one in Derbyshire, for she had 'set her heart on seeing the Lakes'. Incidentally, no lover of Jane Austen can help wishing she had visited the lakes and written a description of the society there to her sister Cassandra, even if she had not used it as a background for a novel. As both Coleridge and Southey were admirers of her works, and Jane's school-friend, Miss Wither, had married Southey's much-loved Uncle Hill, she would surely have paid a visit to Greta Hall, and added her own inimitable touch to its many delightful associations.

The Rev. Joseph Wilkinson, a Norfolk rector, who had no relationship with Wordsworth's friend at Yanwath, was a visitor at Keswick whilst drawing his pictures of the Lakes, whose only merit was that Wordsworth was induced to write his *Guide to the Lakes* as an introduction to the folio volume of the views when they were issued in 1810. Other issues of the Guide, without the views, have been published since, and it has been re-issued in the present day by the Oxford Press. It contains some of the loveliest prose descriptions of the Lake scenery ever penned.

There is one literary association of the Lake District, and of Keswick in particular, that has so far escaped notice: the many visits of the Manx poet, T. E. Brown, which were not even included in Canon Rawnsley's *Literary Associations of the Lakes District*, possibly because the Manxman's genius, although recognized by the literary critics of the day, had not then gained the more widesgread appreciation it deserved and has since achieved. Brown's maternal grandmother was a Cumbrian girl whose maiden name was Birkett, and when Brown was a master at Clifton College he spent a part of every summer vacation at Keswick, from 1873 until his retirment in 1892, first at St. John's Terrace, and after at Lake View. In the *Epistola ad Dakyns*, written in memory of his friend Dakyns, he speaks of Derwentwater as one of the three places which he will haunt after his death because of the love he bears them.

Brown's collected works contain three poems on the Lake District, but it is in his letters that his love for Lakeland is more particularly expressed. He was as great a lover of nature as ever Wordsworth had been, and agreed with the Lake poet that the district was at its best in spring or autumn. One September he wrote of Derwentwater: 'We have just had our last row on the lake. We left it jet, and steel and gold. . . . I do believe your autumns are the very soul of the lake year.' Two of Brown's letters to Canon Rawnsley are included in his published correspondence, showing his appreciation of a sonnet by the Canon, and his interest in the preservation of public footpaths. During the Canon's vigorous campaign in defence of Lakeland rights of way he quoted a saying of T. E. Brown's that 'the meanest thing a man can do is to shut up a footpath'.

Keswick's only really ancient building is Crosthwaite church, but there are one or two sixteenth and seventeenth century houses in which Keswick's most notable sons lived, still surviving. The most celebrated native of Keswick was Sir John Bankes, born at Castlerigg above the town, in 1589, and brought up in a house near Keswick Town Hall. He became the Chief Justice of Common Pleas, and was a man of such integrity that although a professed Royalist, he was continued in office by the Parliamentarians. The celebrated Lady Bankes who defended Corfe Castle for three years, and only yielded through the treachery of one of the garrison, was the wife of Sir John. The Chief Justice died and was buried at Oxford in 1644, but showed in his will that he had not forgotten his native town. He left money to found almshouses there, and although they were pulled down to make way for the post office, the charity is still administered. An inscription on the wall of the modern building records the foundation of the almshouses, and a bust of Sir John in Fitz Park shows he has not been forgotten by the townsmen.

Robley Dunglisson, who achieved fame as a lecturer in the United States, was born at Keswick in 1798, and became a surgeon-apothecary in 1819. One of his publications attracted the attention of an agent of the University of Virginia, and he was appointed Professor there in 1825. He afterwards gave lectures and held appointments in the University of Maryland, and the Jefferson Medical College, and spent thirty-two years in Philadelphia, during which time he wrote and lectured on medical subjects. He was the most prolific writer of his day in America, and a complete list of his medical writings printed in the Index Catalogue of the Library of the Surgeon-General's Office, U.S. Army, shows his amazing industry. In later life he wrote *Legends of the English Lakes*.

Jonathan Otley, although born in Grasmere, came to Keswick as an apprentice and lived there until his death, following his trade as a basket and swill-maker and a mender of watches and clocks, but gaining lasting fame as a geologist and author of the first really reliable guide to the Lakes. He lived in a house in the King's Head Yard, and was visited there by many famous men. He interested Professor Sedgwick in Cumbrian geology, and the Professor paid high tributes to his knowledge. In 1815 Otley gave Dalton the first accurate account of the phenomenon of the Floating Island of Derwentwater, and three years later he published the first accurate map of the district. His correspondence with Sedgwick, Dalton and other distinguished geologists has been preserved, and Dr. Lietch, his friend and biographer, has described how he marked the levels of the lake on Friar's Crag from the dry summer of 1824 annually until the still lower level of 1852. He died in 1855, at the age of ninety.

Otley's successor as a geologist was Clifton Ward, whose excellent work in surveying the Lake District gives him a high place among field geologists. He wrote valuable papers on the geology of the Northern Lakes and on the glaciation of the district, and took a leading part in founding the Cumberland Association for the advancement of Literature and Science. He became curate of St. John's Church, Keswick, and was buried in the churchyard in 1878.

Frederic William Henry Myers, the poet and essayist, was also born at Keswick in 1843. In addition to his distinguished intellectual accomplishments, he was a fine athlete and whilst on a visit to the United States and Canada swam across the river below Niagara Falls, being, it is believed, the first Englishman to perform this feat. He wrote one of the most illuminating monographs on Wordsworth, published in 1881 in the 'English Men of Letters' series, and also wrote an admirable essay on Shelley for Ward's English Poets. He was one of the founders of the Society of Psychical Research, and wrote a considerable number of articles and books on the subject. He was buried beside his parents in St. John's Churchyard, and within sight of the Library founded by his father, who had been the first incumbent of the then newly-formed parish of St. John from 1838 to his death in 1851. The Rev. Frederic Myers was also a scholar of distinction, and among the best known of his published works were *Catholic Thoughts*, and *Lectures on Great Men*.

It was at 3, Derwentwater Place, opposite St. John's, that William Smith, the author of *Thorndale* and *Gravenhurst*, was living when he first met Lucy Cumming his future wife, and wandered with her in the valleys round Keswick and Patterdale which they loved so well.

In modern times Keswick has been the home of the late Sir Hall Caine, and other celebrities; Sir Hugh Walpole settled there some years before his death, and the town has figured in several of his novels.

Portraits of all the local celebrities, and specimens of their works, are to be seen in the Keswick Museum, which also contains the great relief map of the Lake District made by Joseph Flintoft. Also plans of the Lakes drawn by Peter Crosthwaite, who was born at Keswick in 1735. He had served in the Navy and was noted for his careful observations and drawings. The museum has a unique attraction in its Musical Stones, which make practically a full pianoforte keyboard of seven octaves. The stones were collected by Joseph Richardson, who spent many years in chipping and carving them. He commenced the work in 1827, and after experimenting with stones from various mountains round Keswick, found those of Skiddaw the most successful. When the work was completed, Richardson and his sons toured all over England and the Continent. They gave three command performances before Queen Victoria, and also played at almost every royal palace in Europe. Mr. Davey, the curator of the museum, who plays delightfully on the stones—which have great sweetness of tone—has refused the most tempting offers to tour

Britain, America and Europe, so that those visitors to the museum who have the good fortune to hear Mr. Davey perform, have the additional satisfaction of knowing they are hearing a 'turn' which the most famous halls in the world would have been glad to present.

Keswick holds a very popular Sports Meeting on August Bank Holidays, with fell racing, hound trails, wrestling and other events, but the most famous meeting in Keswick is the Convention, an annual summer reunion held for the main purpose of 'Promoting practical holiness' by meetings for prayer, discussion and personal intercourse. The Convention was started privately in 1874 by Canon Harford-Battersby, then vicar of St. John's, and Mr. Robert Wilson, and had its first meeting in 1875. It has no denominational limits, and in spite of attacks on some of the ideas of its leaders and the novelty of its methods, has grown so greatly both in numbers and influence that practically the whole of Keswick is given over to the Convention members, and any holiday-maker wishing to visit Keswick during the weeks in July that the Convention is held must take the precaution of making an early booking for accommodation.

II

It is curious that although Keswick has been a market town for centuries, it formed part of the parish of the diminutive village of Crosthwaite, whose church is most certainly large enough to do duty for both places, but lies a mile away from the town.

Crosthwaite church is one of the most beautiful and interesting in Lakeland, hallowed by the legends and stories associated with its foundation by the famous St. Kentigern, also known as St. Mungo, in the sixth century. Crosthwaite is also intimately associated with St. Herbert, since the Bishop of Appleby, in a mandate dated 1374, enjoined upon the Vicar of Crosthwaite to visit St. Herbert's Isle and hold a commemoration service annually on St. Herbert's Day. The full story of these two saints is told in a booklet containing the five addresses delivered by Canon Rawnsley in Crosthwaite church on successive years to commemorate St. Kentigern's Day—13th January—and St. Herbert's day—13th April.

Alice de Romilli, Lady of Allerdale, mother of the celebrated 'Boy of Egremont', rebuilt Crosthwaite church in the twelfth century, and in 1198 Richard Cœur de Lion gave the rectory of Crosthwaite to the Cistercian Abbey of Fountains, who established some monks at Monks' Hall, a grange in what is now Fitz Park. The hollow way at the bottom of Vicarage Hill indicates an old causeway which connected the Hall with the church.

Parts of the twelfth century church survive in the present building which is chiefly of Perpendicular date, and it was restored under the direction of Sir Gilbert Scott in 1844, when subscriptions were being raised for the Southey memorial, a beautiful effigy of the poet carved by Lough, a self-taught Newcastle sculptor. Wordsworth's extreme conscientiousness in writing the epitaph may be gauged by the fact that even after it was carved he had the last line erased and re-cut with different wording. Among the very early features of the church are a small stone carved with a rough cross, and possibly a 'pillow stone' of great antiquity; a late fourteenth century window brought from Furness Abbey at the Dissolution of the monastery; a fourteenth century bell, formerly at the chapel of Loweswater and one of the earliest examples of Cumberland bells; an ancient sundial incised on the south-west buttress of the tower, and another in the nave clerestory; and a unique feature in its complete set of twelve external consecration crosses, dating from the last important rebuilding of the church, during the reign of Mary Tudor. A number were also discovered in the interior of the church in 1915, hidden under a heavy layer of plaster placed there by Gilbert Scott. Two consecration crosses of earlier dates can also be seen on the walls. An interesting account of the Crosthwaite consecration crosses was given by Canon Rawnsley in *Past and Present at the English Lakes*.

Among the earliest monuments in the church is the brass to Sir John Radcliffe, who probably led the Keswick men at the Battle of Flodden Field and died on Lord's Island on Derwentwater, and to his wife Dame Alice, who survived him and is buried in Salisbury Cathedral. The fifteenth century alabaster effigies of an unknown civilian and his wife are still beautiful, although most wantonly cut during the nineteenth century restoration in order to force it between the pillars below the Radcliffe brass.

Not the least interesting feature of the church is the skilful blending of the old and the new in an appropriate memorial to the work of Canon Rawnsley during the time he was Vicar of Crosthwaite. It consists of a baptistry of local stone and coloured marbles, and a font originally given to the church in the fourteenth century by Lady Derwentwater and Lady Maude, wife of the first Earl of Northumberland who was one of the heroes of Chevy Chase. Appropriately enough, the font was also given to record a long and valuable record of work by a Vicar of Crosthwaite—Sir Thomas de Eskhead, who was appointed Vicar in 1362, and it is a beautiful example of late Decorated work whose inscription can still be read. The font ewer was made at the Keswick School of Industrial Art, and was given to record the work of Edith Rawnsley, the first wife of the Canon.

Among the graves in the churchyard is that of Southey, neighboured by those of Nurse Wilson, James Lawson, William Jackson, and Betty Thompson, all members of Southey's household at Greta Hall. Jonathan Otley; Charles Wright, Ruskin's guide and instructor; Bishops Goodwin and Diggle; Canon Rawnsley and his wife Edith; and Mrs. Lynn Linton, are also buried there.

The vicarage of Crosthwaite has many literary associations. It was the unhappy childhood home of Mrs. Lynn Linton, the daughter of the Rev. James Lynn, who was born in 1822. She lived there until her departure for London at the age of twenty-three. Mrs. Lynn Linton has left a description of the vicarage in her novel, *Christopher Kirkland*, in which there are many autobiographical details, as the hero is most curiously identified with her own life and opinions. The vicarage was also described by the poet Gray on his visit in 1789.

The vicarage took on rich and happy memories during the long occupation by the late Canon Rawnsley and his wife Edith, who came from the vicarage of Wray on Windermere in 1883. Both of them accomplished a prodigious amount of work and took a leading part in the life of Crosthwaite and Keswick, and still found time to originate or support schemes in other districts.

In 1884, as a result of the teaching of Ruskin, they formed classes for metal work and wood carving, the first humble beginning of the Keswick School of Industrial Art which had amongst its subscribers Walter Crane, Holman Hunt and G. F. Watts. It is now a most flourishing and important concern, turning out beautiful specimens of handicraft. The great square of specially designed linen used for a pall at the funeral of Alfred Lord Tennyson was woven at the school, hand-spinning and weaving having been added to its activities by that time.

Canon Rawnsley resuscitated the Keswick and District Footpaths Association, and on one occasion led a large party of the townsmen to remove the barriers of a footpath on Latrigg. The veteran Samuel Plimsoll came especially from London to accompany the party. The Canon acted as master of ceremonies every May Day, and was the prime mover in bonfire celebrations on the Jubilee and Diamond Jubilee of Queen Victoria. He helped to establish the Newton Rigg County Farm School; was a pioneer of secondary education and originated the Secondary Schools Association. He was also concerned with the building of Keswick High School, and the provision of the Sanatorium on Blencathra, and sat for many years on the Cumberland County Council. Nothing came amiss to him. He inspired the memorial to Caedmon at Whitby; organized relief for the Armenians; was largely concerned in the formation of the Cumberland and Westmorland Nursing Association, and instituted the schemes for memorials to the Venerable Bede at Roker Point, Sunderland, and to Tennyson by the restoration of Somersby Church. He became Honorary Canon of Carlisle in 1891 and was appointed to the Second Canonry in 1909, and became Chaplain to the King in 1912.

In addition to all this he was constantly writing valuable papers on the natural history, literary associations and history of the Lake District of which many have been published in book form, and although now out of print are a valuable source of detailed information charmingly written. His *Literary Associations of the Lake District*, in particular, might well be reprinted. In 1896 he went to Moscow to report the coronation of the Czar, and in addition to many summer holidays spent abroad, visited the United States in 1899 and lectured there, making many friends.

Among those who stayed at the vicarage during the time the Rawnsleys were living there were Dr. Temple, Bishop of London; Phillips Brooks of Boston; Rhoda Broughton; Edna Lyall, who dedicated her novel *Hope the Hermit* to Canon and Mrs. Rawnsley; and Mr. Walter H. Page, the American Ambassador, and his daughter, to whom the Canon acted as guide in a tour of the district. The work for which he will be longest remembered, however, is his almost superhuman endeavours, in conjunction with Miss Octavia Hill and Sir Robert Hunter, to interest people in the preservation of natural beauty, which finally resulted in the creation of the National Trust, in 1895. He acted as the Hon. Secretary of the Trust to the end of his life. His work in the preservation of the Lake District, and other beauty spots and historic buildings of Britain, cannot be too highly valued, especially as it was never his practice to oppose any scheme which was good in itself. He recognized the necessity of the water-works at Thirlmere and Haweswater, much as he regretted them. He was the first chairman of the Society for the Safeguarding the Natural Beauty of the Lake District, formed in 1919. His wife died on the last day of 1916 and soon afterwards he gave up his work at Crosthwaite and retired to Allan Bank at Grasmere, which he had bought in 1915 and used as a holiday home. He died there in 1920, and two years later Friar's Crag, Lord's Island, and a part of Great Wood on the shore of Derwentwater, were given to the National Trust as a memorial. His widow, Mrs. Eleanor Rawnsley, has written a sympathetic and appreciative account of his life and work which reveals the charm of both the Canon and Edith Rawnsley, and the amazing scope of their activities.

III

Both Keswick and Crosthwaite are dominated by Skiddaw, which seems so intimately bound up with every thought of the town and village that Southey's references to 'my neighbour Skiddaw' seem not only natural but inevitable. Southey gave a most hilarious account of the expedition made by the Southey and Wordsworth families, accompanied by James Boswell, son of the biographer, and others, to light a bonfire in celebration of the victory of Waterloo. Southey is particularly amusing in recounting the fact that it was Wordsworth, the water-drinker, who upset all the water when they were on the summit of Skiddaw, with the result that everyone had to drink their rum neat, and got very cheerful indeed. In 1888 Skiddaw flamed again to celebrate the tercentenary of the Armada, and in the same century was one of the chain of beacon fires celebrating the Jubilee and Diamond Jubilee of Queen Victoria.

Skiddaw is now considered far from one of the most intimidating of the Lakeland climbs, although it ranks third in order of height among the English peaks, and there has been a well-defined path for more than two hundred years, but Mrs. Radcliffe, fresh from writing the *Mysteries of Udolpho*, thought it distinctly an adventure to climb Skiddaw, and Harriet Martineau, in her Guide, solemnly implores everyone to be sure to take a guide; and as for Gray, it apparently never even crossed his mind that it was possible to do anything so terrifying as scale its peak. Nevertheless the town-bred and town-loving Charles and Mary Lamb managed to climb up in 1802. Charles, in one of his letters, speaks of Skiddaw as a 'fine creature', and one suspects that his reference to the view from the summit as 'making you giddy' was merely his sense of fun breaking out. John Keats, ten years later, climbed Skiddaw before breakfast. Canon Rawnsley wrote many delightful descriptions of the mountain, and also a testimony to the fine character of Joseph Hawell, a Skiddaw shepherd who died in 1891.

Although Skiddaw is so close to the popular holiday

centre of Keswick, the 'tourist' track is well defined, and for the rest it is as lonely as the most remote fells. The meet of the shepherds of Skiddaw and the Saddleback range is held in Wylie Ghyll in the heart of these fells, and is a vigorous survival of the centuries-old custom of meeting annually for the identification of strayed sheep, with the pleasant accompaniment of refreshments and an exchange of news.

Skiddaw House, one of the loneliest dwelling places in England, is set at the foot of Skiddaw, close to the source of the Caldew, and neither from the house nor its neighbourhood is it possible to see a single human habitation. It was the place used by Sir Hugh Walpole for the background of the murder in *The Fortress*.

Carrock Fell, which forms the north-east buttress of the Skiddaw group, has an ancient hill-fort on its summit. In 1857 Dickens, accompanied by his friend Wilkie Collins, came by way of Ullswater to climb the fell, and an account of the outing appeared in *Household Words* under the title of 'The Lazy Tour of Two Idle Apprentices'. Forster's *Life of Dickens* gives other details from Dickens' letters, written in a characteristically amusing vein.

On Skiddaw, as on all Lakeland fells, is one of the stone walls which are so characteristic of Lakeland that they seem to have sprung from the soil, scoring their long lines high up the mountain-side. These dry-stone walls require an expert hand, for every stone has its proper 'face', and there is an art in building them without mortar to withstand wind and rain, and to ensure that ice and snow cannot form inside. The old dry-stone waller, like the thatcher, is dying out, and those who remain are much in demand. One man who died comparatively recently used to live on the fells for a month or more at a time, building and repairing the walls, and shifting his little tent as the work progressed.

The once famous Skiddaw Hermit, whose life story was published in 1891, was George Smith, of a Banffshire family, who was born about 1825. He left home to wander in a vagabonding style which caused him to receive unmerited suspicion from landowners, and finally came to Keswick and made his home on the Dodd of Skiddaw, earning his living by painting portraits in oils, and small water-colours. Towards the end of his life he wandered over southern lakeland, and became a familiar figure at Ambleside, where he attended the neighbouring chapels. He died in Banffshire in 1875 and was much missed in the Lake District, where he had won respect by the fact that although poor, he never asked for alms, and was scrupulously honest.

Chapter XII

BASSENTHWAITE, DERWENTWATER AND THIRLMERE

I

DERWENTWATER is so closely associated with any thought of Keswick that the very existence of Bassenthwaite is sometimes forgotten or ignored, and although it cannot claim the exquisite perfection of Derwentwater, it has a very real charm of its own and a wealth of interesting associations. It has a special appeal for motorists and cyclists in the splendid road which encircles the whole lake, making an eighteen mile round from Keswick of constantly changing scenery, alternating between the rugged beauty of the mountains which close in at its southern end, and the quieter charm of flowery meadows and woodlands at the north.

Keswick is one of the few places in England where there are regular tours all through the summer in four-in-hand horse brakes, and the 'Bassenthwaite Round' on a hot summer's afternoon re-creates the days of the Lake poets with its pleasant, steady progress along the shores of the lake. The coaches also make the journey 'round Skiddaw' to Caldbeck, and there is a day-long 'Buttermere Round' over Honister and Newlands passes.

With the exception of Wythop Hall, built by the Fletchers

in the seventeenth century on the site of the hall which had been fortified by the Lowthers in 1319, the chief literary and historical associations of Bassenthwaite Lake are to be found along the road which skirts Skiddaw, but there are lovely viewpoints by both routes, and for walkers there are fine panoramas from the top of Barf and Lord's Seat, on the western shore of the lake, where is also that curious piece of rock, whose shape has gained for it the name of Bishop of Barf, and which it is the delight of the coachmen to point out.

Those who wish to avoid the highroad for at least a part of the way can take the road by Applethwaite Terrace, one of the finest viewpoints in the neighbourhood, and passing close to several places of interest. Ormathwaite, where the Brownriggs had been settled since 1677, was the home of Dr. Brownrigg, the chemist, who died in 1800 at the age of eighty. He was born at High Close, Cumberland, and after many years in practice as physician and chemist at Whitehaven, retired to Ormathwaite, where he continued his valuable research work. It was in 1772 that he carried out experiments on Derwentwater with Benjamin Franklin. He knew personally or corresponded with many of the most eminent scientists of his day, and his careful and original research work not only resulted in valuable discoveries, but laid the foundations for experiments by later chemists. He was the first to give detailed accounts of platinum, which was brought to him by his relative, Charles Wood, from the West Indies in 1741, and he was probably the first person to realize the acid nature of fixed air, or carbonic acid gas.

It was in Applethwaite village that Sir George Beaumont of Coleorton Hall, the devoted friend of Wordsworth and of many other poets and artists of the day, bought a plot of land and presented it to Wordsworth, in the hope that he would build a house and live there, close to Coleridge and other Keswick friends. The now disused mill of Applethwaite was built just after the generous gift, and its appearance in the beautiful view, taken in conjunction with the growing waywardness of Coleridge, led Wordsworth to abandon the project until over forty years after, when he built a cottage there, on which the date is still to be seen over the door.

Nearby is the vantage point which Southey so loved, just north of the beck flowing down to the disused mill, where he once found the artists Glover, Nash and Westall painting. Lower down the road is Millbeck Hall, a fifteenth century pele-tower with additions made in the sixteenth century, which was described by Sandford in 1675 as the seat of the family of Williamson, and birthplace of 'that most ingenious Monsir Sir Joseph Williamson, now Principall Secretary of State'. There is a Latin inscription above the door with the date 1590. Sir Joseph appears to have been baptized at Bridekirk near Cockermouth, where his father was vicar, and there seems to be no definite record of his birth at Millbeck, and in after life his connexion with the manor must have been extremely slight, as he spent much of his time in London or on estates purchased with the enormous fortune of his wife, the daughter of Lord d'Aubigny and heiress of the Duke of Richmond and Lennox, who was an amazingly brilliant match for a country squire—even one who had achieved a career in politics and gained the favour of Charles II.

Mire House, which lies on the north-westerly edge of the woods covering the Dodd, has collected in that one building literary associations which would give a town distinction, for it is filled with memories of Alfred Tennyson, who paid more than one visit to the Speddings, and on his first visit in 1835 as a young man discussed with young James Spedding the manuscript of the *Morte D'Arthur*, whilst his fellow guest, Edward Fitzgerald, the translator of *Omar Khayyâm*, played chess with their hostess. Tennyson's poem to 'J.S.' was written to James Spedding on the death of his younger brother. Carlyle's letters contain references to a visit to Keswick in 1818, when he visited Mire House, and thought the eldest Spedding one of the best men he had ever known, and his daughters 'three beautiful young ladies'. Carlyle used to say that Tom Spedding was the only man who really understood him. He paid his last visit to Mire House in 1865.

Spedding's counsel was valued by some of the greatest

literary men of his day, and he gave much good advice to the founders of the *National Review*. James Spedding, famous as the editor of Bacon's works, was equally valued by the literary men of the day, and numbered among his friends Thackeray and Lord Houghton. Tennyson called him 'the wisest man I know'. His thirty years' study of Bacon was only interrupted by his appointment as secretary to Lord Ashburton's mission to the United States in 1842, and a civil service commission in 1855; and he refused the office of Permanent Under-Secretary of State for the Colonies rather than abandon his studies.

Bassenthwaite Station lies on the north-west shore of the lake, but the parish stretches between Skiddaw and the eastern shore, with the old church lying close to the lake, between Mirehouse and Bowness, and the new church nearly two miles to the north, beside the Chapel Beck.

Armathwaite Hall, formerly a seat of the Vane family, and, later, of the Bowsteads and Hartleys, has been modernized into an hotel. The view south from this neighbourhood is enchanting, with the mountains framing, but never dominating, the great stretch of water. There are many Roman and Norse sites on the shores of Bassenthwaite, described in some detail by Canon Rawnsley in *Lake Country Sketches*. The beautiful iron sword, jewelled on the hilt and sheathed in bronze, which is now in the British Museum, was found at Embleton, on the western side of the Wythop Fells.

Although the country north of Bassenthwaite Lake is not, strictly speaking, a part of the Lake District, it attracts many tourists in the present day, for at Caldbeck there is the grave of the immortal 'John Peel', and more recently the district has been sought for Ireby, Uldale, and other places which have figured in the 'Herries' novels, where they are described with a master touch.

Orthwaite Hall, an ancient house with Elizabethan windows, on the way to Ireby, was once the home of William George Browne, the oriental traveller, who although born in London was descended from a Cumbrian family. He first set out on his travels in 1792, and in 1812 incurred the unfounded suspicions of the Persian Government, and was

CASTLE RIGG STONE CIRCLE, NEAR KESWICK

murdered. His most valuable writings were published after his death by Horace Walpole in *Travels in various Countries of the East*.

It is a curious fact that although the ballad *D'ye Ken John Peel?* is so widely known, incorrect versions are frequently printed, and the substitution of 'Troutbeck' for 'Caldbeck' in some of the later editions is misleading. Although John Peel spent the greater part of his life at Ruthwaite, he was born at Caldbeck, and was buried in the churchyard there in 1854, at the age of seventy-eight. The composer of the song, John Woodcock Graves, was born at Wigton, but settled at Caldbeck for some time after his second marriage and followed his trade as a woollen weaver, until he quarrelled with the manager of the woollen mills and in a fit of temper decided to emigrate to Australia.

It was during his stay in Caldbeck that Graves composed the ballad, in the year 1832, whilst he was sitting with John Peel by the fireside, fitting its rhythm to the tune of *Bonnie Annie*, which was being sung at the time by an old woman nursing one of his children. The melody was set to music by Mr. Metcalf, then choirmaster of Carlisle Cathedral, and it is said that when he composed it, Graves sang it through to Peel who 'smiled through a stream of tears', and the composer, carried away by enthusiasm, exclaimed with more truth than he realized 'By jove, Peel, you'll be sung when we're both run to earth'. Graves lived in his self-imposed exile until the age of ninety-one, and was buried by the side of the Derwent river which runs beneath Mount Wellington at Hobart Town in Tasmania.

Since 1929, sports have been held annually at Caldbeck on 'John Peel Day' in October. Caldbeck village is of much interest, apart from its associations with the ballad. It grew up round a hospice built by Carlisle Priory for the entertainment of travellers journeying through the forest of Inglewood, and the rectory hall is said to have been the hall of this hospice, which was dissolved during the reign of King John. The ancient church of Caldbeck has some interesting features, and there is a holy well nearby. In the churchyard are the graves of John Peel, and of Mary of

Buttermere, who married a Caldbeck farmer after her first disastrous marriage. There is a portrait of John Peel in the Oddfellows' Arms.

II

The most famous viewpoint for Derwentwater is Castle Head, but the lake is so supremely lovely that every fresh glimpse serves to intensify the first impression of its rare beauty, and make the visitor rejoice that so much of Derwentwater is now in the care of the National Trust, either as a memorial to Canon Rawnsley, or to others. Grange Fell was bought by H.R.H. the Princess Louise as a memorial to her brother, King Edward VII; Scafell Pike was given to the Trust in memory of the men of the Lake District who fell in the War; and Castle Crag was given in memory of Lieut. John Hamer and the men of Borrowdale.

Friar's Crag was possibly the place where the monks of Lindisfarne and other pilgrims were ferried to St. Herbert's Isle when they came as pilgrims to the shrine of the saint. Ruskin declared the view from the Crag was one of the three most beautiful in Europe. It is one of the most photographed views in Lakeland, and is said to have been used as a background for an illustration of a Redskin and his canoe in one of R. M. Ballantyne's stories for boys. In a dry summer Jonathan Otley's marks, recording the varying levels of the lake in his day, can be seen cut in the rock.

The first recorded name of Derwent Island was Hest Holme, in the thirteenth century, when it was given by Alice de Romilli to the monks of Furness Abbey, who held it under the name of Vicar's Island until the Dissolution, when it was granted to John Williamson, who in his turn sold it to the German miners. After the departure of the miners it came to the Radcliffes, who had owned Lord's Island for centuries, and had their home there. They obtained the manor in the time of Henry VI through marriage with the heiress of the Derwentwater family, who had been lords of the district since at least the time of Edward I, and possibly much earlier. It was one of the Derwentwater Radcliffes who died with Richard III on Bosworth field. The Radcliffes built up a fortune as mine-owners during the reign of James I and were created Earls of Derwentwater by James II. They repaid their debt of gratitude to the Stuarts not only with their whole-hearted support but with their lives. The last Earl, having joined the rising of 1715, was beheaded in spite of every effort of his friends and his young wife to save him.

For several nights after the Earl's execution there was a great display of Aurora Borealis, which were afterwards known locally as 'Lord Derwentwater's Lights'.

A romantic story of the escape of the Countess from Lord's Island, in a fruitless journey to save her husband, during which she lost her jewels on Lady's Rake, has been discredited, and certainly appears improbable in view of the fact that the family mansion on the island had been abandoned to ruin about the time of the Civil War. Possibly the story belongs to some earlier escape, for about the middle of the nineteenth century a hoard of silver coins dating from the time of Edward I and II, was discovered, and there is reason to believe that similar finds were made there during the eighteenth century. The bell which hangs in Keswick Town Hall probably came from the Radcliffes' mansion; it has been conjectured that the date 1001 on the bell was an error in casting, and was probably intended for 1601.

All these islands are well wooded, and there is a fourth and much smaller one, Rampsholme. There is also a phenomenon known as the Floating Island, a curious spongy mass which appears periodically in the bay off Lodore, usually about the middle of October, and has attracted the attention of many writers and geologists, who describe it as a thick peaty carpet composed of the water-plants of the lake, which is forced to the surface by gases formed by decomposition.

Borrowdale has a sublime beauty which has inevitably attracted the attention of descriptive writers, particularly since the days when Gray trembled at its 'terrifying' mountains, and in our own time it has been brought vividly before the mind's eye of those who have read *Rogue Herries* and *Judith Paris*, the latter of which also gives vivid descriptions of the hidden valley of Watendlath in sunshine and in storm. Sir Hugh Walpole has unwittingly sowed the seeds of discord in these lovely valleys, for no less than three houses in Rosthwaite claim to be the 'original' of Rogue Herries' farm, and at Watendlath each of the two farms has a sign stating that it is the home of Judith Paris. In the case of Watendlath the truth seems to be that the writer stayed at one farm and described the other.

The chief tourist sight of Borrowdale is the curious geological feature, the Bowder Stone, a poised block of stone 36 feet high which is reckoned to weigh 1,970 tons. The Lodore Falls after heavy rain are as turbulent as they are described in the famous poem Southey wrote for the children of Greta Hall, but in the dry season Lodore is only too apt to justify the postcards sold locally to illustrate the time-honoured story of the man who inquired where the Falls could be found and was told he was sitting on them!

All this lovely valley and its surrounding hills is full of memories. Turner and Rogers rowed on the Lake; Southey, in his *Colloquies*, met with Sir Thomas More when seated under an ash tree hanging over the stream of Cat Ghyll, half-way up the ascent between Falcon and Walla Crags; Faber wrote a poem *Castle Hill, Keswick;* Dr. Arnold and his son walked across the fells from Armboth to Watendlath; a trip which the boy described ten years later in his poem *Resignation;* Keats visited Lodore; William Smith and Lucy Cumming lived in the house opposite the Borrowdale Hotel; and Wordsworth and Dorothy are, of course, there too, finding inspiration in the Floating Island and again in the Yew Trees of Seathwaite and, almost needless to say, in the story of St. Herbert; rich memories these, all threaded on the silver chain of the exquisite river Derwent, which drops down from the fells at the head of Borrowdale and makes its way to the sea in a wide sweep which takes it through Derwentwater and Bassenthwaite, and gathers up the Greta on its way. In the Jaws of Borrowdale is the picturesque hamlet of Grange-in-Borrowdale, with its grey stone bridge across the Derwent, which is on the site of a grange of the monks of Furness Abbey, and at the head of the dale the motor road climbs over the famous Honister pass to Buttermere, and the track, which all lovers of walking are ever alert to defend from conversion into a motor road, climbs over Styhead pass to Wasdale, through scenery which is a sheer enchantment of wild harmony.

III

The 'Druid's circle' which is probably the most popular short excursion from Keswick, lies in an appropriately lonely and beautiful setting on a hill-side east of Keswick, in the midst of fields massed with wild flowers and ringed with stately fells. Immediately below the stone circle are the twin valleys watered by the St. John's Beck and the Naddle Beck and divided by the hause running southward to Thirlmere. Although the main road to Grasmere and southern Lakeland runs through the Naddle valley, and a good road through the Vale of St. John's links Thirlmere with Threlkeld on the Penrith road, these valleys are extremely sparsely inhabited, and there are only a few scattered farms, and a tiny school and church on the dividing ridge is shared by the dalesfolk of both valleys. The little church once belonged to the Hospitallers of St. John of Jerusalem, and in its graveyard is buried John Richardson, one of the most famous writers of Cumbrian dialect poems. Born at Piper House in Naddle in 1817, he became schoolmaster at Bridge House, under the church, where he died in 1886. He had been bred to his father's trade of mason originally, and many of Keswick's houses of that period were built by him, and he also built the parsonage and school at St. John's Vale, and rebuilt the church. Much has been made of the 'difficulty' of understanding his dialect poems, but the difficulty is largely imaginary and the context is sufficient to give the meaning of the occasional unfamiliar words, whilst there is a wealth of detail about the old Cumberland ways, and the 'auld fashint weddins and buryins' and other quaint customs and local beliefs which have long died out, but which he got first-hand from his mother-in-law, Mrs. Birkett of 'Wythburn City', who lived to the age of ninety-five. Richardson's *Cummerland Talk* and *Thowts by Thirlmere* should be read by all who are not content with a merely superficial knowlege of Lakeland.

Better known, and containing splendid descriptions of the scenery, although not so truly characteristic of the district, is Scott's *Bridal of Triermain*, in which he takes the Castle Rock for his subject, although there are traces of a far more interesting ancient fort on Shoulthwaite.

Thirlmere, like Haweswater, is a place of memories, although the Manchester Corporation has spared no effort to make it beautiful and attractive in itself. Beneath its waters lie the old road that the poets knew, and the cluster of cottages pretentiously known as the 'City' of Wythburn. The Cherry Tree Inn and the Nag's Head are no longer inns, and there are only fragments of the stone which was the trysting place of the poets, on which Wordsworth and his wife and sister, his brother John, and Sarah, his sister-in-law, and their beloved friend Coleridge all carved their names. Canon Rawnsley obtained the permission of the Corporation to remove the stone before the valley was flooded, but unfortunately found it immovable. He collected the fragments after it had been blown up, cemented them together, and placed them just beyond the Straining Well on the Keswick road, near the incline which descends steeply to the vale of Legberthwaite.

The stone seat at Wythburn erected to the memory of Matthew Arnold can still be seen there, and other interesting associations are with Dante Gabriel Rossetti, who completed his last volume of poems at Fisher Place, and Sir Hall Caine, who worked the country round Legberthwaite and Thirlmere into his novel *The Shadow of a Crime*, which was inspired by the story of a haunted house at Armboth.

Dalehead, too, had its stories of weird and supernatural fires which flamed brilliantly but left no sign of burning, but the district has a modern and more charming romance centring round an ancient land-owning family, the Jacksons of Armboth. Miss Jackson married the Russian Count Ossalinsky, and also received an enormous sum of money from the Manchester Corporation as compensation for the flooding of her property.

Wythburn church, being on higher ground, was fortunate enough to escape the flooding of the valley and remains the little building with a bell-turret which Wordsworth, Coleridge and Matthew Arnold knew, and which was mentioned by Wordsworth in *The Waggoner* and sympathetically described by Hartley Coleridge. Many quaint stories cling to the church, the best known being the story of the clergyman who accidentally dropped his sermon down a crack between the pulpit and the wall, and after vainly trying to recover it turned to his congregation and said cheerfully that he would read them a chapter of the Bible which was 'worth a dozen of his sermon, anyway'! A less familiar tale concerns the sexton, who was discovered by the vicar standing on the roof of the church just before the church service was due to begin, and explained that as the harvesters had taken the bell-rope for some necessary purpose, he had to ring the bell by hand and did not think it worth while to climb up and down between each peal!

Across the lake from the church is the track over the Fells to Harrop Tarn, Blea Tarn and Watendlath, and beside the churchyard wall is the starting point for the easiest route up to the summit of Helvellyn. Among the fells which surround the summit are the curiously-named Dollywaggon Pike, the origin of whose name is unknown, and Catchidecam, which means the comb or ridge of the cat's ladder, and indicates that it is extremely steep. Swirrel Edge, and Striding Edge are twin buttresses below which lie the Red Tarn where Gough and his dog were found. A monument was erected by Canon Rawnsley and Miss Power Cobbe to mark the place where the accident occurred. A cairn just below the summit on the Wythburn-Grisedale track is inscribed: 'The first aeroplane to land on a mountain in Great Britain did so on this spot on December 22, 1926. Bert Hinkler and John Leeming in an Avro-Alpha landed here and after a short stay flew back to Woodford.'

The view from Helvellyn is as widespread and splendid as befits the second highest point in Lakeland. The immediate neighbourhood of Grisedale Tarn is so barren that Mr. T. S. Tschiffeley in his *Bridle Paths Through England* said it brought back memories of the highlands of Bolivia and Peru, but beyond there is a glorious stretch of fells, lakes and wooded dales, and on a clear day it is possible to see the Solway Firth and the Dumfriesshire Hills to the north, and the distant line of Morecambe Bay to the south.

Helvellyn has a particular interest for geologists as one of the principal places in Great Britain where manifestations of the Arctic and sub-Arctic frost phenomena of 'stone-stripes' and columnar ice needles can be observed. Other places on the Lakeland fells where the stone stripes have been seen include Low Man in the Skiddaw group. Interesting papers have been written on the phenomena by Dr. S. E. Hollingworth; and by Mr. Thomas Hay, for the *Geographical Journal* in January, 1936.

The county boundary, which crosses the summit of the Helvellyn range, leaves the tarns over on the Westmorland side, and drops down on the south of Seat Sandal, crossing the main road at the summit of Dunmail Raise, where there is a cairn of stones said to mark the burial place of the last King of Cumberland, but more probably marks the scene of his defeat in the tenth century by Edmund of England, after which he lived for another thirty years, and died on a pilgrimage to Rome.

Chapter XIII

SOUTHWARD FROM COCKERMOUTH

I

COCKERMOUTH is another of those Lakeland towns which so pleasantly prove that it is not necessary to blot out all beauty in order to be prosperous. It has been a market town since 1226 and a Parliamentary borough since 1295, and in the present day has a considerable trade and manufactories, yet the gardens round the ruined castle and the walks beside the Cocker and the Derwent are preserved in all their fresh green beauty, and the busy main street is wide and attractive, as befits the street in which stands the dignified old house where Wordsworth was born.

The fame of William Wordsworth and his sister Dorothy has so overshadowed the rest of the family that 'Brother John', who lived with them at Dove Cottage, is the only one known even by name to many of the poet's admirers, yet his brother Christopher was a brilliant scholar who became master of Trinity College, Cambridge and had three sons, all of whom achieved distinction. John, the eldest son, became Classical lecturer at Trinity College, Cambridge; Christopher became Bishop of Lincoln, and Charles, after splendid work as a Master at Winchester College, was appointed Bishop of St. Andrews. All three wrote many valuable papers as a result of original research work, and Charles's book *On Shakespeare's Knowledge and Use of the Bible* has a permanent place in Shakespearean literature. Christopher's eldest daughter, Elizabeth, was the first principal of Lady Margaret Hall, Oxford. William Wordsworth's eldest son, John, was at one time vicar of the neighbouring village of Brigham.

Cockermouth, in addition to its associations with the Wordsworth family, was the birthplace of the Rev. Fearon Fallows, an exceptionally distinguished astronomer who established an observatory at Capetown to which he had been appointed director by the Commissioners of Longitude at the Cape of Good Hope in 1820. He carried out observations there until his death in 1831, cataloguing 425 stars and making nearly four thousand observations. He is buried near the South African Observatory where he worked, but there is a tombstone to his memory in All Saint's churchyard at Cockermouth.

Joseph Sutton, R.A., was born in 1762 in the Main Street. His most famous picture was 'The Blind Beggar of Bethnal Green and his daughter', suggested by the old ballad of that name. The Rev. John Whitelock, born in the Blue Bell Inn about 1777; Isaac Wilkinson, born in South Street in 1752; Jonathan Wilkinson, Stanley Martin, James Alexander Slevan, and Robert Barnes, were natives of the town who achieved a local celebrity as writers of prose and verse. Isaac Wilkinson is of particular interest in the present day as he was for seven years the schoolmate of Fletcher Christian of 'Mutiny on the *Bounty*' fame, who was born at Eaglesfield nearby. Wilkinson at one time addressed a poem to Lord Byron, defending the character of Christian, which had been adversely criticized by Byron, adding a note in which he finishes: 'I can with truth say, a more amiable youth I never met with; he was mild, generous and sincere.'

Cockermouth has a special interest for film enthusiasts, for in addition to the association with Fletcher Christian, it numbers among its visitors Raphael Sabatini, the filming of whose novels, *Captain Blood* and *The Marriage of Corbal*, has increased the already wide popularity of his historical novels, and who made the town his summer home for many years; Ouida, whose old-time popularity is recalled by the filming of *Under Two Flags* as a silent film and more recently as a talkie, spent a holiday at Oakhurst on a hill above the Cocker river; and Sir Hall Caine, whose novel *The Manxman* has also appeared as a silent film and a talkie, stayed several times as the guest of the late Colonel Edwin Jackson.

The writers who have visited Cockermouth at various times show a most catholic range of interests. Robert Louis Stevenson, in his *Essays of Travel* describes his stay in the town and a talk with Smethurst the hatter, who carried some of his goods on his head, one on top of the other. John Woodcock Graves spent six years at the old Lamb Inn, kept by his uncle; and Roger Quinn, the Scottish 'Tramp Poet', also visited the town. Cockermouth also figures in several novels, of which the Herries series and Edna Lyall's *Hope the Hermit* are the best known.

Mr. J. M. Denwood, author of *Red Ike*, sponsored in the literary world by Sir Hugh Walpole, was born in Cockermouth, and was the son of John Denwood, a Cumbrian poet born in the town in 1845. Both John Denwoods spent some years in the United States before finally settling in England, and one of the younger man's best known poems is *Thowts on seĕan a Daisy at Niagara*. The lives of John Denwood and other Cockermouth versifiers of their time are given, with specimens of their work, in *The Cumbrian Caroller* written by E. R. Denwood, who has also written a very full account of the historical and literary associations of Cockermouth and district in the small book *Round Wordsworth House*.

Part of Cockermouth Castle is used as a residence by Lord Leconfield, but the remainder, which is in ruins, is open to the public. The first mention of the castle was in 1221, when the Sheriff of Westmorland was ordered by Henry III to besiege and destroy it, but its then owner, William de Fortibus, Earl of Albemarle, later regained the King's favour and was allowed to rebuild the ruined walls. It was again partially rebuilt in the fourteenth century, and enlarged towards the end of the same century, traces of all the periods being discernible in the surviving portions.

Warlike memories cling to the walls, and it has sheltered many famous people. In 1269 it came by marriage to Edmund Crouchback, Earl of Lancaster, the Crusading brother of Edward I. It was besieged and taken by Robert Bruce in 1315, and two of its constables—Piers Gaveston and Sir Andrew de Harcla Earl of Carlisle—were beheaded in the same century. Harcla appears to have been convicted of treason on very inadequate evidence, and a paper read by Cornelius Nicholson, based on careful research, vindicated his character very successfully. Harcla's captor, Anthony de Luci, received Cockermouth as his reward, and it was his descendant, Maud, the heiress of the Lucies, who brought Cockermouth to Henry Percy, Earl of Northumberland. The Earl took much of the material for his reconstructions from the Roman building at Papcastle, and a Roman altar can be seen on the north side of his gatehouse. Nearly two hundred years later the castle sheltered Mary, Queen of Scots, for a night, after the defeat of Langside. She landed at Workington, in May, 1568, and was entertained by the Curwens at Workington Hall, where it is said she left an agate cup known as the 'Luck of Workington' behind her in appreciation of this hospitality. During her short stay in Cockermouth there was a charming incident. Sir Henry Fletcher, noticing how soiled her garments were, presented her with thirteen ells of rich crimson velvet to make herself another gown—a kindly act which evidently touched the Queen, for her son acknowledged her pleasure years later, when he became King of England.

Some accounts of her stay in Cockermouth give the Old Hall as her lodging, but in the opinion of W. G. Collingwood the room supposed to have been her bedroom is of later date than her visit.

The last outstanding episode in the castle's history was an unsuccessful siege by the Royalists, when it was relieved by Colonel Ashton after a few weeks. Its later owners, the Wyndhams, allowed all but the gatehouse, courthouse and a few rooms adjoining to fall into ruin. An old house near the castle has an Elizabethan plaster ceiling, and bears the arms of the Percies and Lucies on the fireplace.

The castle overlooks the Derwent, not far from the point where the river Cocker flows into the greater river, giving the town that rather misleading name which suggests it is on the sea coast. The church of All Saints, in whose graveyard William Wordsworth's father is buried, was rebuilt in 1852.

Cockermouth claims to have the first Congregational Church established in Cumberland, which owes its origin to the Rev. Thomas Larkham. Their first pastor was his son, the Rev. George Larkham, who was pastor at Cockermouth for forty-nine years until his death in 1700, and was buried at Bridekirk. It was the Rev. George Larkham to whom George Fox refers in his journal as 'priest Larkham', when the Quaker delights in his victory over the Congregationalist and speaks of the large numbers who were brought to join the Society of Friends. An extremely interesting *History of the Congregational Church, Cockermouth*, by the Rev. W. Lewis, which prints many extracts from Larkham's own notes, and from the Church book, shows that the Congregationalists were more moderate in their comments, and the eminently fair entry under the date 1653 merely reads: 'Mr. Larkham and Mr. Fox met at Cockermouth and opposed sentiment to sentiment, each with the ardour of one conscious of the exclusive justness of his own cause.' The record further shows that although so many joined the Society of Friends under the immediate influence of Fox's burning words, a very large number returned to the Congregational fold within a year, and the number of those from the Cockermouth church who finally seceded to the Friends was only five. Nevertheless the transparent honesty of purpose and fiery zeal of Fox won many to follow his precepts, and it was only the fanaticism of a section of his followers which prevented the number of converts being far greater.

II

There is an ancient fort with an oval rampart and a ditch at Fitz Wood, just west of Cockermouth, and a Roman fort, now nearly obliterated by new buildings in the village of Papcastle, but the most interesting antiquity in the neighbourhood is the celebrated font in the modern church of Bridekirk, and the pre-Norman and medieval monuments in the graveyard, beside the ruins of the old church of St. Bridget.

It is interesting to compare the eighteenth century opinion of the font and its runic inscription with modern ideas on the subject. A *Description of England and Wales*, published in 1749, says that the font was discovered among the ruins of Stapcastle (Papcastle) and that there are 'some characters in this font, which long puzzled the learned to interpret. This difficulty has, however, in great measure, been removed in a letter written by the learned Bishop Nicholson to Sir William Dugdale. He supposes . . . that the inscription . . . should be thus read: "*Er Ekard han men egrocten, and to dis men red wer Taner men brogten,*" i.e. "Here Ekard was converted; and to this man's example were the Danes brought." The doctor's letter, together with an accurate copy of the inscription, is at large inserted in the last edition of Gibson's Camden'. W. G. Collingwood renders the inscription: '*Rikarth he me wrokte, and to this merthe gernr me brokte*'—'Rikard he me wrought, and to this beauty eagerly me brought.'

Collingwood further suggests that Rikarth was Master Richard of Durham, the greatest craftsman of the north in the later part of the twelfth century. The work is of marvellous richness, depicting dragons and all manner of strange beasts; a representation of the expulsion from the Garden of Eden; and of the baptism of Christ; and a presumed portrait of the artist with chisel and mallet above his runic signature.

Thomas Tickell, the poet and friend of Joseph Addison, was born at Bridekirk Vicarage. Dr. Johnson considered Tickell's poem on the death of Addison the finest funeral poem in the English language. Sir Joseph Williamson, of the Millbeck Hall family, was also born in Bridekirk Vicarage.

North-east of Cockermouth are Isel, in lovely woodlands beside the Derwent, with its interesting little twelfth century church; Isel Hall, an Elizabethan extension of an earlier pele-tower, and Hewthwaite Hall, with an inscription over the door recording that John Swynburn and his wife 'did make cost of this work in the dais of their lyfe. 1581'. In Setmurthy village between Isel and Lake Bassenthwaite, was the school, since pulled down, where Thomas Farrell, the author of the ever-popular *Betty Wilson's Cummerland Teals*, was master for several years. He is buried at Aspatria. The Rev. Charles C. Southey, son of the Poet-Laureate, was Vicar of Setmurthy from 1842 until about 1850.

Among the many other places of interest in the neighbourhood of Cockermouth is Whistling Syke, the house on the road between Broughton and Dearham which was built by the grandfather of the famous Josiah Wedgewood in 1708, who carried on a manufactory of earthenware there.

Both the Cumbrian John Daltons who achieved fame were born in the near neighbourhood of Cockermouth—John Dalton, D.D., the poet, at Dean Vicarage in 1709, and the chemist in the village of Eaglesfield. The poet Dalton, among other works, adapted Milton's *Comus* for the stage, and gave the profits to Milton's grand-daughter, whom he had found in great want.

Canon Rawnsley expressed a wish in his *Literary Associations of the Lake District* that the cottage in which John Dalton the chemist was born should be marked with a slab commemorating the fact, and this has since been done, but the most intimate associations with the chemist are those at Kendal and Manchester. The home of his cousin, Elihu Robinson, the friend of Wilkinson of Yanwath, who did much to encourage and help young Dalton, is also at Eaglesfield.

Moorland Close, the birthplace of Fletcher Christian, stands on the Cockermouth side of the village. The family had been settled in Cumberland for three generations before the birth of Fletcher, but was descended from the famous Manx family at Milntown. Mr. Edgar Christian, one of Fletcher Christian's descendants, has been the Chief Magistrate of Pitcairn Island for many years. Fletcher Christian's elder brother was Edward Christian, the jurist, among whose numerous literary publications—all of which showed considerable research into antiquarian law—was an appendix giving a full account of the causes of the mutiny, which was attached to the Minutes of the Proceedings of the Court-Martial and provoked a reply from Captain Bligh.

Eaglesfield was also the birthplace of Robert of Eglesfield, the chaplain of Queen Phillipa, who in 1340 founded Queen's College, Oxford. It was Eglesfield's express wish that scholars from Westmorland and Cumberland should be given preference for fellowships there which led to the close relationship between the College and those counties.

A mile or two south of Eaglesfield is Pardshaw Crag where George Fox preached to a crowd of people and which, although it undoubtedly does not give that impression at first sight, has natural acoustic properties that make it a perfect platform for an orator. Canon Rawnsley records that when Neale Dow, the American temperance reformer, addressed a meeting there in 1857 there were 5,000 people in the audience—and that the occasion was memorable for the amount of beer sold and drunk!

Although Cockermouth is not so closely invested by the fells as Keswick, it is essentially a Lakeland town, for not only is it within easy reach of some of the finest scenery of the district, but owing to the configuration of the fells and dales it is the best centre for Buttermere, Crummock Water, Loweswater and Ennerdale, and is on the principal highway to the coast and to Wastwater. The greater part of the road traffic from Keswick to the western fells passes by way of the Cold Fell or Distington Moor—the former route giving magnificent views seaward—and any motorist wishing to avoid the steep ascents of Honister, Newlands or Whinlatter Passes must necessarily go through Cockermouth.

III

Directly south of the town the Vale of Lorton, watered by the Cocker, stretches away into the Lakeland fells—a rich pastoral valley in a noble setting, which provided Mr. O. S. Macdonell with the background for his fascinating novel, *Thorston Hall*, which re-creates the life of the estatesmen on the Cumbrian farms at the period when Wordsworth and the Lake poets were alive, and also gives a sympathetic and illuminating picture of the Quakers of the period, and of local customs, traditions and economic difficulties.

The Yew Tree which Wordsworth described as the 'Pride of Lorton Vale' was the one under which George Fox preached in 1653, and recorded in his Journal that the tree 'was so full of people that I feared they would break it down', and although it survives to-day, it is decaying with age.

The Keswick Museum has a relic of a merry-making in Lorton Vale—one of many—the printed handbill of a 'Public Wedding or Bridewain' held at High Lorton in May, 1807. These public weddings were also known as 'Penny Weddings' as each guest contributed one or more pennies to the expenses of the occasion which included competitions, races and sometimes a play or pantomime afterwards. Many of the 'Notices' are still in existence, and some break into verse, as in the case of a Wedding Notice at High Lorton in 1811 which ran:

> ''Tis Love, immortal Power! give birth
> To healthful Sports and Sprightliest Mirth.
> Awhile your Drudgery and Pains
> Forego, ye jocund Nymphs and Swains.
> We think it only Right to acquaint ye,
> That each sort may get Sweethearts plenty!
> For those who Pastime love and Fun,
> We've Horses, Dogs, and Men to Run;

MUNCASTER CASTLE

Athletic Sports we'll set before ye,
And Heats renown'd in Ancient Story:—
Leaping and Wrestling for the Strong,
Enough to please you—*Come Along!*'

A Lamplugh effusion of 1786 ended with the confident claim:

'And you'll all go home happy—as sure as a gun,
In a word—such a Wedding can ne'er fail to please,
For the Sports of Olympus were trifles to these.'

The Bridewain, a ballad describing a Public Wedding, is one of the best-known works of John Stagg, the blind fiddler and poet born at Burgh-by-the-Sands in 1770.

At the little village of High Lorton a road branches off over the steep Whinlatter Pass to Keswick, giving a magnificent view of Bassenthwaite Lake. The Pass is one of the districts which have been planted out with conifers by the Forestry Commission, and the contrast between the beautiful contours of the unplanted fells, ever-varying through the day with sunshine and cloud-shadows, and the 'set' look of the trees planted in regular rows will make every beauty-lover thankful to remember that a large area in the heart of Lakeland has been exempted from afforestation.

The village of Loweswater, so happily set between the pretty little lake of that name and the larger Crummock Water, was for eighty-one years the home of Jonathan Banks, huntsman to the Mellbreak Hunt, who died in January, 1928, after having accounted for over 1,800 foxes, a record which entitles him to take his place among the most famous huntsmen of the district. A picturesque cottage at Crabtreebeck was the birthplace of John Burneyeat, a Quaker, who travelled and preached through England and Ireland, and in 1660 went to Barbadoes and from there to Virginia and Maryland, where he did notable work for the Society of Friends, and wrote many books expounding the teaching of George Fox, which were collected and published in 1691 under a long and discursive title beginning *The Truth Exalted in the Writings of that Eminent and Faithful Servant of Christ, John Burneyeat.*

In 1805 John Walker, author of the poem, *A Village Pedagogue*, who had been teaching at Newlands for a salary of £10 a year with board and lodging, came to Loweswater school at a slightly higher salary. He was a cousin of the Rev. George Walker of Hawkshead.

Crummock Water, fed by little becks from Buttermere and Loweswater, and by the great Scale Force, and drained by the Cocker, can be seen to perfection from the road which skirts its eastern shore to Buttermere. In spite of the tourists who pass through Buttermere every year, it remains a diminutive and peaceful hamlet. Its small church has been rebuilt since the days when 'Wonderful Walker' was curate there, and the present incumbent certainly fares better than his eighteenth century predecessors, of whom West reported in 1789 that although twice augmented with the Queen's bounty, their stipend did not exceed twenty pounds per annum, and he was of opinion that the 'perquisites of the clog-shoes, harden-sark whittle-gate, and goosegate, have no better support than in some ancient and, probably, idle tale'. Nevertheless some such payment in kind of clog shoes, clothing, meals, and room for his goose on the common, with some sort of recompense for acting as the village schoolmaster must necessarily have been made to eke out the meagre stipends which were customary in the dales, and which were seldom augmented by any private income, for the vicars were usually local boys who had received their education as the result of sacrifices on the part of their parents.

It is usually assumed that Mary of Buttermere was unknown outside the valley before her first marriage, but she had been brought into public notice by Budworth, the author of *A Fortnight's Rambles to the Lakes*, in 1792, as the charming daughter of the proprietor of the Fish Inn. Nevertheless, it was her marriage in 1802 which brought her the celebrity which has lasted to the present day, for Coleridge, Southey and Wordsworth helped to make the story known to the public, and chap-book versions 'sold like hot cakes'. John Hatfield, who married her whilst staying at the inn as the 'Hon. Col. Hope', proved to be a confirmed rogue—an impostor of the worst type who, curiously enough, was not hung for his heartless crimes as a bigamist, but for the franking of letters as a bogus M.P.—in modern eyes a far less important crime. There is some reason to suppose that the 'Beauty of Buttermere' after she had survived the first shock, rather enjoyed the nation-wide sympathy she received, and the 'nine days wonder' ended happily enough with her marriage to a farmer of Caldbeck, where she lived to an advanced age. An engraved portrait in *Echoes of the Lakes and Mountains*, published about the end of last century, like so many such portraits, does not convey much idea of beauty beyond curling hair and large eyes, but in actual fact Mary's youthful charm must have been considerable. The Fish Inn still exists, and incorporates part of the centuries-old original building which Mary knew.

Buttermere Lake is perfection itself—heart-stirringly beautiful in every mood of storm and sunshine in its splendid setting of mountains. Scale Force, the loftiest waterfall in the district, drops between perpendicular rock walls in a single leap of 120 feet, and is within easy reach of the village by a path through the flowery meadows and woods which separate Crummock Water and Buttermere. Among the many lesser falls which cascade down these fells is the conspicuous Sour Milk Ghyll, which those readers of mystery stories who have followed the investigations of Mr. H. C. Bailey's detective will remember figures prominently in one of the tales in *Clue for Mr. Fortune*.

There are two roads into Keswick from Buttermere, both intimidating to nervous motorists. Honister Pass has magnificently wild and lonely fells before Seatoller is reached, and Newlands Pass is also hemmed in with great bracken-clad fells before the road drops down to the smiling vale of Newlands, where the Prologue of that most fascinating book *The Dalesman*, by Mr. A. W. Rumney, is laid. In the words of the author's own preface '. . . the book does not aspire to the status of a novel, but I believe it to be the only attempt to describe a dales farmer's life and attitude to the world *from the inside*'. Mr. Rumney, who is the descendant of a long line of Cumbrian statesmen, has a specialized knowledge of his subject which he has used to such good purpose that

Sir Hugh Walpole wrote of the book '... it is as though the Cumbrian ground becomes vocal'.

Newlands church, rebuilt in 1843, stands at the fork of the valley, half-way up its length. The Goldscope mines worked by the German miners during the time of Elizabeth, and still worked up to the earlier part of last century, are in the branch of the valley running south of Dale Head. On the Keswick side of the road branching off to the church is Emerald Bank, once the home of Robert Southey's sailor brother Tom, and later the place where the famous Master of Balliol, Dr. Jowett, spent many summer holidays.

At the pretty little village of Stair, whose houses are grouped on either side the Newlands Beck, is the picturesque farm-house marked with the initials and date, 'F. F. 1647', in which the Parliamentarian General Fairfax is said to have lived for a while. Beyond Swinside the road plunges into the enchanting woodlands which border the western shore of Derwentwater to Portinscale, where in 1901 a hoard of stone tools and weapons of Neolithic man was found, which can now be seen in the Keswick Museum, two miles away.

Chapter XIV

THE WESTERN DALES

I

ENNERDALE WATER is so 'off the beaten track' that even the ubiquitous charabanc tours merely view it from a distance as they drive down from Cold Fell to Loweswater, and its solitudes are usually only penetrated by the really hardened walkers and the most expert climbers. Edwin Waugh, the Lancashire poet, wrote an appreciative description of this lake in sunlight and in moonlight in his *Rambles in the Lake Country*, and in watching the cloud shadows most truly said: 'If there be magic in the world, it is this!' In some moods Ennerdale is as blue as a sea-loch but in storm it can be lashed to fury by the wind.

Cumberland's own poet has not neglected such a scene of beauty, remote from his home in the Grasmere Vale though it might be, and his poem *The Brothers* has cast its spell over Ennerdale and the Pillar Rock, although the scene of the fall he describes was in reality a rock a mile farther up the dale, and his picture of the churchyard with 'neither epitaph nor monument . . . only the turf we tread. And a few natural graves', is an example of poetic licence, as some of the monuments in the churchyard at Ennerdale Bridge undoubtedly date from a time before Wordsworth could have visited it. The poet evidently had in mind the well-defined Cumbrian dislike for tombstones which persisted among the dalesfolk up to the end of last century and probably had its origin in the strong Quaker influence.

How Hall, a modern farm-house which lies between the village of Ennerdale Bridge and the foot of the lake, has barns which show traces of earlier buildings on the site, and was once a mansion of importance.

North of Ennerdale Bridge is Lamplugh, where only a gateway, with arms dated 1595, survives from the old Hall. The Lamplugh Cross and the pele of the Lamplugh family have been destroyed. William Dickinson, one of the nineteenth century dialect poets of Lakeland, wrote an account of the Lamplugh Club meetings. The village was once known for the 'Lamplugh Pudding', consisting of biscuit soaked in hot ale with seasoning and spirits to taste. Among Cumbrian 'specialities' which have survived is rum-butter which is generally served with tea in Cumbrian farm-houses, and always puzzles visitors when they first encounter it.

Above Ennerdale-water is the river Leesa, whose name, W. G. Collingwood suggests, is derived from the same source as the Icelandic river Lysâ, meaning 'the bright water', and proves that this district was one of those originally settled by the Norsemen. The limpid waters of this stream, cascading in a series of waterfalls half-hidden in luxuriant ferns and trees, is in exquisite contrast with the wild, bare fells by which it is surrounded.

There are two tracks over the fells from Ennerdale to Wasdale, one over Windy Gap; and the other over the

Pillar Mountain, the latter giving superb views, without incurring the difficulties involved in the ascent of the craggy pinnacle of the neighbouring Pillar Rock, which should be avoided by all but experienced cragsmen.

The Pillar Rock is separated from its parent mountain by a deep cleft, and juts out like a great rock column, true to its name. In the second edition of Otley's Guide, published in 1825, the rock was described as unclimbable, but by the time his 1827 edition was being prepared for the Press it was necessary to alter the reference, for in 1826 a shepherd named Atkinson, who lived at Croftfoot, in Ennerdale, had climbed up the western side of the crag by the route now known as the 'Old West Climb'. The modern route up the Pillar Rock is believed to have been discovered in 1863 by a Cambridge party, and by 1870 the first lady had scaled the 'unclimbable' Pillar Rock. Four years later, another lady had scaled the rock and had her feat celebrated in verse in the *Whitehaven News*, which so piqued the veteran Rev. James Jackson, who prided himself on his athletic feats, that in May, 1875, at the age of seventy-eight, he too conquered the rock and proudly adopted the title of 'Patriarch of the Pillar'.

In the present day, when members of the Alpine Club, the Climbers' Club, and the Fell and Rock Climbing Club, come year after year to these wild western fells, and every climb has been thoroughly explored and charted, and such well-known mountaineers as Mr. George D. Abraham have written exhaustively on the subject, the Pillar Rock no longer takes first place, but it is numbered by Mr. W. P. Haskett-Smith among the four finest climbing grounds in England, the other three being the Gable, Mickledore, and the Wastwater Screes. Mr. Haskett-Smith also considers that 'few places can teach one so much about "chimney sweeping" in a month as Cumberland can in a week'.

Although Scafell Pike is the highest mountain in England, it is generally conceded that there is no mountain in the Lake District better worth climbing than Great Gable, whose summit, nearly 3,000 feet above sea level, commands a widespreading view. It is an easy climb, especially from Styhead, but the detached rock of Napes Needle is a challenge to skilled cragsmen. Great Gable was one of the peaks given into the care of the National Trust by the Fell and Rock Climbing Club in 1923, in memory of those members of the Club who fell in the Great War. The bronze tablet with a memorial inscription and a group of the neighbouring peaks shown in relief, is on a boulder near the summit cairn on Great Gable.

II

It is but too rarely that there is perfect agreement between those who delight in physical prowess and those who are more wedded to intellectual pursuits, but they are in perfect agreement in their appreciation of Wasdale Head. The famous Wastwater Hotel is one of the chief centres of the Alpine Climbing Club, and the heavy calf-backed visitors' books there have the signatures of all the pioneers of English Rock Climbing, and like all the best Lakeland inns, reserves its warmest welcome for the true climbers and fell walkers, who return year after year, rather than for the wealthier but less understanding type of tourist.

Round the walls of the Wastwater coffee-room are photographs of the most renowned climbers who have conquered the fells, all of which have their interest, but the one which has pride of place is that which shows the grand head of Will Ritson, the most celebrated landlord of the inn. Edwin Waugh, who stayed there in 1860, devotes a chapter of his *Rambles in the Lakes* to Will Ritson, who had known Wilson, Wordsworth, Professor Sedgwick, De Quincey and others of that famous company. Waugh recounts the often-quoted story of the trick played on Will and his friends by Wilson, who went out boating with them on the lake, and pretended to topple into the water in a faint. As Ritson said: 'Wilson was a fine, gay, girt-hearted fellow, as strang as a lion, and as lish as a trout; an' he hed sek antics as nivver man hed. Whativver ye sed tull him ye'd get your change for it gaily soon.'

Ritson was a perfect example of the old type of Cumbrian estatesman, and was as warm-hearted and talkative with his friends as he was reticent with strangers. He could be extremely caustic on occasions. A cockney who said disparagingly of Wasdale Head: 'Fancy living here all your life. Why don't you come up to London and see the sights?' to which Ritson crushingly replied: 'Ah, m'lad, theer's nea 'cashion for us t'cum up t'Lunnon t' see t'seets, 'cos sum of t'seets cums doon here t'see us.' He had a small opinion of rock-climbing as a sport, and once said to some climbers: 'What's makkin' ye fellas fash yer-sels seea mich aboot climming t'crags? Isn't t'fells big eneugh for ye?'

There were many merry gatherings of friends at Wasdale Head when Ritson was the life and soul of the party, however, for he was a noted humorist and especially proud of his power of inventing 'tall stories'. There is a splendidly drawn description of Ritson, and of a visit of Wilson to Wasdale Head in Mr. O. S. Macdonell's enthralling novel *George Ashbury*, which many people consider gives the most understanding interpretation of the Cumbrian character that has yet been written. The author was born in the Lake District, and had that inner knowledge of the dalesmen which no true Cumbrian will ever believe can be acquired by any 'off-come', however gifted, and he has woven into his thrilling tale the local traditions of the smugglers who used Moses Trod on Great Gable, and many incidents which actually took place in Wasdale in the early eighteenth century.

Ritson came of a long line of estatesmen of Wasdale Head, and his wife was one of the Fletchers of Nether Wasdale, who had owned land in the valley for seven centuries. It was Will's fame as a wrestler and raconteur, and his friendship with Professor Wilson that first drew travellers to the secluded dale, and inspired Ritson and his wife to build a wing on to their small farmhouse of Rowfoot, procure a licence, and open it as an inn, about 1856. Ritson remained as landlord until 1879, and died at Strands in 1890 at the age of eighty-three, but his memory will endure as long as there are visitors to Wasdale to recount the time-honoured anecdotes. His name is further perpetuated in the delightful little waterfall, half a mile above the inn, which was named 'Ritson Force' by the late Mr. Baddeley.

Another novel which takes Wasdale Head for its setting

is Mrs. Lynn Linton's *Lizzie Lorton of Greyrigg*, which gives an interesting and accurate picture of the changes which took place in the remote dales at the end of last century, when the old type of vicar, frequently ignorant and always poverty-stricken, but often liked as a friend by his parishioners, was being replaced by zealous and well-educated young men who, whilst they were of the highest possible character and filled with good intentions, had a hard struggle to reconcile their flock to the new ways. That the change was necessary, however much it was regretted by the older dalesmen, can be gauged by the stories told of some of the older clergymen which, whether true or not, show the general trend of opinion.

A poem 'Written at Mr. Rawson's Wastwater Lake' has put on record the appreciation of Walter Savage Landor for the dale, and Wastwater is also pictured in *Red Screes*, by Cecil Headlam; *Halfway House*, by Maurice Hewlett; *The Odd Women*, by George Gissing, *Rogue Herries*, and other novels.

The maximum population of Wasdale Head has been less than fifty for a long period, and its church is correspondingly small, and if it cannot claim to be quite the smallest in England, it can undoubtedly claim to be one of the quaintest, with its great wooden beams in the roof making the interior look even smaller than it really is. In the tiny graveyard are monuments to those who have been killed on the mountains, as a reminder to the expert, no less than the novice, that not only skill but care also is needed in climbing the great fells walling in the dale, and that it is folly not to take the possibilities of mists into consideration.

Harriet Martineau records in her *Guide to the Lakes* that the schoolmaster of Wasdale was entertained on 'whittlegate' terms, that is, he boarded at the farm-houses in turn, and an old man told Miss Martineau that he got the children on very well 'particularly in the spelling. He thinks if they can spell, they can do all the rest'. Miss Martineau also mentions the curious superstition, which was very strong in her day, that if a child's arms were washed or its hair and nails cut before it was six months old, it would be a thief.

Nether Wasdale, at the foot of Wastwater, though but a tiny place, has much interest, for in its ancient little chapel is oak carving from York Minster, and the mansion of Wasdale Hall looks out from the trees beside the lake. It was at Nether Wasdale that the last of the Fletchers died at Church Style, in 1897. It is said that although the last of the direct line, he had over two hundred and fifty cousins!

In the fells which lie between Wastwater and Eskdale is Burnmoor Tarn, and the source of the River Mite, and in the wooded country which lies between the river Irt and the Mite is Irton Hall, which has grown out of an ancient pele-tower. In Irton churchyard is a cross 10 feet high and richly carved, which probably dates from the ninth century.

III

The Eskdale fells come right down to the sea at Ravenglass, and every mile of the way between the mouth of the Esk and its source, far away between the Scafell Pikes and Bowfell, increases in beauty until the great fells close in at its head. It has the quaintest and most delightful little narrow-gauge railway running for the first seven miles from Ravenglass to Boot; it has a famous inn of the best type, hospitable farms, the finest waterfall in Lakeland, and other scarcely less attractive falls; the great Roman station on Hardknott, and fifteenth century Dalegarth Hall to give it historic interest, and even a haunted house, and yet it has not achieved the fame to which it is surely entitled. It is true that for a few short weeks in the height of the season the baby engines of the railway are kept puffing busily up and down the track, but the passengers seldom go farther than Dalegarth Force, and the wild and splendid region at the head of the dale is neglected by all but the faithful few who can be relied upon to penetrate the most remote and neglected corners of Lakeland.

Those who avoid the Lake District because they fear it is overrun with tourists would do well to visit Eskdale. It is so sparsely inhabited that there are only three shops at Eskdale Green and two at Boot. The peace of the upper valley is absolute, whilst the sea-breezes blowing in from the coast dispel any possibility of feeling 'shut-in'.

Although the valley has no lake of its own, there are innumerable tarns on the fells above, and the lakes of neighbouring dales are easily reached, whilst the rugged Muncaster Fell which closes in the foot ensures that although the best way to explore the valley is to go up to the head, there is no 'tameness' in the view of those who come down the valley. Any regrets that it has no lake must needs be lost in the greater pleasure of its preservation from a 'popular' development that might have marred its seclusion.

There are direct tracks across the fells to Wastwater, and from there to Ennerdale or Borrowdale; to the Langdales; and over Hardknott Pass to the Duddon Valley, and there are good second-class roads by way of Devoke water to Ulpha and other places in the Duddon Valley, and to Ravenglass and the coast, and branching off to skirt Irton Fell into Miterdale and Wasdale.

The valley itself is cultivated as much as possible, and some of its farms have endured for centuries, but on the heights above there is a wilderness of fells stretching away to the blue haze of distance in utter loneliness and grandeur.

In the whole length of the valley there are only two hamlets—Eskdale Green and Boot. A ruined farm-house at Eskdale Green is pointed out as the place where a woman who had been left alone in the farm with her baby, having given hospitality to a gypsy-woman, was alarmed to realize it was a man in disguise. Waiting until he had fallen asleep, she killed him by pouring boiling tallow down his throat, and ever since the farm has been haunted. The true setting of the story is Miterdale; it has been told by Miss Alice Rea in her book, the *Beckside Boggle*, in which she also recounts the legend of the escape of a horse which was being brought over the corpse road across the fells with a dead body strapped to its back for burial. It was never recaptured but still haunts the fells.

The old King of Prussia Inn at Eskdale was renamed 'King George' in a burst of patriotism during the Great War.

The terminus of the railway is at Dalegarth station,

within a quarter of a mile of Boot, and not far from the beautiful woods in which Dalegarth Hall and its waterfall are hidden.

Dalegarth Hall was a seat of the Stanleys until about 1690, when John Stanley built Ponsonby Old Hall, and moved there. A great part of the building was pulled down in 1750, but some oak beams and a ceiling dated 1599 remain. Guide books dating back as far as 1852, if not earlier, have emphasized the necessity for obtaining a key at Dalegarth Hall before viewing the waterfall, but in 1936 the delightful woods in which the fall is situated were thrown open to the public. Dalegarth Fall, which is sometimes called the Stanley Ghyll, is a 60-foot drop of a tributary of the river Esk between precipitous cliffs, and is reached by a path through the woods beside the river, and there is another winding track zigzagging up from a point near the foot of the fall to a gate high on the fells above, close to the road winding away to Devoke Water. The widespreading view of the bracken-covered fells, rising and falling for miles around, is a fascinating contrast to the rich beauty of the woods in the cleft where the view is concentrated on the picture of sunlight dancing through the leaves and sparkling in the falling water.

Devoke Water, lying 766 feet above the sea, is the largest of all Lakeland tarns and is set in a wild and beautiful situation among the fells. It is famous for its red trout which it is said were originally imported from Italy for the tarn by the abbots of Furness Abbey. One of Faber's sonnets was inspired by a view in sunshine after storm 'On the Heights near Devoke Water'.

IV

Boot is a small cluster of houses grouped round a picturesque stone bridge across the Esk. The waterfall and the old corn mill with its overflow water-wheel, are a favourite subject with artists who visit the village. Bridge-end Farm, a substantial grey stone house beside the river, is three hundred years old, and in one of the rooms is a fitted press of elaborately carved wood with the date 1703 on it.

In the churchyard which lies some distance from the village is the grave of Tommy Dobson, who died in 1910. He was a notable Master of the Eskdale and Ennerdale Pack for fifty-three years, and his likeness is carved on his tombstone together with the heads of a dog and fox and a hunting crop and horn.

Boot is a famous centre for sheep fairs, and has been a resort of shepherds and flock-masters for centuries. The Woolpack Inn, beloved by Lakeland climbers, remembers in its name the days of the pack-horse trains of the wool-merchants which came over the fells on this short cut between Kendal and Whitehaven. There are delightful short walks in the neighbourhood of Boot and the Woolpack, up the Whillan Beck with its many cascades, or to the Birker Force, whilst for the keen fell-walker and climber there is the glorious route to Burnmoor Tarn and Wasdale, and the veritable maze of tracks at the head of the Dale beyond Butterilket, where the fells have not been 'developed' in the slightest, and remain as gloriously untamed as in the days when the Romans came to build their camp on Hard-knott.

The excavation of the Roman Camp was commenced in 1889 and carried on until 1894, disclosing a fort about 360 feet square partly enclosed by a deep ditch. There were towers at each corner of the stone walls, and a gate on each side, and inside were the barracks, store-house, home of the commandant and other necessary buildings. Outside the fort was the levelled area for drilling the troops, and the remains of a Roman bath-house and other buildings. Among the many relics were some bones, so brittle as to be difficult to identify, but generally believed to be those of a small dog and its puppies or a cat with its kittens, killed by the fall of the walls of the bath-house. A Roman pottery and tilery has also been discovered at Park House, a mile from Eskdale Green.

The ancient farm which the monks of Furness Abbey, writing in the thirteenth century, spelled 'Brotherilkeld', and the origin of whose name is unknown, lies immediately below the great fell of Hardknott. It figures in Agnes Hilton's novel, *The Hermit of Eskdale*, which successfully recreates the life in Eskdale during the fourteenth century, when the superstitions, loyalties and customs which are now only a memory were a living force. Witches, Beltane or Need fires, May Day ceremonies, the gaieties attendant upon the brewing of the Whitsun Ale, the gathering of the St. John's wreath, to scare away evil spirits on St. John's Eve, these and many other familiar sights and scenes of the days when paganism still lingered in the dales to struggle with the ever-growing influence of Christianity, are woven into the touching story of the hermit whose beautiful ideal of Christianity was so unacceptable to the orthodox churchmen of his day. Early Saxon times figure in the popular novel, *Shelagh of Eskdale*, edited by Mr. Nicholas Size, from a story by the late Dr. Parker. Mr. Size has also depicted the dalesmen in the eleventh and following centuries in *The Secret Valley*.

Beyond Butterilket the scenery becomes increasingly wild and lonely, until above the Esk Force the valley branches into two, one branch leading to Bowfell or Langstrath and the other into the grandeur of the inner valley walled by the splendid crags of Scafell, the Pikes, and Great End.

V

The beautiful Duddon, which Wordsworth made the most famous of all Lakeland rivers, marks the boundary between Cumberland and Lancashire during the whole of its course from a point near the Three Shires Stone on Wrynose to the gleaming golden sands of the wide tidal estuary. Great bare fells rise and tower over the upper course of the stream—Hardknott, Greyfriar and Harter Fell dominating the many lesser heights until the woods begin on the lower slopes of Birker and Ulpha Fells on the Cumbrian side, and on the Seathwaite and Dunnerdale Fells of Lancashire, whose majesty heightens the captivatingly gentle beauty of the river where rowan trees bend lovingly over the water. Its pageant of wild flowers through the year opens with the golden glory of the wild marsh asphodel, which turns the banks of the river into molten gold triumphantly flaunting over the delicate beauty of

SKIDDAW

wild anemones, violets and stars of the primroses round Bleasley Banks and then in due season makes way for the heaven's own blue of great swathes of bluebells. Spring in the Duddon Valley is the very soul of that joyous season, when Cumberland and Lancashire unite in a blaze of beauty to proclaim that summer is on its way.

The only village on the Cumbrian bank of the river, before the estuary is reached, is Ulpha, with its church on a hill, its Old Hall and its legend. The Old Hall is a ruined sixteenth century pele-tower, in the delightful little ravine of Holehouse Ghyll. The little waterfall is known as the 'Lady's Dub', and tradition tells that a lady of the hall was drowned there as she fled from a wolf. Frith Hall, south of Ulpha, is now a farm-house, but according to a local tradition, was built on its lofty height by one of the lords of Millom, who used it to watch the deer-hunting in his park of Ulpha, on the Cumbrian bank of the river. The road across the fells from Eskdale Green drops down into the Duddon Valley at Ulpha. A mile lower down the valley is Duddon Hall, where the Logan Beck flows into the Duddon, and a road crosses the moors to Bootle on the sea coast.

Chapter XV

THE CUMBRIAN COAST

I

THE chapter which Edwin Waugh wrote in 1861 on the 'Seaside Lakes and Mountains of Cumberland' is still so applicable in the present day that it is worth quoting. He says: 'Of all our English lake scenery no part is less known than that which skirts the sea, from the ruins of Peel in Furness to Whitehaven in Cumberland; and there is none which less deserves neglect. Shut out on the east by England's wildest mountains and on the west by the Irish Channel . . . this tract of country possesses interesting relics of every race which has left a name in our history.'

Whitehaven and Workington, although on the coast, and extremely interesting historically, do not claim to be ideal holiday resorts, but the amusements they offer and the shops, too, are acceptable to those to whom holiday joys do not spell complete freedom from town life, and it is they who organize the coast tours and ensure that the motor bus services shall be good and frequent so that they have their place in the scheme of things, whilst such places as Bootle, Whicham, Silecroft, Ravenglass, Drigg, Seascale, Braystones and St. Bees have a simplicity which makes them the delight of all who can appreciate a completely care-free, unconventional holiday.

The most southerly of the coastal towns of Cumberland is Millom, a modern town which takes itself seriously as a holiday resort, in spite of the handicap of its tall chimneys where the rich hæmatite ore is worked in pockets which are frequently found far under the sea. So beautiful is the town's setting on a low promontory jutting out into the Irish sea and a long stretch of golden sands sweeping round into the vast expanse uncovered by low tide in the Duddon estuary, and green, smiling fields stretching to the foot of the great fells of Lakeland, that its plans for development as a centre for holidays have been justified by a growing popularity with those who like to season their appreciation of untouched natural beauty, with man's handiwork in the shape of golf links and tennis courts.

The ruins of a castle are a reminder that although the town and its mines are modern, Millom Castle was the seat of the Lordship of Millom, which passed by marriage from the Boyvilles to the Hudlestons in the time of Henry III, whilst the Gallows Hill has a pillar whose inscription records that 'Here the Lords of Millom exercised Jura Regalia'. This power of life and death over their tenants was exercised until early in the sixteenth century. The castle was largely rebuilt after a Scottish invasion in 1322, by Sir John Hudleston, and the tower was added late in the sixteenth century. The parish church of Millom contains an altar-tomb, two marble effigies, and other memorials of members of the Hudleston family.

II

Silecroft is chiefly notable for its good bathing and as the station for Whicham, Kirksanton, Whitbeck and Black Combe, all of which are well worth exploration.

The school of Whicham has produced many notable scholars, and a delightful story is told of a party of students from St. Bees College who paid a visit to the 'John Bull' Inn at Whicham at the beginning of last century, and amused themselves by endeavouring to impress the landlord with their intellectual attainments. He made no comment, but on their departure presented them with a bill written in Hebrew, Greek and Latin, which none of them could read! A similar story has been attributed to a dalesman at Ulpha. Near Whicham Hall is a field called Scots' Croft, where tradition tells a fierce and sanguinary battle was fought between the English and the Scotch. Whicham figures largely in Faber's poem, *Sir Lancelot*.

Kirksanton is traditionally believed to derive its name from a church which sank suddenly into a peaty tarn nearby, complete with minister and congregation, but the tarn is now drained and nothing has been discovered to support the tradition. There are similar beliefs in other parts of England, and remembering the close connexion between Cumbria and the Isle of Man it is more likely the name has a similar derivation to its namesake on the Island, which was the church of St. Sanctan. At the farm of Standing Stones is the Giant's Grave, two standing stones with cup markings on the larger one. Lacra farm also has prehistoric remains.

Whitbeck has a church of very ancient foundation which was given by Gamel de Pennington to the Priory of Conishead. It is said that on one occasion when smuggling was rife in the district the cargo of spirits was concealed in the church, but as the smugglers were unable to remove it in time for Sunday service a hint was conveyed to the minister, and he obligingly gave out that there would be no morning services as he was too ill to perform his duties! The so-called Cockpit at Monk Foss, a mile to the north of Whitbeck, may have been the fish-ponds of the monks of Furness Abbey, who had a grange there.

Black Combe, the most southerly of the mountains of Skiddaw Slate, is an easy climb from any of the villages at its foot, but the view is so rewarding that Wordsworth, in speaking of it, declared that an experienced surveyor of his acquaintance had said it commanded a more extensive view than any point in Britain. On a clear day not only the Isle of Man, but Ireland also may be seen on the seaward side, and Jack Hill in Staffordshire inland, with the Welsh mountains to the south and the Scottish heights of Galloway on the north.

Black Combe was one of the principal Beacon hills of Cumberland, the others, so far as the Lake District Coast is concerned, being Newton Knott, above Muncaster; St. Bees Head; and St. Michael's Mount, Workington, with Hardknott in Eskdale to carry the message inland. So many disastrous Scots forays made their way south round Black Combe that it gave rise to a traditional saying in Furness that 'Nowt good ever comes round Black Combe'.

John Linton, who wrote a guide book published in 1852, was told by a member of the 'Muncaster Mountaineers', one of the numerous corps raised for home defence during the Napoleonic Wars, that the company marched to the top of Black Combe for their manœuvres, which so struck him that he wrote: 'It must then have presented an impressive spectacle—bristling with bayonets, and enveloped in the "dark red smoke" of war, while the "swift and deafening peals" of musketry rang in countless echoes among the hills. It was, to our thinking, conceived in a profoundly poetic spirit, and would have been worthy of some Roman general, intent on rousing the martial ardour of his soldiers on the eve of a great battle—that mustering of the gallant mountain-band on this elevated spot, in full view of the "pleasant fields" for whose protection they had assembled.'

On Swinside Fell, north-east of Black Combe, is the third largest megalithic circle of the Lake District.

III

The complete contrast between the Cumbrian town of Bootle and its more famous namesake in Lancashire can be imagined easily when it is realized that the population of the former is about 1,000 and of the latter is in the neighbourhood of 80,000. Wordsworth once spent a holiday at Bootle with his wife and two of his young children, during August, 1811, and it is strange to find that in spite of the magnificent sunsets over the Isle of Man and the immediate neighbourhood of his beloved mountains, the nature poet did not appreciate his seaside holiday, and complained in his poem, *Epistle to Sir George Beaumont*, that they were 'stunned by Ocean's ceaseless roar', but the truth was, apparently, that they were unfortunate in their choice of a lodging and were further depressed by bad weather.

Bootle was a part of the great lordship of Millom, and received its charter as a market town as far back as 1347. The ancient church was considerably enlarged in 1837 but retains its beautiful old octagonal font of marble, carved with shields and various devices. There is a sixteenth century brass of a knight in armour on the chancel wall, with an inscription to 'Sir Hugh Askew, Knyght, late of the seller to King Edward VI'.

Sir Hugh's home was at Seaton Hall, which was originally a thirteenth century Benedictine nunnery about a mile to the north of Bootle. Askew had been yeoman of the cellar to Queen Catherine, and when the Queen was divorced he was left destitute. The manner in which he acquired Seaton Hall is told in Sandford's MS. *History of Cumberland*: '. . . he applied for help to the Lord Chamberlain . . . who knew him well . . . but told him he had no place for him but a charcoal carrier. "Well," quoth this Monsir Askew, "help me in with one foot and let me gett in the other as I can." And upon a great holiday, the King looking out at some sports, Askew got a courtier, a friend of his, to stand before the King; and Askew gott on his velvet cassock and his gold chine, and baskett of chercole on his back, and marched in the King's sight with it. "O," saith the King, "now I like yonder fellow well, that disdains not to doe his dirty office in his dainty clothes what is he?" Says his friende that stood by on purpose: "It is Mr. Askew, that was yeoman of the seller to the late Queen's ma[tie], and now glad of this poor place to keep him in y[r.] ma[tie's] service, which he will not forsake for all the world." The King says, "I had the best wine when he was i' the celler. He is a gallant wine-taster, let him have his place againe", and afterwards knighted him; and he sold his place, and married the daughter of Sir John Hudleston; and purchased this religious place of Seaton, nye wher he was borne, of an ancient freehold family, and settled this Seaton upon her, and she afterwards married Monsir Penington, Lo: of Moncaster, and had Mr. Joseph and a younger son with Penington, and gave him this Seaton.'

IV

Eskmeals, beside a ford across the river Esk, is the station for Waberthwaite and the hamlets on the southern bank of the river Esk. Countless rabbits have their home in the sand dunes at Eskmeals, and John Linton, who was roused to martial thoughts on Black Combe, became playful at Eskmeals, of which he says: 'As we cross the Warren, which covers a subterranean city crowded with inhabitants, we shall probably catch flying glimpses of some of them peeping from the doorways—breakfasting on the tender herb—or scampering, with all a gossip's haste, to and from their neighbours' houses. The construction of the railway has not been unproductive of benefit, even to this graminivorous colony, inasmuch as the bridge across the Esk has tended very much to facilitate their access to the well-stored fields of Muncaster (to which they were formerly in the habit of *swimming*) whenever they are disposed for a little foreign travel, or ambitious of a rather more luxurious style of living than their own homes afford them.'

The little church of Waberthwaite was for centuries a chapel of Muncaster. The shaft of an elaborately carved pre-Norman cross has been re-erected in the churchyard, and in the vestry is the fragment of a still earlier carved stone which probably dates back to the ninth century. The floods of the river Esk defeated many attempts to build a bridge across the river at Waberthwaite, and the sturdy stone bridge which carries the highway across the river now owes its existence to men from Grasmere, whose special knowledge of the art of building bridges across mountain torrents stood them in good stead. Carved on the east side of the bridge is the inscription, 'This bridge built by men of Grasmere MDCCCXIX'.

V

No one could ever complain of feeling stifled at Ravenglass, which thrusts out on its level promontory into a waste of waters and sand dunes and is freshened by sea-breezes guaranteed to 'blow the cobwebs away'. This tiny town is so small that only the fact that it has had a charter for a market since 1209 entitles it to rank as a town, for it has no Town Hall, and its church is two miles away in Muncaster Park. The population does not equal that of some villages, but the two short rows of houses set well apart across a wide road and surrounded on three sides by water and on the east by the wooded slopes of Muncaster Fell, have a charm for anyone who can appreciate a sturdy simplicity, and they have a history which unrolls the pageantry of the ages.

The famous gullery, a bird-sanctuary where beautiful sea-birds breed in countless thousands, was in all probability there long before any human beings made their appearance, but men came early to Ravenglass and Romans, Norsemen and Normans have all left their mark to tell of the great days of this almost forgotten port, where the sand bar now prevents any but small craft from entering. According to one tradition Ravenglass is also the place where Herdwick sheep first came into the Lake District, forty having landed there from the wreck of a Spanish ship. Another tradition attributes them to the Norse settlement.

Only the eye of the expert can trace the remains of the Roman fort of Clanoventa beside the railway line, but the so-called 'Walls Castle' which stands beside the private drive to Walls House, is the best preserved Roman building in the north of England, for nowhere else in the north is there a Roman house still standing to the full height of its walls. The 'castle' was actually a Roman bath-house attached to the nearby fort and whilst its interest to archæologists can hardly be too strongly urged, it cannot be denied that the less expert visitor will be apt to mistake it for a comparatively modern house falling into ruin! The remains consist of an irregular block about fifty feet long by forty feet wide, forming two rooms and part of two others, and the hardness of the mortar, the internal rendering with pink cement, the relieving arches of the doors and other features which have survived nearly two thousand years of wind and rain are a spark to set the imaginative mind on fire, and the perfect roundheaded niche in one of the rooms seems to cry aloud for the statue that once stood there.

The full description of the Roman remains at Ravenglass, and a reconstruction of their history is given in a booklet, *Roman Eskdale*, by Prof. R. G. Collingwood, who has the rare gift of making the Roman times 'alive' to those with no specialized knowledge. He traces the course of the Roman road from Ravenglass to Hardknott, in Eskdale, and Ambleside. The illustrations are from the photographs of Miss Mary C. Fair, the Eskdale archæologist whose excavations have done so much to clear up doubtful points in the Roman story of Eskdale.

The Penningtons came to Ravenglass as lords of the manor some time during the twelfth century, and apparently used the Roman bath-house as their dwelling until they moved into the pele-tower which was enlarged into a castle about 1325. The present castle was built in 1800 on the same site. The Penningtons succeeded each other at Muncaster until the death of the late Lord Muncaster. When Henry VI left the 'Luck of Muncaster' with his host, in gratitude for hospitality after a defeat in 1461, the tradition was born that 'whyllys the famylie shold kepe hit unbrecken, they shold gretely thrif' and never lack a male heir. The tradition has been fulfilled to the letter; there have always been male heirs, but the lords of Muncaster must have often wished that the royal donor had added the word 'direct', for it has been their misfortune that they have so frequently lacked a direct male heir. The property passed time and again to younger brothers, and the present owner, though undoubtedly a 'male heir', with Pennington blood in his veins, has broken the centuries-old connexion of the Pennington name with Muncaster castle.

The Luck of Muncaster, which is a curious bowl of greenish glass, about seven inches in diameter, enamelled and gilt, is still preserved at the castle, together with the bedstead used by the King and a portrait of him with the Luck in his hand. The portrait of Tom Skelton, the Muncaster fool, who is said to have lived during the time of the Civil Wars, also hangs in the castle.

Muncaster Church, which stands in the park, is of very early foundation, and was given about 1190 to the Priory of Conishead by Benedict de Pennington. It was granted back to the family at the Dissolution. An eleventh century cross-shaft stands in the pretty churchyard. There are many interesting memorials to the Penningtons, of which the earliest are two brasses dating from the fourteenth century. Many of the Penningtons were distinguished soldiers. Sir John Pennington, who died in 1470, accompanied the seventh Earl of Northumberland on expeditions into Scotland. He remained faithful to the House of Lancaster during the Wars of the Roses, and it was he who gave refuge to Henry VI. A grave slab in the church records that another Sir John, who died in 1518, 'stoutelie headed his souldiers at Flodden Field'; and a brass dated 1533 records that 'Syr William Penington Knight' married 'Frances Pagrane, nighe-kinned woman unto Charles Duke of Suffolk'. William Pennington was created a baronet in 1676, and his grand-daughter married Robert Lowther, Governor of Barbados, and became the mother of the first Earl of Lonsdale. Her brother John, the third baronet, was a colonel of the Cumberland militia during the siege of Carlisle by the rebels in 1745. The title of Baron Muncaster was conferred on the Penningtons in 1783, the first Lord Muncaster being the Col. John Pennington who met Dr. Johnson at Fort George in Scotland in 1773 and worsted him in an argument about the comparative merit of discipline in semi-savages. On retiring from the army he had a distinguished political career and was the intimate friend of Pitt and Wilberforce. His only son, Gamel, who died at the age of eight, is commemorated by a wall tablet in Muncaster church:

> 'Yes, thou art fled, and Saints a Welcome Sing
> Thine Infant Spirit soars on Angel wing,
> Our dark affection led to hope thy stay
> The voice of God has called his Child away
> Like Samuel early in the temple found
> Sweet Rose of Sharon, Plant of Holy Ground,
> Aye, and as Samuel blest, to thee 'tis given
> Thy God he served on earth, to serve in Heav'n.'

Sir Lowther Pennington, the younger brother of the first Lord Muncaster, succeeded to the title in 1813, after a career in the army during which he served in America, where he fought a duel in New York, and later became colonel of the 131st foot, called 'Penington's Regiment'.

In Wordsworth's day the Lord Muncaster locked his gates against the intrusion of tourists, and the poet could not see the glorious view from the terrace, but in the present day anyone who cares to pay the modest fee of sixpence can walk the terrace on Fridays, as most guide books tell, but it is not generally known that the terrace is also open on Bank Holidays and that any party of twenty or over that cares to make a prior application, can see the view at any time: a privilege which, if more widely known, would doubtless draw many sightseers. The view is so enchanting, and the approach through the beautiful, well-wooded park so delightful, it is a matter for wonder that more people do not visit the terrace. The beauty of the view is heightened by the skill with which the approach has been arranged to shut out every sight and scene but that of trees and flowers and castle walls until the wide, grassy terrace with its low, clipped hedge and its colourful flower-beds is reached. Then, with all the suddenness of the highest artistic effect, the eye is carried away across the valley, with the river winding far below, to the bracken-clad hills, and rocky peaks of Lakeland.

VI

The country which lies between the coast and the fells has many interesting manor-houses and towns. The largest of the seaside resorts is Seascale, which is especially popular for its sands, sea-bathing and golf, and its Horticultural Show held in August. All its buildings are modern, with the exception of the Herding Nebb Cottage on the shore road, which has a quaint figure-head above the porch, said to have been taken from one of the vessels wrecked in a great storm. The cottage was originally an inn largely patronized by local poachers who, when the Lord of the Manor prevented the renewal of the licence, declared they 'wadna leeav him a hare aboot t'spot'. Seascale Hall lies inland, nearer Calder than the coastal town. It was the ancient manor-house of the Senhouses and although modernized as a farm has some old fireplaces, a stone bearing the ancient arms of Senhouse quartering Ponsonby, and another stone dated 1606. The stones of the megalithic circle which stood on the Hall farm are now buried. Drigg, also on the coast, is a village with a celebrated chalybeate spring, and a huge boulder on the sandy shore, known as Carl Crag, and said to have been dropped by the Devil in an unsuccessful attempt to build a bridge between the Isle of Man and the mainland.

About a mile inland from Drigg is Holmrook, set beside the River Irt where in olden times there was a pearl fishery, from which one owner of How Hall in Ennerdale is said to have gained £800. In the present day the salmon and trout fishing in the river is excellent, but the shell-fish containing the pearls are no longer found. Holmrook Hall is famous for its beautiful gardens.

St. Bees Head rises over 300 feet, above a sandy bathing beach which is the delight of visitors to the attractive little town set in a valley between green hills, only five miles from Whitehaven.

The legend of St. Bees tells that Saint Bega came from

Ireland with her nuns in the seventh century, and the lord of the land mockingly said they should have as much ground as the snow covered at midsummer—and although presumably taken aback when snow fell over a large tract on Midsummer Day, kept his word. It has since been demonstrated that no St. Bega had any connexion with the site, although there was undoubtedly a pre-Norman church there.

The Priory was founded by William de Meschines in the twelfth century as a cell of St. Mary's of York, and although burnt by the Scots in 1315, became the third richest in Cumberland. After the Dissolution it was left to decay, but the church was reconstructed in 1611 to serve as a parish church. The Norman arcades, and the great west doorway with its splendid carvings were retained, and among the ancient monuments are carved fragments of crosses dating from the eighth to the tenth centuries. Among the entries in the parish register at the end of the seventeenth century is one believed to refer to the baptism of Ellen, the daughter of Robert Washington of Whitehaven.

Opposite the church is the Grammar School founded by Edmund Grindal, a native of the neighbouring village of Hensingham, who was successively Archbishop of York and Archbishop of Canterbury in the reign of Elizabeth. It was reconstituted in 1881, but a considerable portion of the original Elizabethan buildings remains. The Theological College established at St. Bees in 1817 by George Henry Law, Bishop of Chester, was closed at the end of the same century.

VII

Inland, interest centres chiefly round Egremont Castle, Gosforth Cross and Calder Abbey, but there are also many notable manor-houses and villages.

Egremont has been a market town since 1267, and its modern parish church contains two Norman windows and some early medieval sculptures. Part of the remains of its great castle dates back to 1170. The 'Boy of Egremont', young William de Romilli, nephew of David I of Scotland, was the sole heir to wide lands, and might have been king of Scotland, and so many fair hopes perished with him that there was 'endless sorrow' when he was accidentally drowned, and his fate was the theme of innumerable ballads of the time. The famous legend of the Horn of Egremont, which was said only to sound for the rightful lord of the castle, has been retold by Wordsworth, who, according to the Cumberland and Westmorland Antiquarian Society made 'every possible historical mistake'.

Egremont Castle was besieged by Robert Bruce and by Lord James Douglas, but it survived until all but the court-house was destroyed in 1578. South-west from Egremont is the village of Beckermet, with its two interesting churches, and the site of Carnarvon Castle, the twelfth century seat of the Flemings.

Gosforth's ancient church has been restored, but two pre-Norman hog-backs and other fragments of carved stone have been preserved. The famous cross, which stands 14 feet high, is in the churchyard. Its magnificent carvings date from A.D. 1000 and closely resemble those on the Norse crosses of the Isle of Man. It is one of the comparatively few survivals to show how closely Cumberland and the Isle of Man were once linked under the Norse Kings. Even the Cumbrian folk-lore of the Norse era is rare, although it is possible the tales of horses which escaped from the 'corpse roads' to haunt the fells, are a later version of the ancient belief in the Cabbyl-Ushteys or water-horses, and other spirits, of which the tradition survives to this day on the Isle of Man.

In the countryside round Gosforth and Calder Bridge are the interesting manor-houses of Ponsonby Hall, on the site of a manor-house of the Stanleys, who settled there in 1388; Sella Park, dating back some three hundred years; Gosforth Hall, a seventeenth century seat of the Copleys; and Calder Hall, once the manor-house of the lordship of Calder.

The Abbey of Calder was founded by the Lord of Copeland in 1134 for a colony of monks from Furness. Within four years they were driven out by an invasion of the Scots, but another band of monks came from Furness, and remained in possession in spite of a second Scottish raid in the fourteenth century. After the Dissolution it passed through many hands, and the fabric suffered severely, not only from the weather, but from the depredations of those who built the mansion which now occupies the site of the monks' dining-hall and dormitory. The red sandstone ruins, lovely in decay, are set in a charming pastoral valley, and are carefully preserved by the present owner.

The west door of the twelfth century church, parts of the thirteenth century nave, and of the fourteenth century chapter house, remain. Of the four effigies, one with joined hands and a fret on his shield is probably that of Sir John le Fleming of Beckermet, who died in the thirteenth century; the figure with the lions on his shield is probably a Leyburne of Cunswick, and one of the others may be Sir Richard, son of Sir John le Fleming; but the other knight, with his hand on his sword-hilt, has not been even tentatively identified.

PART III

LANCASHIRE

Chapter XVI

ON THE SHORES OF MORECAMBE BAY

I

THOUSANDS of people arrive in the Lake District every year by the trains which skirt the shores of beautiful Morecambe Bay to Ulverston, Windermere and Coniston, but it is probable that not more than one in every thousand realizes there is a centuries' old coach route across the sands, which saved a fourteen-mile detour round the head of the Bay, and that a guide still exists to prove the route and accompany anyone who wishes to approach or leave the Lake District by the sands which, with their complete freedom from motor traffic, and their glorious views of the Lakeland Fells, afford the nearest approach to the conditions of Wordsworth's time which can be found in any route to the Lakes.

Most guide books ignore the route across the sands, or, if they mention it, dismiss it as 'dangerous' or 'uninteresting'. It cannot be too strongly urged that the route is dangerous to follow *alone*, but in company with the guide, it is a great deal safer than the high roads with their toll of accidents, and it is an experience which has the additional charm of novelty. Scarcely a hundred people a year take the route, but they are of the goodly company who are willing to 'try anything once', and they return to repeat one of the most delightful experiences even the Lake District, with all its lonely dales and unspoiled beauty, can offer.

The guides were originally appointed and maintained by the Prior of Cartmel, and the sands are known as the 'Cartmel', 'Kent', or 'Lancaster Sands'. The first record of a guide is during the reign of Henry VIII, when it was stated that about the beginning of the sixteenth century a man named Edmondson held a tenement and lands called 'Carter House' and held the office of 'Carter upon Kent Sands'. A local tradition that there were guides over the sands as far back as the thirteenth century may, or may not, be true, but it is certain that such a guide was needed, for the Abbot of Furness petitioned King Edward II for the appointment of a Coroner because so many people were drowned in the crossing. When Cartmel Priory was dissolved, the Duchy of Lancaster took over the appointment of the guides, and to this day part of the guides' salary is paid out by the Duchy revenues, although administered by the Charity Commissioners. So little is known of this service being available, that inquiries locally will not always yield information, but anyone who wishes to cross the sands can get in touch with the guide at 'Guide's House', Cart Lane, Kent's Bank, near Grange-over-Sands. It is best to make the journey from the Kent's Bank side at the first attempt, when the guide will accompany the traveller either to Arnside—a four-mile walk—or to the old terminal of the route at Bolton-le-Sands, or Hest Bank, which involves a ten-mile walk. The guide proves the route three times a week, and farms the land which is part of his perquisites as guide, but is always ready to make the journey. The proving of the route is a very necessary part of his work, as the constant shifting of the bed of the River Kent causes quicksands to form, and in its most recent phase, it is necessary to cross the first channel on the Kent's Bank side by boat, as the river is now flowing between 10 and 12 feet deep, although a few years ago it was so shallow that it was possible to make the crossing in a pony cart!

The fullest and most interesting account of the guides and their work, and of the ancient industries of fluke-fishing, cockling and mussel-gathering still pursued in Morecambe Bay, is to be found in a booklet, *The Sands of Morecambe Bay*, by Mr. J. Pape, which is published at Morecambe, and deserves to be far more widely known than it is at present. The booklet also gives full details of the route across the Leven Sands from Flookborough to the house of the Leven Sands guide, at Canal Foot, Ulverston—another interesting trip which is much shorter and can be made by pony-trap when the tide is out or by boat when the tide is in. The illustrations include a reproduction of Turner's painting, 'Lancaster Sands', which shows the coach arriving at Hest Bank about 1828.

There are some delightful towns and villages on the shores of Morecambe Bay, and of these the largest and most popular holiday resorts are Morecambe itself, which is a keen rival of Blackpool in its amusements and illuminations, and boasts of being a centre for Lakeland tours, and Grange-over-Sands on the northern shore of the bay, which delights to be called 'The Torquay of the North'. Grange cannot claim either the size or the range of amusements of the Devonshire Torquay, but the nickname sufficiently indicates the ambitions of Grange-over-Sands, and is completely justifiable on the score of climate; man-made charm of flower-filled gardens; and a superbly beautiful setting of sea and mountains.

The county boundary between Northern Lancashire and Westmorland follows the course of the Winster nearly to the mouth of the river. A highroad runs direct from Grange to Kendal, which is thirteen miles away. There are also two main roads running north to Newby Bridge, Windermere and beyond, one of which goes direct and the other by way of Cartmel and Cark, and there is also a road into the fascinating district of Furness, all these routes from Grange opening up a district which is comparatively little known, but supremely interesting.

The fells rise so close to the shores of Morecambe Bay near Grange that the visitor can walk to the heights in a very short while and gain a view so widespreading that, as a local guide says of the view from the neighbouring Hampsfell, 'if you have a fine day you may almost scream with delight'.

On the curious high cone of Castle Head, rising from the flats at Lindale, north of Grange, is the mansion which was built by John Wilkinson, the famous ironmaster and inventor, who was born at Clifton, Cumberland, in 1728. He revolutionized the whole of the iron industry and amassed a colossal fortune, before his death in 1808. He built the first iron ship, which floated on the River Winster to the amazement of all beholders, and he built the first iron bridge, made many of the cannon used in the Peninsula Wars, built iron barges which carried the castings from his foundry at Broseley down the River Severn, and soon outstripped his rivals in the excellence of his manufactories and the enterprise of his schemes. By his own wish he was buried in an iron coffin and is commemorated by an iron column which bears his portrait in relief. The column, which has been moved several times since it was first erected, now stands beside the road between Grange and Lindale. When the foundations were dug for Wilkinson's house in 1765 a large deposit of flint implements, Roman and Northumbrian coins, and bones of buffalo, deer, and human beings was found.

The direct road to Newby Bridge from Grange runs by the foot of the Cartmel Fells, and close to Buck Crag where, in a farm-house fallen into ruin, Edmund Law was born in 1703. He became Bishop of Carlisle, and four of his sons achieved distinction and were themselves fathers of notable men. One of the Bishop's sons, Edward, became the first Baron Ellenborough; John became Bishop of Elphin; George was successively Bishop of Chester and Bishop of Bath and Wells; and Thomas, who went to the United States in 1793 out of admiration for American institutions and reverence for Washington, had a distinguished career there. He married Anne Curtis, grand-daughter of George Washington's second wife, Mrs. Curtis.

There is a closer link with America at Warton, about a mile from Carnforth which, although not actually in the Lake District, is within easy reach of Grange, either across the sands, or by the road round the head of the estuary. There was a branch of the Washington family settled at Warton centuries ago, and the arms of Robert Washington were carved on the tower of Warton church, where they are now protected from the ravages of weather and tourists by a sheet of glass. Lawrence Washington left Warton in the reign of Henry VIII for Northampton, and later settled at Sulgrave, but a branch of the family remained at Warton, and Thomas, the last of the Warton Washingtons, was vicar from 1799 to 1823 and is buried there.

WASTWATER TOWARDS WASDALE

II

A two-mile walk from Grange through the fields beside the shores of Morecambe Bay leads to the delightful little village of Kent's Bank, bowered in trees and a haunt of peace; and a walk over the fells above leads to the noble Priory Church of Cartmel.

Cartmel is the name not only of the town and priory, but of the district which lies between the River Leven and the River Winster. The earliest reference to Cartmel was in the seventh century, when the last King of Northumbria gave St. Cuthbert 'the land called Cartmel with all the Britons in it', and a church was probably built there shortly afterwards. W. G. Collingwood, in his story of the Norse settlers of the Lake Country, *Thorstein of the Mere*, suggests that the early building was at Kirkhead, near the southern end of the valley, but nothing is known definitely until the twelfth century, when the great William Marshall, afterwards Earl of Pembroke, founded the Priory of Cartmel on its present site, for the Canons Regular of St. Augustine.

According to the local legend the monks came to Cartmel from foreign parts, and resolved to build their church on a hill above the valley, but when they began to clear the site, a voice from the air commanded them to build 'in a valley between two streams, one flowing north and the other flowing south'. They obediently set out to search for the valley and after wandering through the whole of the north for many months, they returned to Cartmel, and in crossing the valley, forded the streams and realized one flowed north and the other south. They built their great priory and on the hill where they had heard the voice, set a chapel to St. Bernard, and although the chapel has long since disappeared, the hill is still called Mount St. Bernard, and the priory stands between the two rivers to this day.

Benefactions flowed in upon the priory for centuries after its foundation, and its growth of power and property was only checked by two devastating Scots raids in the fourteenth century, which laid waste its lands without injuring the priory itself. Subsequently the monks probably suffered some apprehensions in June, 1487, when Lambert Simnel passed through Cartmel with his troops, but they were left undisturbed until their Dissolution in the following century.

An ancient gatehouse, and the great priory church are all that remain of the old priory, but the disappearance of the rest of the buildings is compensated by the splendid condition of the church, which is used as the parish church. The greater part of the fabric dates from the twelfth century, but it fell into disrepair after the Dissolution, until George Preston of Holker Hall carried out extensive restorations in 1618, a fact which is recorded on his epitaph: 'the said George out of his zeale to God at his Great Charges repaired this Churche being in greate decay with a new roofe of Tymber & Beautified it within very decently with fretted Plaister Works adorned the Chancell with curious carved wood-worke And placed therein a pair of Organs of Great Valewe'. The church was again restored in 1855, and although its east window of stained glass was removed to Bowness centuries ago, the tombs of some of the priors, and the monks' seats with their exquisitely carved canopies and quaint misericords are still to be seen. The wonderful Renaissance screens of richly-carved black oak were added by George Preston, and are among the finest of the kind in England. Among the many tombs is the Harrington monument, which shows the effigies of a knight in chain armour and a lady in contemporary dress with veil and wimple, under an elaborately-carved canopy; it is generally believed to commemorate John, first Lord Harrington, who died in 1347, and his wife, but has no inscription to confirm this. There is also a life-size effigy, in white marble, by Thomas Woolner, R.A., of Lord Frederick Cavendish, who was assassinated in Dublin in 1882. Cartmel church is not only rich in monuments, but what is more unusual, rich in curious and quaint inscriptions on these monuments. One to Nicholas Barrow, who died at the age of eighty-three, says non-committally: 'What sort of a man he was the last day will discover'; William Myers' inscription says he died on February 30*th*, 1762; and one to Thomas Garrett, a stonemason, was carved by himself, and originally crowned by a coat of arms, but now only has a blank space showing chisel marks owing, it is believed, to the visit of an official of the Heraldry Office, who said with more truth than charity: 'This man has no right to armorial bearings,' and removed the design, there and then.

Judging by many of the inscriptions the inhabitants of Cartmel parish were a godly race; William Robinson, who died in 1677 at the age of twenty-eight, is commemorated by an inscription which reads '. . . whose full-blown youth left such a pattern of Charity and liberality as may raise Emulation in some, Envy in others, but be outdone by few. He having eternized his name by building the Vestry of Cartmel and given for ever £100, the interest of which sum to be emploued for ye Use of a Schoolmaster or Reader at Staveley Chappel towards the repairs of which he gave £5 and £5 more the interest of which to be given yearly to the poor of that place, also £20 the Interest of which is to be yearly given to the Guide of Lancaster Sands.' The wife of his eldest brother, Edward, commemorated her husband —evidently another pattern to humanity—with the inscription:

> 'The Blessing which she did most prize
> and soonest ravished from her eyes.'

Dame Katharine Lowther, who died in her twenty-fifth year, in 1700 was

> 'the comfort of S^{r}. William Lowther Bart., only daughter and heiress of Thos. Preston of Holker Esqr., and Elizabeth daughter to S^{r}. Rog^{r}. Bradsghaugh of Haigh Kt. and Bart. She was a Dutifull Child and an Endearing Wife, a Compassionate and carefull Mother, Charitable to ye poor, Hospitable to Strangers, Courteous to all, sweet in her temper, sincere in her Conversation, Serious and Devout in ye Profession & practise of her most excellent Religion. She left two sons, Thomas & Preston, & two daughters, Katharine & Margret.'

Unlike so many husbands of the period, who put up appreciative commemorative slabs and went off to marry again, Sir William only survived his wife five years, and died at the age of thirty.

A small memorial dated 1600 bears a rhyme composed with more goodwill than success:

> 'Here before lyeth interred
> Ethelred Thornburgh corps in dust
> In lyfe at death styll fyrmely fixed
> On God to rest hir stedfast trust
> Hir father Justice Carus was
> Hir mother Katharine his wife,
> Hir husband William Thornburgh was
> Whylst here she ledd this mortall lyfe
> The thyrd of Marche a yeare of grace
> One thousand fyve hundred nyntie six
> Hir sowle departed this earthly plase
> Of aage nighe fortie yeares a six
> To whose sweet sowle heavenlye dwelling
> Our Saviour grant everlastinge.'

As if Cartmel Priory had not sufficient interest with its richly carved doorways and arches, its glorious woodwork, its monuments, and its antiquity as a place of worship, it also has a veritable little museum in the vestry, where there are medieval manuscripts, including part of the Book of Isaiah, written about 1200; fifteenth century manuscript music with four staves; old prints and photographs of the church; a cumbersome umbrella 250 years old, which used to be held over the clergyman when he conducted a funeral in wet weather; and a library of over 300 books, most of which were bequeathed to the church in 1697. They include a book printed at Venice in 1491 and a first edition of three folios of Spenser's *Faerie Queen*. The folios were stolen some years ago, and the thief took them to New York, where he tried to sell them, but as he was unable to do so returned them a year afterwards to Cartmel. There are some pieces of silver and pewter church plate, a fifteenth century chair adapted as a parish chest, and a copy of the Lord's Prayer painted in 1700 with quaint embellishments. The Churchwardens' Account Books from 1597 to 1674, have many curious entries; and the Parish Registers, which begin in 1559, are of such interest that the entries up to 1661 have been printed. There are only too many relating to people drowned crossing the Cartmel, or Lancaster Sands, usually by name but on one occasion entered as 'One little mann Rownd faced wch was Drouned at Grainge'. Some of the entries recall local tragedies: in 1583 'Richard Wilsonn de Allythwat hanged himselfe'; in 1576 Richard Taylor was buried 'whoe suffered the same daye at Blacragge Bridge end for murthering wilfullye Richard Kilner of Witherslack' and on another occasion 'Edward Brokbank' was 'killed in his owne wood with a tree'.

The old market town of Cartmel, scarcely larger than a village and drowsing beside the placid River Eea with the most delightful air of repose, has a market square which is given stateliness by the great gatehouse of the priory, whose upper room was used as a Grammar School from 1624 to 1790, and has also been used as a Court Room. The market cross dates from the eighteenth century. Those who delight in local delicacies should try the 'Cartmel Fair Cake', a large square turnover of pastry filled with a special kind of mincemeat, and very delicious.

Cartmel is set in a district of the utmost charm, of woods and meadows, and low, rolling hills, and there are innumerable ancient manor-houses and villages in the near neighbourhood. Hampsfield Hall, to the north, was built in the early seventeenth century. Holker Hall, although practically a modern mansion, having been largely rebuilt after the fire of 1871, has been a seat of the Cavendish family since 1756, and was before that date the seat of the Prestons. Cark Hall, which has title deeds dating back to 1582, was the home of Christopher Rawlinson, a once famous antiquary and Anglo-Saxon scholar, who died in 1733. He remodelled the front of the Hall, and his arms are still to be seen there, but the manuscripts he had collected were sold to the villagers of Cark in bundles, for a few pence, and his valuable collection of documents on the history of Lancashire, Westmorland and Cumberland has been completely lost, with the exception of a few extracts which had been copied by Sir Daniel le Fleming for his library at Rydal Hall.

Wraysholme Tower, a ruined pele-tower commanding the bay, was once a seat of the Harringtons of Gleaston Castle, but when they forfeited their possessions after the battle of Bosworth Field it was granted to the Stanleys. The Stanley crest on a piece of stained glass was long preserved at the farm. Immediately south of the tower is Humphrey Head, where, it is said, the last wolf in the country was killed by the Sir John Harrington believed to be buried at Cartmel Priory, although there is no definite evidence by which any date can be fixed for the hunt, which traditionally originated from the rivalry between two suitors for the hand of Adela of Wraysholm, ward of Sir Hugh Harrington, the successful huntsman being Sir Hugh's son, John, who was married to her by the Prior of Cartmel, in a cave on Humphrey Head. Even without the legend Humphrey Head is interesting, for it has a Holy Well which Camden mentioned in his *Britannia* as enjoying great popularity, and which is still celebrated locally for its curative properties. Its composition is very similar to the waters of Wiesbaden and the Bavarian Spa of Kissingen.

Flookburgh lies south of Cartmel on the eastern shore of the Leven estuary, and is to-day the sleepiest of places, but it is the restful sleep of age. It received a charter for a market from the Prior of Cartmel as early as 1278, and in 1412 Henry IV granted a second charter to his very dear son, Thomas of Lancaster, Duke of Clarence, empowering him and his heirs for ever to hold a market every week on Tuesday in his manor at Flookburgh, and also two annual fairs. Charles II confirmed the charter to the town, and the sword, halbert and regalia are still in the possession of local people, and the last of the charters is preserved, with its little portrait of Charles II in one of the corners and a beautifully-decorated border on vellum. Flookburgh was one of the chief centres of the cockling trade of Morecambe Bay for centuries, and at one time over 3,000 tons of cockles were sold in a year, at an average of 48*s*. a ton, at Flookburgh alone, but both the cockling and the mussel industries are gradually dying out in the present day, although the local fishermen still set their fluke nets with considerable success.

The vast stretch of sands uncovered in the Leven estuary

when the tide goes out is variously known as the Leven, Cartmel, or Ulverston Sands, and is broken only by the tiny wooded Chapel Island, which still has slight traces of the ancient chapel or oratory founded by the monks of Conishead, where it is said that services were performed for travellers who wished to return thanks for a safe crossing of the sands. The genuine ruins are confusingly mixed up with a sham ruin built in 1823 by an owner of Conishead Priory. Wordsworth described the chapel in the *Prelude*, and Mrs. Radcliffe also referred to it in her description of Furness. The marshy stretch of grass-land which edges the estuary is one of the sources of the famous 'sea-washed turf' which is so greatly in demand for first-class bowling greens.

Chapter XVII

LANCASHIRE'S WINDERMERE

ALTHOUGH Westmorland owns that lovely and frequented stretch of Windermere's shores which lies between Storrs Hall and the head of the lake, Lancashire has no cause to be discontented with its share, which is not only larger, but equally beautiful, as the thousands of Lancastrians who descend upon Lakeside station every summer would testify—yet those thousands are usually content to take the steamer up the lake and return by way of Windermere station, and they leave all the enchantment of Cartmel Fell and the glory of the woods on the western shores to those who can appreciate their sweet solitudes.

Cartmel Fell, caught between the charming valley of Winster and the lake, has many a picturesque old farmhouse and inn, but the gem of them all is the ancient chapel of St. Anthony, restored with a just perception of its charm. This is the 'Browhead Chapel' of Mrs. Humphry Ward's *Helbeck of Bannisdale*—and is even more notably attractive than her description, for the windows and walls are venerable with the passing of 400 years, and the low stone seat outside the south wall is still in position. A deep porch leads into the interior, which is beautified with rich woodwork and ancient stained glass. The wooden figure of Christ taken down from the old roodbeam is preserved in the vicarage. It is one of the only two pre-Reformation Crucifixion figures surviving in England.

About a mile to the south of this beautiful chapel is another, scarcely less interesting although it has only the natural beauty of the surroundings, for it is an abandoned Meeting House of the Society of Friends, known as the Height Chapel, which was built in 1667 during the time when the Five Mile Act was in operation, and no Nonconformist minister could live or teach within five miles of a town. The wooded slopes on which these chapels are set sweep up to Gummer's How, over a thousand feet above the sea, from which there are glorious views of the lake and the Furness Fells.

Great Tower Plantation, which was presented to the Boy Scouts Association by Mr. W. B. Wakefield in 1936 and opened by Lord Baden-Powell with due ceremony, lies north of Gummer's How, on the lake shore and is an ideal national camping ground with its woods and lake frontage.

The little hamlet of Staveley with its seventeenth century church lies at the foot of the lake, and must not be confused with the larger Staveley-in-Kendal. Among the curates who have served in this remote parish are two with splendid records of service—Martin Lamb, who was there for fifty-six years, and Edmund Law, father of the Edmund Law who became Bishop of Carlisle, who was there for fifty years, and must have been a notably sturdy old man, for throughout that half century he took the services and taught in the village school, walking over from Buck Crag, four miles away, in storm and shine, and all for about £20 a year.

Newby Bridge is a picturesque bridge spanning the Leven as it flows from the lake on its short but very lovely journey through woods and meadows to its vast estuary. Half-way along the course of the Leven is Backbarrow, the little hamlet where John Wilkinson as a young man helped to make flat-irons in his father's foundry. Backbarrow was

WATENDLATH

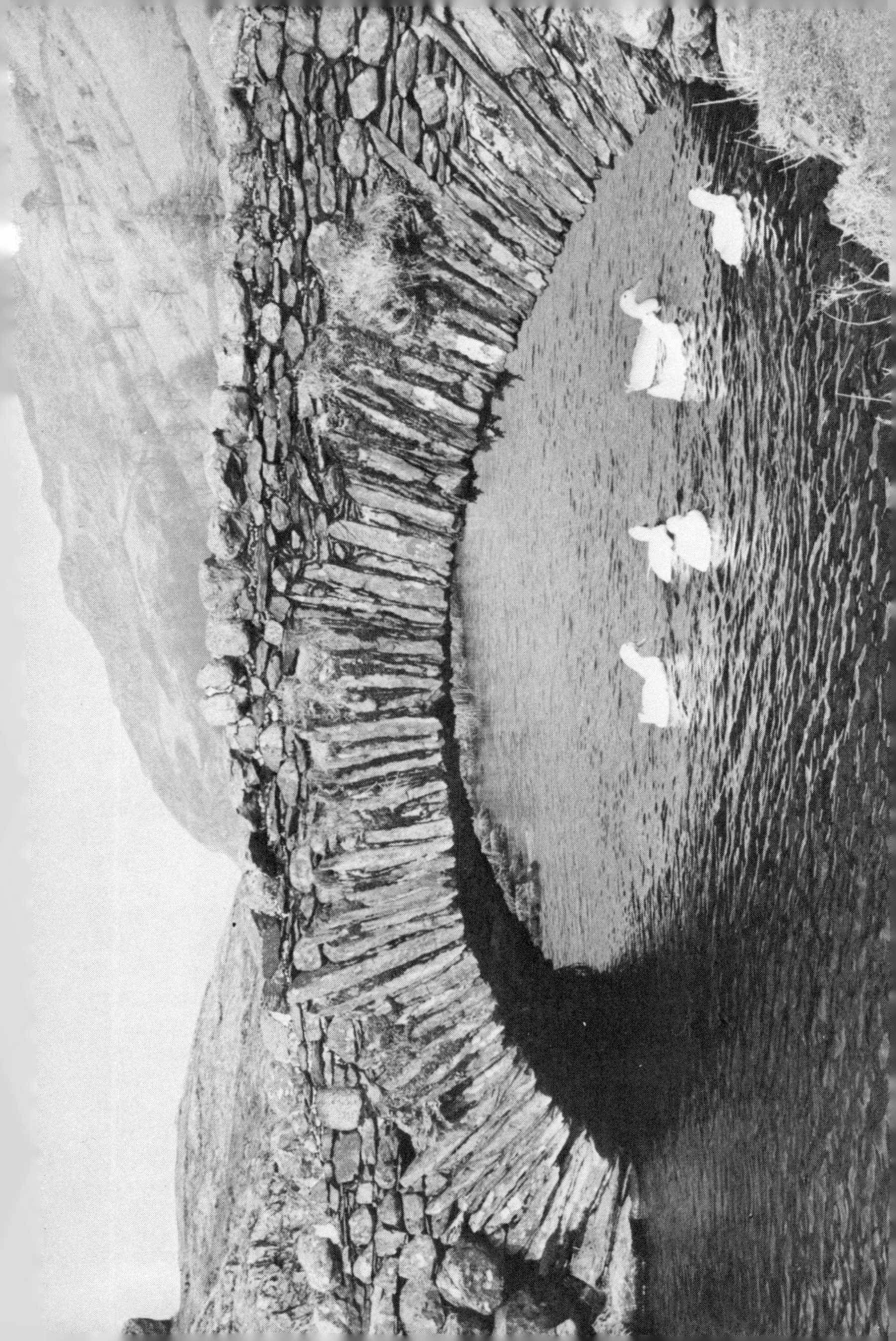

the last place in the country to use charcoal for smelting, and the old furnace is still to be seen with the date 1711 on it.

Woods stretch northward from Newby Bridge along the western shore of the lake, and completely cover Finsthwaite hill, which is crowned by the tower built in 1799 to commemorate the naval victories and 'the officers, seamen and marines of the Royal Navy, whose matchless conduct and irresistible valour decisively defeated the fleets of France, Spain and Holland, and promoted and protected liberty and commerce', and probably was intended especially to commemorate the Battles of Camperdown, Cape St. Vincent and the Nile. In the village of Finsthwaite, which lies in a little dell behind the hill, there are memorials to soldiers who fought in the Great War which has apparently wiped out the remembrance of the naval victories of so long ago, for the tower on the hill has been allowed to fall into ruin. In the modern church of Finsthwaite are treasured some unusual relics of the Great War, consisting of a cup and two patens made from shells, and a wooden cross cut from a plank in the pontoon bridge built to carry troops across the River Piave, all four of which were made by British soldiers in Italy that they might receive Communion on the Christmas Day after the Armistice. They were brought to Finsthwaite by the Padre who had used them on that occasion, when he was appointed vicar of this secluded parish, whose peace must have seemed to him like a heaven on earth after the battlefields.

In Finsthwaite churchyard is buried a Polish princess. The mother of Prince Charles Stuart was the Princess Maria Clementina, grand-daughter of King John Sobieski of Poland, and the Princess Clementina Johannes Sobieska Douglas was presumably a relative, but the tradition that she was a daughter of Prince Charles is considered improbable by Mr. Compton Mackenzie, who studied the question for his book *Prince Charlie and His Ladies*. A comparison of dates confirms this view, for Clementina is said to have come to the seclusion of Waterside House in 1745. She died there in 1771.

In the immediate neighbourhood of the Lakeside station, sheltering under Finsthwaite Hill and looking up the lake to the great mountains ringing Ambleside, twelve miles away, there are a few houses and an hotel, but for the most part there are miles of woods whose solitudes are undisturbed by the excursionists, who step from their train on to the landing-stage and so away to more populous haunts.

Both the lake shores are in Lancashire as far as a point just south of Storrs Hall, and the western shore is all in the County Palatine, and offers a refuge full of interest and beauty to those who wish to escape from Bowness or Lakeside during the 'tourist hours' of the summer days. One of the most interesting places on the west of Windermere is Graythwaite, where there are High Hall, the seat of the Sandys family, and the Elizabethan Low Hall of the Rawlinsons.

High Hall, usually called Graythwaite Hall, has been the home of the Sandys family for many generations, and their first written record is dated 1305. There have been many soldiers in the family; among others Myles Sandys, who fought under Wellington in the Peninsular War, and his descendant, Major Sandys, who was with his regiment, the Royal Scots, during the Great War. The Sandys have also been great huntsmen, and on the walls of the billiard-room in the Hall are the heads of deer that have been shot in recent years, the largest of which weighs 27 stone, and none less than 22 stone—all from the deer forest round Graythwaite, where the deer have run wild for many generations.

Low Hall, or Old Hall, also confusingly known as Graythwaite Hall, was built by the Rawlinsons in the sixteenth century, and is set appropriately in a garden with many clipped yew trees. A mansion built early in the nineteenth century is now called Silver Holme.

The island of Silverholme, which lies opposite the Graythwaite woods, is traditionally the hiding-place of a hoard of silver. Other legends tell of dreadful boggles that haunted Basswick and Beech-hill—the former being particularly troublesome to Graythwaite folk returning from the Ferry on Saturday nights! The Ferry itself was long haunted by the 'Crier of Claife', who continually called for the ferryman, but finally a priest from Lady Holme laid the ghost for 'as long as ivy should be green'.

The Ferry Inn was for many years the scene of an annual sports day instituted by Professor Wilson and kept up until about 1861, after which the sports were transferred to Grasmere. The Ferry sports of 1857 were described by Dickens in *Household Words*, and J. Wilson's *Reminiscences of Thomas Longmire*, the Troutbeck wrestler, quotes Dickens' tribute to the prowess of Longmire, who was then nearly forty years of age and still a champion wrestler. In the winter of 1785, wrestling contests took place on Windermere Lake itself, which was so thickly frozen over that a fire was kindled on the ice, and a whole ox roasted.

Although the wrestling contests no longer take place on the banks of Windermere, it is still a haunt of sportsmen, and on 2nd September, 1911, Joseph D. Foster, the Oldham Champion, swam the length of the lake, the only known occasion when this feat has been accomplished, as Captain Webb, the famous Channel swimmer, contented himself with giving an exhibition of swimming opposite Millerground on his visit in July, 1877.

Since 1918, motor-boat racing has become a popular sport on the lake, much to the annoyance of lovers of peace and tranquillity. It claimed two victims in 1930 when Sir Henry Seagrave and his engineer, Victor Halliwell, were drowned.

The road from the Ferry to Esthwaite Lake rounds the wooded hills, passing near High Satterhow, a restored Jacobean farm-house with mullioned windows, and running through the picturesque villages of Far Sawrey and Near Sawrey—respectively farther from and nearer to Hawkshead, and dating from the days when Hawkshead was a flourishing town and centre of learning, long before Windermere village was thought of, and before Bowness had much more than a church and vicarage.

Immediately above the Ferry Hotel is the 'Station' which was built towards the end of the eighteenth century by one of the Curwens who owned Belle Isle, and excited widely differing comments from guide-book writers and travellers of the nineteenth century, some of whom could not praise it sufficiently, and others of whom shared the opinion of M. Simon who wrote that '... this station affords no favourable specimen of the proprietor's taste, notwithstanding the coloured panes of his windows, which are considered as symptomatic of it'.

North of the Ferry sixty-four acres of the woodlands beside the lake are now in the care of the National Trust—one of the few places along the lake shore to which the public have free access. At Low Wray, between Claife Heights and Brathay, is Wray Castle, a modern building with the tower and battlements of an ancient fortress now mellowing with the passing years, which is also in the care of the Trust for the wonderful views it commands. It is tenanted by the Fresh-water Biological Research Association.

It was at Wray that Canon Rawnsley began his long association with the Lake District, for after his ordination in 1875 he was offered the living of Wray by his cousin, who was then living at Wray Castle. In the following autumn he married Edith Fletcher, of The Croft at Clappersgate, and the vicarage became a holiday centre for many of the most brilliant intellects then at Oxford. Edward Thring came from Uppingham, and Professor Knight, J. M. Shorthouse, and others of like celebrity, were among their guests during the four years before they removed to Crosthwaite, and they themselves were frequently at Wray Castle to meet their cousins' guests, among whom was John Bright, the great statesman.

Three years after they left Wray, the living was offered to the Rev. T. E. Brown, who refused it on the ground that he wished to continue his work at Clifton College. Had he accepted, he might have developed as another Lake poet, rather than in his own distinctive line as a Manx poet.

The Braithwaites were living at Brathay before their removal to Burneside in the sixteenth century, but no trace of their home survives. It was Thomas Braithwaite, who lived at Brathay during the reign of Elizabeth, who made a valuable collection of coins from the site of the Roman fort at Ambleside, which was presented to the University of Oxford by one of his descendants.

High and Low Brathay, and Brathay church, stand on the

Lancashire side of the Brathay river. High Brathay, built about the beginning of the nineteenth century, is usually known as Brathay Hall. It was the home of the Hardens from 1804 to 1834, during which time the Lake poets were frequently entertained there. It is also said to have been the home of Jane Penny, who married Professor Wilson, although other accounts mention Gale House in Ambleside as the home she shared with her married sister.

The Hardens were followed at Brathay Hall by the Redmaynes, and in 1836, soon after he had settled there, Giles Redmayne founded Brathay church. Owing to the difficulties of the site, the church is one of the very few in Britain which are not properly orientated, but the difficulties were more than compensated by the beauty of the situation, which Wordsworth praised in a letter to a friend at the time of the consecration, writing: 'There is not a situation outside the Alps, or among them, more beautiful than this.' It was for the wedding of Dr. Hugh Redmayne, a grandson of the founder, which took place in the church in 1883, that the hymn 'O perfect Love' was written at Brathay Hall by Miss Dorothy Blomfield, the bride's sister.

The Lodge of Brathay Hall was the birthplace of William Purdom, who accompanied the late Reginald Farrer to Tibet in 1913. On his return to Pekin in 1915, Purdom was offered and accepted the post of Forestry Expert in the Ministry of Agriculture of the Chinese Government. He carried out much important work before his death in 1921.

Low Brathay, or Old Brathay, is close to Brathay Bridge, and was another great resort of the Lake poets, when Charles Lloyd and his family were living there. De Quincey, especially, was a frequent visitor, and all that gifted company delighted in the brilliant intellect and lovable ways of Charles Lloyd, of whom Charles Lamb once wrote: 'I am dearly fond of Charles Lloyd, he is all goodness.' Lloyd's poems have never achieved any great fame, yet they have a charm, and his name will live as long as the letters of Charles Lamb, and the *Reminiscences* of De Quincey are read, and few who know the story of that bright, laughter-loving and devoted young couple and their children, can pass the home where they spent their happiest years without remembering the tragic sequel when Charles Lloyd was sent to the mental asylum. His gentle son Owen, who was born at Old Brathay, and was equally beloved by all, also fell eventually under that terrible cloud.

Chapter XVIII

FURNESS

I

THE name of Barrow-in-Furness is to many people a synonym for all that is dreary—most unjustly, for there are many less pleasant places—and the stigma seems to have attached itself to the name of Furness also, for it comes as a surprise to these people that the great district bearing the name stretches north to the Brathay River, and includes the valley of the Duddon, the lakes of Coniston and Esthwaite, and the glorious wooded fells which lie between Windermere and Coniston.

All visitors to Lakeside, Windermere, or Coniston who travel from the south by railway must go through Ulverston, for it is an important junction, but it is to be feared that like so many junctions it is known and judged solely from its railway station, and few of its visitors realize that the Ulverston townsmen have a pride in their town equal to that of any 'Babbitt'. Affectionate references to 'Bonny Lile Oostan' are so much a part of their life that even the booklet issued by the local bookseller begs you to 'Shop in Bonny Lile Oostan'. It is very evident that the people there pity visitors for having been born elsewhere, and still more for continuing, of their own free will, to live elsewhere, although forced to admit that one of Ulverston's most notable sons in the present day—Mr. Norman Birkett, K.C., has achieved his fame and fortune elsewhere. However, they are consoled by the knowledge that he has not forgotten his home, for in the Foreword to that excellent handbook for walkers, *Lakeland Passes*, he has said that

'. . . it is endeared by a thousand associations and now enriched by lengthening memories', and pays Lakeland other compliments no less deserved. Ulverston can further congratulate itself that Mr. Birkett's cousin, Mr. H. F. Birkett, has been inspired to write those delightful short stories of local life, *Overton* and *The Isle of Dreams* in which Ulverston appears under the name of Overton.

Ulverston has cause for pride. It belonged to a king long centuries ago and although he gave it away to the abbots of Furness early in the twelfth century, as part of their endowment, its importance grew rather than lessened, for it obtained its charter for a market in 1280 and was quite definitely the chief town in Furness. The early foundation of its parish church is proved by a twelfth century doorway and a late Perpendicular tower, which have survived the numerous rebuildings, together with seventeenth century brasses and monuments. An effigy of William Sandys, who died in 1558, is said to be a 'modern antique'.

Ulverston has yet another source of pride in its associations with Sir John Barrow, who was born in 1764 in a little cottage beside the Dragley Beck, which had been in his mother's family for nearly 200 years, and is still standing. The fascinating story of his life, with its constant search for knowledge brightened by an instinctive love of adventure, makes it possible to understand how the boy who had been born in this cottage achieved a fame which made his friendship valued by the greatest men of his day, and led his proud fellow-townsmen to build the conspicuous Hoad Monument on the hill above Ulverston in his memory.

He accompanied Lord Macartney's great expedition to China and the book which he wrote on this journey, and on another to South Africa, brought him immediate fame, and increased his own interest in explorations. He became Secretary to the Admiralty in 1804, and held the post for forty years, during which time he also used his influence to encourage Arctic exploration, and may be regarded as the founder of the Royal Geographical Society as, although the idea was not of his conception, it was he who proposed its formation and took the chair at its first meetings. He was created a baronet in 1835. Sir John was throughout his long life the personification of mental and bodily activity and, as the *Dictionary of National Biography* says, 'The subsidiary enterprises on which he expended his inexhaustible energy might have been the main occupations of another man's life'. Among other useful schemes which he promoted was the plan he suggested and assisted to carry out when in South Africa for supplying Cape Town with water from the Table Mountain. Each of the innumerable books and articles he wrote is of value. Southey, himself such a brilliant and successful biographer, said that he had never read any book of the kind so judiciously composed as Barrow's *Life of Lord Howe*, and he also wrote an account of the 'Mutiny of the *Bounty*', which has been reprinted in the *World's Classics* in recent years. His name is on the map in polar lands where Point Barrow, Cape Barrow and Barrow Straits were named in his honour.

Ulverston is also the centre from which the Society of Friends spread its influence to such distant corners of the earth, for without the refuge of Swarthmoor Hall, and the help of its mistress, so gracious and lovely in all her ways, the teaching of George Fox might not have spread nearly so rapidly or taken such a firm hold. If Ulverston cannot claim that Margaret Fell was born there, they can claim her as practically a native for she lived there from the time she came to the Hall as a bride of seventeen until her death at the age of eighty-seven and is buried in the nameless grave of a Quaker in the burial ground at Sunbreck, beside the estuary.

In the story of Margaret Fell, the name of Judge Fell should be remembered and revered, for although he never became a Quaker himself, he allowed his wife to keep open house for her persecuted Quaker friends, and used all his influence to protect them. It was not until eleven years after the death of Judge Fell that Margaret married George Fox, but all the time she was working for the cause he had at heart, and suffering for it too. When he was arrested she saw the King and pleaded his cause. When other Quakers were arrested she again pleaded for royal intervention and obtained it. She endured imprisonment, and only used her liberty to visit and comfort other Quakers thrown into jail; and always Charles II, appreciating her utter fearlessness and honesty, stood her friend, although his orders were sometimes set aside by his bigoted subjects for as long as they dared to ignore them. Born in 1614 and received into the Society of Friends in 1652, she maintained her convictions through all the changes which took place between the last year of Charles I's reign to the accession of Queen Anne, and left behind her the memory of a brave woman of whom Leonard Fell wrote so charmingly: 'Thou whose voice is so pleasant, and into whose mind no dark spirit enters.'

Beside the Elizabethan hall of Swarthmoor is the Meeting House which George Fox built in 1688, and relics of the three noble personalities associated with the Hall are preserved there.

Both Ulverston and Greenod, at the head of the estuary, were actively engaged in ship-building during the nineteenth century, and in addition to ships of the prevailing type they evidently made experiments, for one named the *Elephant*, mentioned in the Ulverston Shipping List in 1847, was shaped like a square box with little or no difference between the shape of bow and stern, the removable bowsprit sometimes being out at one end and sometimes at the other! This queer vessel did good service until broken up.

Ulverston not only has itself that indefinable air of antiquity which clings to towns of ancient foundation, however much modernized, but is a centre for many ancient sites set in the rolling hills and woodlands of Low Furness. Castle Hill, where the great earth ramparts overhanging the ravine show signs of having enclosed early medieval houses, long since vanished, was a seat of the Pennington family down to the fourteenth century, and the village half a mile away has borne the family name since before Domesday. In the neighbouring mound of Ellabarrow 'Lord Ella sleeps with his golden sword', and weapons and implements of the Iron Age have been found nearby.

Great and Little Urswick share a beautiful medieval church in which is the ancient tomb of Amicia, daughter of John le Fraunceys, and between the villages lies the tarn into which, it is said 'lile U'ston' sunk beneath the waters in past ages. W. G. Collingwood suggested that this and similar legends indicate that there was a lake village on the site in prehistoric times. Stone Walls, half a mile away, has been explored and proved to be a site dating back to 100 or 200 B.C.. and there are other ancient sites and stone circles in the neighbourhood. Aldingham has a twelfth century church containing the medieval tomb of Godith de Scales. Aldingham Mote-hill, on a cliff overlooking Morecambe Bay, was probably the site of the first house and farmstead of the Flemings, who lived in Furness during the time of William Rufus, and also held Gleaston, where the site of their pele is marked by the picturesque ruins of Gleaston Castle, built by their successors, the Harringtons, in the fourteenth century.

II

Low Furness had no less than three religious houses—Bardsea, where there was a hospital of St. John of Jerusalem; Conishead, which had a priory of Austin Canons, and Furness Abbey, founded by the Order of Savigny and shortly afterwards forcibly absorbed into the Cistercian order.

The village of Bardsea figured in Domesday Book, and the monks came there in the twelfth century. The monastic buildings have long disappeared and perhaps it is just as well in this case, for Bardsea now has ambitions to develop as a holiday resort for sea-bathing and the ghosts of shocked monks might have risen to haunt the ruins. There is an ancient seat of the Gales, and numerous prehistoric sites in the neighbourhood.

The foundations of Conishead Priory underlie part of the grounds of the mansion built in 1821, which is now a convalescent home for Durham miners, returning to its original purpose as a hospital after an interval of nearly eight hundred years.

Conishead Hospital was founded by Gamel de Pennington during the twelfth century, and was shortly afterwards made into a priory, and it was the priors of Conishead who maintained the guide across the Leven Sands until the Dissolution, when the responsibility was transferred to the Crown.

Immediately after the Dissolution, the priory and its possessions passed through a succession of owners.

The Doddings gained the Conishead estate by marriage, and in the seventeenth century the heiress of the Doddings carried it to John Braddyll of Portfield, and the Braddylls continued in possession for nearly two hundred years, during which time the Prince Regent, William IV when Duke of York, and Queen Adelaide, stayed at Conishead Priory as the guests of Colonel Braddyll. But the family which had held such wide lands and given princely benefactions to the district, was forced to part with Conishead in 1854, and by an ironical turn of fortune, had the family retained it only a few years longer, they would have been the possessors of the mines which have since yielded rich stores of ore.

The splendid remains of Furness Abbey more than compensate for the loss of the two smaller houses. Founded originally at Preston in 1123, the monks removed three years after to the larger but more distant lands of Furness, all of which were given to them, with the exception of the possessions of Michael le Feming. How lonely and how desolate it must have seemed to those monks so newly arrived from the fair land of France and their parent house at Savigny may be imagined, and the name of the Vale of Deadly Nightshade hardly sounded propitious, but for the succeeding three or four centuries buildings were continually added to meet the growing needs of the great centre of religious life and learning, until to-day, although not all the walls are standing above ground, it is easy to imagine that it must have been a marvellously impressive sight to the people of the district whose highest flights of architecture had been pele-towers and primitive churches. Even those parts of the building which date from the twelfth century are conceived and carried out on a magnificent scale, with exquisitely carved and decorated stonework, and the rose-coloured sandstone walls, rising to their full height, look tremendous against their background of green hills and trees.

The whole building is now, happily, in the care of the Commissioners of Works, who are carrying out the work of preservation with their usual intelligent care.

In addition to the vast church, cloisters, infirmary, chapter house, abbot's house, cellarium, kitchen and other buildings, some of the earliest known freestone effigies of knights in armour are preserved at the abbey, each with the rather peculiar expression which comes from the loss of their noses, but otherwise practically undamaged by their long exposure to the wind and rain.

Every part of the great and glorious building has its special interest, not the least of which, architecturally or historically, is the chapter house, where the second Abbot of Furness sat on those momentous occasions when bands of monks were sent to colonize the daughter houses of Calder Abbey in Cumberland, and Rushen Abbey in the Isle of Man, and where there was the last sad gathering of the Abbot and his monks assembled in full chapter to sign the deed of surrender, and receive the meagre sum of forty shillings to start life afresh in the world beyond their sheltering walls.

The modern Abbey Hotel stands between the ruins of the main gatehouse and its chapel and the main block of buildings on the site of one of the guest houses of the abbey. It incorporates a considerable part of the guest house, including the notable Adam and Eve carving; a supposed original fireplace; two small stained glass windows; a magnificently-carved panel of woodwork, believed to be of Italian workmanship; and other interesting fragments. One of the bedrooms has a curious wall ornament of stone and metal work with Latin inscriptions and ancient niches, which have been filled with some rather unfortunate modern statues, and the adjoining room has an unusually beautiful modern stained glass window.

III

Although the ruins lie in such a peaceful and seemingly lonely valley, there is a very busy world carrying on its multitudinous concerns all around, for on the north is the town of Dalton-in-Furness and on the south is Barrow-in-Furness, and although both are thriving towns, as so often happens where docks and industrial centres are concerned, the youthful Barrow, scarcely a century old, has outstripped

Dalton with its thousand years of existence; but both have interesting antiquities in and around their busy streets.

Dalton's pele-tower was built by the monks and has quaint stone figures at the four corners of the battlements. It contains some ancient armour and part of a primitive cannon dating from early in the fourteenth century. The church, rebuilt in modern times, is on the site of the old earthworks which formed the rampart of the Daltune of Domesday book; the holy well and the park where the ruins of a medieval house were found, neighbour the hæmatite quarry; the little medieval chapel of St. Helen's has been converted into a cottage, and everywhere the old and new are inextricably mingled. Thomas West, the eighteenth century antiquary who wrote the *Antiquities of Furness* and the famous *Guide to the Lakes*, lived at Titup Hall, north of the town. The wooded Highhaume Hill was the beacon where the fires flamed to summon the armed forces maintained by the abbots of Furness against the raiding Scots, and has a special interest for geologists because in the local phrase 'every mack of stone that God Almighty ever made is ligging there'. The mines of Orgrave figured in Domesday as Ouregraue and were probably worked before that time. The little house of Beckside was the birthplace of George Romney, of whom Dalton is rightly proud, and he is buried in the churchyard with a plain stone inscribed 'Pictor Celeberrimus' above. In the east window of the church is one of the local memorials to Lord Frederick Cavendish who was murdered in Phoenix Park, and the church also has some fragments of ancient glass and a medieval font with the arms of Furness Abbey carved on the bowl.

Romney went to school in the village of Dendron, within a mile of Gleaston Castle ruins. His schooling only cost a pound a year and he was boarded and lodged for the sum of threepence a day, but spent so much of his time in sketching that his father thought even this small sum wasted, and took him away from school when he was ten years old. Romney went to school in the seventeenth century chapel, which has been much altered since his day, but still has a brass recording the fact that the founder, Robert Dickinson, a citizen of London, had 'given sufficient maintenance for ever to a minister to have divine service read in the said chapel, and in the week day to have children brought up in learning and taught there in'.

Barrow-in-Furness has developed the lonely stretch of water sheltered by Walney Island into three hundred acres of docks, and has set up a statue to Sir James Ramsden, and others of those who helped to work the transformation, but on the Isle of Foudrey still stands the Pile or Piel of Foudrey, built by the monks of Furness Abbey in 1327 on an earlier site, to guard the harbour from which they exported their wool. A thriving little port was in existence there until some time in the sixteenth century, when there were only a few cottages left to mark the site which was destined to grow into a town greater than the monks ever visualized.

It was on the Isle of Foudrey that, according to the 'Herball' of the sixteenth century naturalist Gerard, the barnacle goose was bred out of barnacles—an engaging spectacle for the loss of which the prosperity of the town can never compensate the sightseer. Lambert Simnel landed on the island with his troops in 1487. It was this 'Piel' tower of Foudrey which inspired Wordsworth's sonnet, and not, as has frequently been said, the Peel Castle on the Isle of Man. He spent a month with his cousin, Mrs. Barker, at Rampside, opposite Piel Castle, during one of his holidays from Hawkshead. The Elizabethan Hall of the Knype family at Rampside has a series of chimneys set cornerwise, which are known as the 'Twelve apostles'.

Barrow, like Dalton, mixes the past with the present. Just outside the modern station is a sight to fire the railway enthusiast—the old 'Copper Nob' engine, which started work on the Furness line in 1846, and ran for over half a century before being honourably retired to the peaceful seclusion of its gigantic glass case. Walney Island, although linked to the mainland by a bridge and largely occupied by the workers' homes of Vickerstown, has a long shingle beach where the Irish Sea thunders, and the seagulls wheel and glide above a tiny, lonely colony of three coastguards with their families, gathered close under the lighthouse and cut off when the tide is high from all communication with their fellow men. Biggar, half-way between Vickerstown and the lighthouse, is both ancient and remote, cherishing many memories of smugglers and wreckers—for Walney Island is quite preposterously long in comparison with its width, and there is room for loneliness as well as for the neighbourliness of modern Vickerstown.

Those who delight in Miss Dorothy Sayer's detective stories will remember that the agreeable Chief Inspector Parker was educated in Barrow Grammar School, which in 'real life' can claim Mr. Norman Birkett as an Old Boy.

Northward from Barrow-in-Furness, road and rail skirt the eastern shore of the Duddon estuary, past the ironworks of Askam and the ravine of Ireleth village, to Kirkby-in-Ireleth, in whose church men have wrought to the glory of God since the days of the Normans, who carved the south door. The nave and chancel date from the thirteenth century; the font was added a hundred years later; and the north arcade in the sixteenth century, whilst the solid silver almsdish was taken from the French and given to the church by Colonel Kirkby in the seventeenth century. Other memorials of the past in the church include a quaint medieval effigy.

Kirkby Hall, the Tudor manor house which was the home of the Kirkbys for ten generations, but is now a farmhouse, has curious frescoes in the room which was once a chapel, and a priest's hiding-hole. In the district around are prehistoric remains and enormous wasteheaps of the blue slate quarries of Kirkby Moor, which are famous for some of the best roofing material in England.

Chapter XIX

THE FURNESS FELLS

I

UNTIL very recent years, when a bus service was established to Ambleside, Hawkshead had no regular communication with the outer world, and remained, as it had been for centuries, self-centred and self-supporting. The earliest known mention of Hawkshead occurs in the Coucher Book of Furness Abbey, at the beginning of the thirteenth century, when the chapelry of Hawkshead is mentioned. Hawkshead church was granted parochial rights in 1219 and the manor house of the monks was fixed at Hawkshead Hall, as a centre for their hunting-ground and timber forest—a region at that time so wild that the scattered inhabitants, with all the independence of their Viking ancestry, evidently resented the overlordship of Furness Abbey, for King John gave the abbot a charter permitting him to use force against refractory tenants.

A farm-house about a mile to the north of Hawkshead, on the Ambleside road, occupies the site of Hawkshead Hall, but the fifteenth century gatehouse, incorporating a fireplace and other traces of thirteenth century work, still stands, and is now in the care of the National Trust.

After the Dissolution the Kendalls took possession of Hawkshead Hall in 1539, to be succeeded about the end of the century by the Nicholsons, who became a family of considerable local importance. Allan Nicholson who married a daughter of Daniel Hechstetter, was a supporter of the mining industry at Hawkshead and is said to have been instrumental in securing Hawkshead's charter for a market. His death in 1616 was commemorated in a poem by Richard Braithwaite of Burneside, who claimed him as a kinsman, and it was one of Allan's descendants who held the Kentmere estate of the Gilpins during the Civil War.

Edwin Sandys, born at Esthwaite Hall, now a farm-house, before the reign of the monks had ceased, became Archbishop in 1575, and ten years later founded the Grammar School at Hawkshead whose religious teaching must have been designed to wipe out all remembrance of the vanished monks, for the Archbishop was almost violently Protestant in his outlook, and by his own two marriages displayed his opposition to the monkish ideal of celibacy.

Early in his career Sandys was one of the supporters of Lady Jane Grey, and spent some time in the Tower of London after the accession of Mary Tudor, but was released and went to Antwerp in 1554. Later he visited Augsburg—another link between that town and the Lake District. It is quite possible that the future Archbishop's talk of his homeland was the origin of the interest shown by the Augsburg firm in Lakeland mines, and the arrival of the German miners at Keswick six or seven years later. At any rate, no reason for this interest has yet been advanced, and the firm was so distant in those days of difficult travel that they would hardly have conceived the venture without some previous information on the subject. Sandys returned to England on the 13th January, 1558, and was actively employed in all projects affecting the establishment of the Protestant religion until his death in 1588.

The Archbishop had seven sons and two daughters by his second wife, of whom the eldest son, Sir Samuel Sandys, was the ancestor of the Barons Sandys of Ombersley in Worcestershire. Sir Edwin Sandys, the Archbishop's second son, was a statesman who took a leading part in the establishment of the colony of Virginia. Two of Sir Edwin's sons fought in the Parliamentarian army, and one founded a branch of the family in Kent. George Sandys, the youngest son of the Archbishop, was a poet and traveller and, like his elder brother, was closely connected with the development of Virginia, where he acquired a plantation. His best known work, the translation of Ovid into English, was completed there.

The Rev. George Walker, who was a kinsman of the Archbishop, was born at Hawkshead about 1581. Fuller says he was a man of 'holy life, humble heart, and bountiful hand'. He was a celebrated divine, and author of many books on religion which were widely read in his day. He allowed the Hawkshead minister £20 a year, and the parsonage house and glebe were long called 'Walker Ground' in his memory. He was also a benefactor of the Sion College Library during the time he was in London.

Hawkshead Church is not earlier than the fifteenth century in its present form, for the so-called Norman arches of the church have been adjudged of later work. Among the memorials are the effigies of William and Margaret Sandys, the parents of the Archbishop; and mural tablets to Daniel Rawlinson of Grisedale Hall and his son Sir Thomas Rawlinson, Lord Mayor of London; Thomas Alcock Beck, a nineteenth century historian of Lancashire; and Elizabeth Smith, who lived at Tent Cottage, Coniston. A book on Lancashire recently published fancifully suggests that Wordsworth may have seen Elizabeth Smith 'toddling about the streets in her pinafore', but she did not visit the Lake District until she was twenty-four years old, in 1801, long after Wordsworth had left Hawkshead. There is a roughly hewn seventeenth century wooden chest in the church, and in the churchyard are a sundial dated 1693 and a modern peace memorial designed by W. G. Collingwood.

Wordsworth came to Hawkshead school when he was eight and studied there until he was sixteen, lodging at Ann Tyson's picturesque old cottage and, in spite of his pre-occupation with the dawnings of poetic genius and nature study, living the life of a very normal small boy, birds' nesting, skating and carving his name on the bench which is still preserved in the now disused Grammar School. Hawkshead has been fortunate in escaping the heavy hand of the 'developer' and although modern ideas of hygiene have caused the open stream down Flag Street to be covered over, and various other alterations have been made, the town remains the quaintest and most captivating cluster of houses, full of unexpected nooks and corners, in a fashion more reminiscent of a Cornish fishing village than of other Lake District towns, except that Hawkshead houses are white-washed and the lake, although near, does not come so close as the sea approaches the Cornish villages.

Esthwaite water has not the ruggedness of some of the lakes, but it has great charm, particularly when its great masses of water-lilies are abloom. Near the northern end of the lake is 'Priest's Pot', a dub which is twenty yards across, and is said to derive its name from the fact that it holds the measure a thirsty priest would like to drink if it were filled with good ale!

Hawkshead was a great centre of the rural woollen industry from 1608, when it received a market charter, to the nineteenth century, and there was a pack horse trail which led to a ferry across Windermere from Wray to Millerground.

Among its other interesting relics, the town treasures a

WRYNOSE PASS

og said to have been the largest ever made, which
a mole catcher named John Waterson who had
large foot. The clog measures 20 inches in
8 inches in width at the bottom, 16 inches
t, 22 inches round the back, and 7 inches
—and even then Waterson had to cut the
ont and make lace-holes to widen it before
Another 'speciality' is the Hawkshead
of puff pastry filled with currants, spice,
eel.

Meeting House and graveyard at Colt-
om about 1688, and a Baptist Chapel
lt in 1678 and since restored.

d are wooded hills and lovely little
Hawkshead moor rising between
iston, and traversed by two roads
isedale and Dale valleys after a
ing to both walkers and cyclists,
ts views.

Park are so shut in by their
e ruggedness of Lakeland is
ty of flowery meadows and
was turned into a deer park
out 1516, who ruthlessly
ts to make himself this
forgotten and the farms
clusion almost as great
the road is good and
ands at Windermere
Park or its equally
sedale, or even the
Valley in which
tterthwaite.
vlinson brought
s his bride in
o London, to
Lord Mayor
s old home,
ad School.
ws under

he
ad,
the
of

toral
even,
es, or
lished
entury,
by the
ers and

osses the
and occa-
t country
l, another
the surrep-
urn copper
ent officials
being warned
into the bog
day. White-
escendants of
from the road,
ll cannon on a
ook How, also
House founded
is an interesting
on and retaining
ghteenth century
e churchyard wall
ers frequently rode
Hall was a home of
ago, and a mile to
tlebank, founded in
Parliamentarian who
its old box pews and
reached for fifty-five
e and others who stood

Adam of Beaumont had their headquarters during t
fourteenth century and, according to an ancient ball
boasted of their misdeeds, which probably gave rise to
line: 'Fellows fierce from Furness Fells' in the balla
Flodden Field.

All three valleys are now entirely given over to pa
pursuits, but from Norman times until about the s
teenth century there were a number of 'bloomeri
furnaces for iron smelting, one of which was esta
beside the pretty Force Forge by the seventeenth c
and slight traces are to be found, nearly obliterated
kindly hand of Nature, which has restored the flo
trees once displaced by slag heaps.

The network of roads which crosses and recr
Rusland Valley holds many delightful viewpoints
sional clusters of cottages and farms, or pleasa
houses. The eighteenth century Rusland Ha
seat of the Rawlinson family, was the centre of
titious manufacture of guineas from the Green
at one time, and when the local magistrates
with a search warrant, the lady of Rusland Hall
in time had the plant and 'guineas' thrown
nearby, where they are said to remain to this
stock Hall was the home of generations of
George Romney and although almost hidden
can be distinguished by a flag-staff and sm
grassy platform overlooking the road. R
known as Abbot Oak, has a Quaker Meetin
in 1725. Colton church on its green hill
church built in 1603 by William Rawlin
its Jacobean altar rails and chair, an e
sundial, and a mounting block outside t
as a relic of the days when the parishion
on horseback over the hills. Colton Old
the Sandys family three hundred year
the south is the Baptist chapel at To
1669 by Colonel Roger Sawrey, a
owned Broughton Tower. It still ha
the pulpit where Thomas Taylor
years. It may well be imagined that

in that pulpit preached against the cock-fighting which went on in the neighbouring Oxenpark cockpit—and as for 'Praying Sawrey', the founder, his very nickname suggests how he would denounce the practice—probably more on the score of sinful pleasure than of cruelty.

II

At Coniston the Furness Fells which are so softly rounded and well wooded in Low Furness, harden into the more imposing rocky crags of Lakeland until at the head of the lake there is the grandeur of mountain scenery to contrast with the softer beauty of the southern end at Lake Bank, making the journey up the lake by road or steamer more beautiful by far than in the reverse direction. There are two little wooded islands on the lake, the larger of which is a mass of bluebells in May, and blends bell-heather with bracken in the summer. W. G. Collingwood's *Thorstein of the Mere* describes the island as it may have been one thousand years ago, and Mr. Arthur Ransome's books, *Swallows and Amazons* and *Swallowdale*, describe its charm in the present day.

Coniston has such beauty and interest that the visitor is apt to find difficulty in deciding 'where to start' even when personal inclination points to any special phase of interest, for historical and literary associations abound and there is a no less strong appeal for climbers and fell-walkers in the Coniston Old Man, the Coniston and Blawith Fells and the peaks guarding the Duddon Valley, and all this variety of interest is not confined to the village, but is scattered far and wide on the shores of the lake and among the fells.

Coniston is so much a part of the Lake District, so completely 'in character' with its buildings and its setting, that many visitors regard it more as a Cumbrian or Westmerian town and consider it an anomaly if they realize that it is a part of Lancashire—yet the most casual glance at the map will show that this seemingly anomalous piece of Lancashire stretching into Lakeland is perfectly justified, for the long length of Windermere, the 'greatest standing water' cuts it off completely not only from the county towns of

Westmorland and Cumberland, but from the great centres like Kendal and Carlisle which are bound up with the progress and development of their respective counties. The Bay of Morecambe, which apparently cuts off North Lancashire from the rest of the County Palatine was for centuries the real reason for binding them together, for the route over the sands was then both well-known and generally used, in journeying between Cartmel and Furness and the county town of Lancaster, and even in the present day the railway runs up from the south from the bay and continues the old tradition of linking Coniston to Lancashire and cutting it off from the rest of the Lake District, a situation remedied only in modern times, by the bus services from Ambleside.

Excavations have proved that the district round Coniston has been inhabited since the earliest times, and finds made at the Banniside Circle and other prehistoric sites are to be seen in the Coniston museum, and it is certain that the land was inhabited again during the Norse colonization, for the lake was known as Thorston Water, or Thorstein's Mere for many centuries, and there are innumerable other Norse place-names in the neighbourhood.

Early in the twelfth century the Furness Fells had become royal property and the greater part was granted by King Stephen to the monks of Furness Abbey. In 1240 the third William de Lancaster, who shared Coniston water with the monks of Furness, granted them leave to have a small boat and twenty nets on Thurstainwater in the same document by which they were granted similar facilities on Winendremer. From that time onwards there were also a number of 'bloomeries' for iron-smelting, and in the late sixteenth or early seventeenth century the German miners from Augsburg opened up the copper mines, which are still being worked.

Coniston Hall, a mile to the south of the church, was built in the fifteenth century by the Flemings, and there are traces of an earlier hall on the site, and the church, which was built in 1586 and restored in the nineteenth century, contains a brass of the Flemings. The Flemings gained Coniston in 1250 by marriage, and made it their principal seat for about seven generations, but after the marriage of

Sir Thomas with the heiress of Rydal in the fifteenth century, one branch of the family settled at Rydal Hall, the other remaining at Coniston until early in the eighteenth century, when Coniston was abandoned and allowed to fall into ruin until finally utilized as a farm-house easily recognizable by its quaint chimneys. Mrs. Radcliffe and several later writers confused Coniston Hall with Conishead Priory.

Coniston's literary associations are numerous and varied, but they are obscured by the greater fame of Ruskin's long association with Brantwood, which has over-shadowed not only the memory of those who lived at Tent Lodge and at Thwaite, but also the earlier owners of Brantwood itself. Brantwood was first the home of Gerald Massey, that son of a canal boatman who began life as an errand boy in London and grew up to be a poet and a thinker, and after him came W. J. Linton, the engraver, poet and political reformer, and close friend of Mazzini. It was there he set up a printing press and published a monthly journal, *The English Republic*, which was discontinued in 1855, two years before his marriage to Miss Eliza Lynn, who afterwards became celebrated as a novelist under her married name. When the marriage proved unsuccessful they disposed of Brantwood to Ruskin and parted amicably, though not before they had published a joint book on the Lake Country for which Mrs. Lynn Linton provided the descriptive matter and her husband did many beautiful engravings.

Linton went to the United States in 1866, settled in Connecticut and devoted the rest of his life to revivifying the art of wood engraving in America by the printing of his own blocks and writing many authoritative books on the subject. He lived in Connecticut until his death in 1898—yet for all his close and useful connexion with the United States, there are few among the hundreds of American visitors to Brantwood who give him a thought owing to the greater fame of his successor there.

When Ruskin bought Brantwood from Linton in 1871, it was a rough-cast country cottage, old, damp and decayed, and adorned on the outside with revolutionary mottoes, but set in five acres of rock, moor and streamlet which Ruskin declared commanded the 'finest view I know in

Cumberland or Lancashire', and had Wordsworth's 'seat' in the grounds to prove that it was one of the poet's favourite viewpoints. During the next twenty-nine years, Ruskin spent thousands of pounds on repairing and extending the cottage until it became the splendid mansion it now is, and in the first twenty years he wrote some of his best works there.

It was during this time that old-fashioned spinning and hand-loom weaving was re-introduced into Langdale by Albert Fleming, a member of the Guild of St. George founded by Ruskin. The industry still flourishes in the Lake District, but its headquarters are no longer in Langdale but at Keswick and Grasmere. There is an interesting description of the cheerful parties and the busy, useful life at Brantwood in the book on Ruskin written by his friend, W. G. Collingwood, who also recounts Ruskin's fondness for visiting his poorer neighbours and the genuine interest he took in them, which was far removed from an impertinent curiosity, whilst his many benefactions were never spoiled by condescension, and even the aloof dalesmen learned to appreciate his genuine goodness of heart and say of him: 'Eh! he's a grand chap, is Maisther Rooskin!'—praise indeed from a dalesman, when speaking of an off-come.

Many were the 'pilgrims' to Brantwood from all parts of the English-speaking world in the years after his death, and although there came a fashion for a while of sneering at his teaching, the fundamental truths he expounded are once again becoming generally appreciated, and there can be no doubt that the 'Friends of Brantwood' who have acquired his home for a centre of study and experiment on the lines he laid down will revive and keep alive the Ruskin tradition. His admirers can stay in the guest rooms of Brantwood, examine his books and original drawings, and enjoy the view he loved. In Coniston's Ruskin Museum they can see innumerable relics; in the parish churchyard the memorial designed by his friend, W. G. Collingwood, to mark his grave, and in the Roman Catholic church they can see the window he gave during his lifetime.

Just north of Brantwood is Tent Lodge, where Alfred Tennyson spent his honeymoon in 1850, and William Smith and Lucy Cumming spent their honeymoon in 1861—two memories of happiness to soften the remembrance of an earlier tragedy—the death of Elizabeth Smith in 1806, at the early age of twenty-nine. She was born at Burn Hall, near Durham. When a bank failure in 1783 reduced the family to comparative poverty she not only did not complain herself, but proved a tower of strength to her mother. The family moved several times until they finally came to the Lake District, first to Patterdale, to be near Thomas Wilkinson at Yanwath. They soon afterwards settled finally at Tent Cottage, which stands in front of the gate of Tent Lodge, which was built by the Smiths after the death of Elizabeth, on site of a tent which had been pitched for her in the garden.

The brilliance of her intellect and the facility with which she learned languages and her extraordinarily retentive memory were such that a memoir in the *Englishwoman's Magazine* in June, 1846, truly said, 'she was a living library', yet she was also an accomplished needlewoman, an able cook, and a horsewoman, and had a most affectionate nature and natural charm. De Quincey, who was not given to over-praising, wrote eulogizing her in his *Reminiscences* and considered that the tablet to her memory in Hawkshead church 'is the scantiest record that, for a person so eminently accomplished, I ever met with'. She was taught French and a little Italian by her governess in the days of their affluence, but taught herself Algebra, Latin, Greek, Hebrew, Syriac, Arabic, Persian, Spanish and German, and excelled in these languages so greatly that she made notable translations, of which the most famous was a new translation of the Book of Job from the Hebrew, acknowledged by the most eminent Hebrew scholars to be one of the best translations known. Among other works she wrote the *Memoirs of Klopstock*, a *Vocabulary of Hebrew, Arabic and Persian*, and other prose and poetic works. Mrs. Fletcher, who was then staying at Belmont, near Hawkshead, records in her *Autobiography* that she met Mrs. Smith soon after Elizabeth's death, and that some years later she rented Tent Cottage from the Smiths for the summer. Tennyson's 'seat' is on the hill above Lanehead, near where W. G. Collingwood lived, a student of Lake District history and a writer of such charm that his death was an inestimable loss to the district for which he worked with such love and intelligent interest. His splendid book on the Lake Counties is but one of a series of writings which have conferred a lasting benefit on every lover of the district and its history, folk-lore, and scenery.

The conspicuous house on the lake-shore almost opposite Tent Lodge is the Thwaite, which was the home of John Beever, the author of *Practical Fly-fishing*, and of his sisters, Miss Mary and Miss Susanna Beever, the well-known botanists, whose companionship was so valued by Ruskin. Coniston also has its local poet, for although Dr. Alexander Craig Gibson was born at Harrington, he lived at Coniston for nine years and most of his dialect poems were inspired by his experiences there. He began his medical career at Whitehaven and after practising in that town and Lamplugh successively, moved to Coniston in 1844 on his appointment as medical officer to the Coniston Copper Company, and shortly afterward married and went to life at Yewdale Bridge, near the head of the lake. His first literary work was *Ravings and Ramblings about the Old Man of Coniston*, which is full of close observations of the scenery, character and customs of the people.

His best known dialect sketches are *Joe and the Geologist*, *T'Reets on't*; and *Bobby Banks' Bodderment*, whilst of his songs, *Lal Dinah Grayson* with its catching refrain 'M'appen I May', is by far the most popular. *Joe and the Geologist* was based on an idea which occurred to the doctor as to what one of the farm lads would think about the labours of a geologist, and tells how Joe lightens his labours by turning out the contents of a geologist's bag, and refilling it when near home from a handy stone-heap!

Dr. Gibson left Coniston in 1851, and settled for a few years at Hawkshead, after which he spent the remaining years of his life in Cheshire. His *Folk-speech of Cumberland* is a rollicking production with excellent dialect, but his antiquarian legends are generally regarded as of doubtful authenticity and his attacks on Wordsworth are mere curiosities in the present day when the comparative celebrity of the two can be more accurately gauged.

Also in the near neighbourhood of Coniston is the house at Hausebank where Lieutenant Oldfield lived on his retirement. He had shipped before the mast, but received his Lieutenancy from Nelson himself in appreciation of his invaluable services at Copenhagen, when he was the only one who would undertake to pilot the fleet through the entrance to the Baltic after the Danes had lifted all the buoys and other navigation guides. James Garth Marshall, M.P. for Leeds, who was one of the first to study the metamorphic rocks of the Coniston district scientifically, lived at Monk Coniston.

III

Southward from Coniston the railway and the road run to Torver, a scattered village whose church was consecrated in 1538, but has been rebuilt. One of its vicars was the Rev. Thomas Ellwood, the great Scandinavian scholar, who translated from the *Landnama Bók* and wrote much on the Viking occupation of Cumberland and Lake Lancashire. The old church, which was rebuilt in 1848, was said to have been the 'first built in England for the exercise of the Protestant form of worship', and the new church preserves a paper signed by Cranmer, authorizing its consecration in 1538.

From Torver a track to the north-west over Torver Common leads to Dow Crags, a precipice over Gaits Water which has some of the most savage rock scenery in Lakeland, and south of Torver is a complete contrast in the pastoral beauty of the valley of the Crake, with the pretty little village of Wateryeat—whose name is a corruption of 'Water Gate'; Blawith, which has interesting prehistoric sites in its neighbourhood; Lowick with its old Hall; and Greenodd, whose Norse name of grœn-oddi, the green point, is still delightfully appropriate, for it is set among wooded hills where the Crake and Leven meet, and its green promontory commands the whole glorious estuary of the Leven.

IV

North and west of Coniston there is scenery to delight with its variety of beauty. The main road from Coniston to Ambleside opens up magnificent and ever-changing views which make it one of the most beautiful in Lakeland and there are footpaths to keep the most energetic fully occupied during the longest stay. There are pretty little cascades set among rocks and trees, pastoral valleys and picturesque farms, a wilderness of mountains and moors, and many tarns, of which the best known and most lovely is to be seen from the farm-house of Tarn Hows, a favourite viewpoint for the moorland Monk Coniston tarns with their mountain background which is now in the care of the National Trust.

The fells which lie between Coniston Old Man and the valley of the Duddon have wild ravines, abrupt precipices, towering peaks and solitary tarns, and are as lonely and as awe-inspiring as the most remote Highlands of Scotland. Walna Scar is traversed by an old pack-horse road dropping down into the beautiful Duddon Valley at Seathwaite, where a tributary river from Seathwaite Tarn flows into the main valley. Seathwaite, ever memorable for the life and labours of 'Wonderful Walker' is much as it was in Wordsworth's day, apart from the rebuilding of the church where the Rev. Robert Walker ministered for nearly sixty-seven years. Born at Undercrag farm in 1709, the youngest child in a family of twelve, he held curacies at Gosforth, Loweswater, Buttermere and Torver before coming to Seathwaite, where he died at the age of ninety-three and is buried in the churchyard.

Innumerable accounts of his life have been written since Wordsworth first eulogized his unremitting toil and the frugality by which he achieved the means to educate his family, maintain a modest hospitality and leave two thousand pounds for their support after his death, on a stipend which at first only amounted to five pounds, but was later increased to £50. There can be no doubt that Wordsworth did not in the least exaggerate the virtues of this hard-working and good old man, but, as a guide to Coniston published in 1849 points out, such examples of frugality and industry were by no means unknown in the dales, either in the case of the poorly paid clergymen or their parishioners. Southey mentioned that the curate of Newlands, near Keswick, was obliged to add to his income by work as a tailor, clogger and butter-print maker, and there were many others.

In the Duddon Valley itself was the example of poor Mary Hird, who was left a destitute widow with a family of small children when she was still a young woman. She brought up her family by hard work, and established them all in life, yet always exercised the most open-handed hospitality. One who knew her said that he believed she gave away more bread, cheese and home-brewed ale than was sold in some public houses. Her house was always most scrupulously clean, and in the heather season she always had a thick sod of purple heather in full blossom in the large grate as an ornament. She met with a sad end, for in February, 1848, she left home to visit some relations in Eskdale, having arranged to be picked up by a friend who owned a gig, but apparently missed him and walked on. She was overtaken by the mist, and when her body was found a week later, the lacerated condition of her hands and knees showed that the poor old woman had struggled on hands and knees after she grew too weak to walk.

North of Seathwaite are the Stepping Stones which, when the river is low, carry the track from Coniston to Eskdale across the stream; the wooded heights of Grassgars; the picturesque Birks Bridge; Cockley Beck Farmhouse and the Three Shires Stone on Wrynose, with the wild, bare mountains of Hardknot, Greyfriar and Harter Fell, a remote and impressively beautiful region seldom penetrated by visitors. A mile south of Seathwaite the river reaches Hall Dunnerdale and the bridge, and flows on past Cumbrian Ulpha, with its ruins and its legends, and beneath hanging woods and shelving banks of wild flowers to Duddon Bridge and the great estuary which is guarded at the head by Broughton Tower and at its mouth by Millom Castle.

Broughton-in-Furness is an ancient market town, delightfully situated. Both its church and its pele-tower have been rebuilt in modern times, but the church has a Norman doorway and traces of Perpendicular work, whilst the embattled fourteenth century pele-tower of Broughton and part of its dungeons is incorporated in the pseudo-Gothic mansion, and there are traces of early earthworks. The tower was built by the family of Broughton, who are said to have settled there in Anglo-Saxon times, and who flourished until Sir Thomas Broughton took part in Lambert Simnel's rebellion and died in hiding at Witherslack, with his estates forfeited to the King, who granted them to the Earl of Derby. Richard Broughton, the Catholic historian, who died in 1635, claimed in his preface to the *Monasticon Britannicum* to be descended from this family. Broughton Tower, after passing from the Stanleys to various owners, came into the possession of the Sawreys of whom the first was the Parliamentarian Colonel, Roger Sawrey, during whose time the tower was a place of refuge for many dissenting ministers.

Standing as it does on the Coniston branch of the railway, only a mile from the Duddon Valley; with roads stretching out like tentacles to grasp the beauty of the Duddon, the Furness Fells and of Cumbrian and Lancastrian Lakeland, Broughton-in-Furness is typical of the unpretentious Lakeland towns, with their roots in the far distant past, their quiet prosperity in the present day, and their outstanding attraction as centres for one of the most fascinating districts in the British Isles.

INDEX